KB264123

TEPS in
TEPS

650청해

박기혁

서울대학교 졸
(현) 메가스터디 어학센터 TEPS 강사
(현) SLA 학원 TEPS 대표 강사
(현) 중앙일보 영자 신문 중앙 데일리 교육 분야 객원 논설위원
(현) 한국 생산성 본부 영어 전임 강사
(현) PTT(Park's TEPS Teacher's Group) 대표 강사
-TEPS의 최고를 지향하는 강사들의 모임

송승룡

성균관대학교 졸업, 경희대학교 대학원 석사과정
영국 Wimbledon School of English 어학과정 이수
(현) 중앙데일리 영자 신문 객원 해설위원
(현) 민중에센스 아동영어/실용영어 연구센터 연구위원
(현) 한국생산성본부 영어 지도위원
(현) PTT(Park's TEPS Teacher's Group) 강사
-TEPS의 최고를 지향하는 강사들의 모임

TEPS in TEPS 650 청해

저자 | 박기혁 · 송승룡
초판 1쇄 발행 | 2009년 5월 25일
초판 6쇄 발행 | 2017년 2월 28일

발행인 | 박효상
총괄이사 | 이종선
편집장 | 김현
기획 · 편집 | 박혜민
디자인 | 손정수
마케팅 | 이태호, 이전희
디지털콘텐츠 | 이지호
관리 | 김태옥

Special Staff

표지 | 장선숙
내지 | 홍수미
편집 | 정선영

출판등록 | 제10-1835호
발행처 | 사람in
주소 | 121-839 서울시 마포구 양화로11길 14-10(서교동) 4F
전화 | 02) 338-3555(代) 팩스 | 02) 338-3545
e-mail | saramin@netsgo.com
Homepage | www.saramin.com

:: 책값은 뒤표지에 있습니다.
:: 파본은 바꾸어 드립니다.

ⓒ박기혁 · 송승룡 2009

ISBN 978-89-6049-119-9 18740
　　　978-89-6049-116-8 (세트)

사람이 중심이 되는 세상, 세상과 소통하는 책 **사람in**

TEPS in TEPS

650 청해

박기혁·송승룡

사람in
saram
in.com

Preface

영어 시험을 둘러싼 여러 가지 환경 변화에 의해서 TEPS의 중요성은 나날이 강조되고 있고 그 특징 또한 뚜렷이 변화를 겪고 있다.

첫째, 갈수록 문제가 다양화되고 있고 더욱더 세련되어지고 있다.
둘째, 시험을 치루는 대상 연령층이 자꾸 낮아지고 있다.
셋째, 특목고나 외고, 로스쿨이나 의학전문대학원 진학 등 그 쓰임새가 더욱 광범위해졌다.

이러한 세 가지 변화에 발맞추어, TEPS 교재도 다양화되고 진화되어야 하는데, 현재의 교재 시장은 그러한 가시적인 변화에 능동적으로 대처하지 못하는 것이 사실이다. 이에, 이번 TEPS in TEPS 시리즈를 통해서 진화하는 TEPS에 가장 적합한 패러다임을 제시하고자 한다.

TEPS는 참으로 복잡하고 미묘한 시험이다. TOEFL처럼 학문적인 점에 초점을 맞추는 것도 아니고, TOEIC처럼 실용 언어적인 측면만을 강조하는 시험도 아니다. 어쩌면 이 둘의 장점만을 모아 놓은 시험이라 할 수 있겠다.

학문적인 내용들을 풀어가되 좀 더 현실성을 부여하여 실용적으로 쓰이는 영어들을 묻는 것이다. TEPS가 최근 시험 시장에 지각 변동을 일으키고 있는 이유는 이런 장점이 토대가 되었다고 볼 수 있다.

TEPS는 실제로 회화를 하다가 혹은 네이티브가 보는 외국 신문 등을 읽다가 느끼는 애로사항을 잘 해결해 줄 수 있는 시험이다. 어휘력의 측면에서 보아도 실생활에서 우리는 이런 어려움을 겪는다. '단어 하나하나의 해석은 되는데 왜 전체적으로는 독해가 안 되고 해석이 안 될까?', '이 상황에서 저 말은 대체 무슨 뜻으로 쓰이는 걸까?'

그것은 바로 간단한 단어라도 초보적으로 배웠던 사전적 지식 외에 실생활에서는 다양한 뜻으로 활용되기 때문이다.

이처럼 네이티브와의 가장 적절한 의사소통에 초점을 둔 TEPS는 지극히 영어수험과 영어실용의 접목이라는 공인영어시험의 목적에 가장 합당한 인증시험이라 하겠다.

TOEIC이 점수 인플레로 상위권 수험생의 변별력을 상실했다는 비판이 많다. TEPS는 TOEIC과 같은 패턴의 지속적인 반복만으로는 해결할 수 없는 시험이다. 이에 학습자들도 이런 TEPS에 대한 관심과 욕구가 더욱 늘어나고 있는 현실이다.

필자는 좀 더 실용적이고 영어 실력 향상에 도움이 되는 TEPS에 대한 관심이 높아지고 있는 것은 고무적인 일이라 생각한다. 그리고 그런 TEPS를 연구하고 학습하는데, 이 'TEPS in TEPS 시리즈'가 선구자적인 역할을 하길 진심으로 바라는 마음으로 문제 하나 설명 하나에 세심한 신경을 쓰면서 작업에 임하였다.

혼자서는 할 수 없었던 작업에 언제나 도움이 되었던 분들께 감사의 마음을 전할까 한다. 늘 미안한 마음이 드는 가족들과, 사람in 출판사의 박효상 사장님, 김상호 팀장님, 조승주 대리님 그리고 이 책의 출간에 물심양면으로 도움을 주신 류건 선생님, 신일섭 조교, 윤이랑 조교에게도 아울러 감사의 뜻을 표하고 싶다.

PPT(Park's TEPS Teacher's Group) 대표 강사

박기혁

TEPS in TEPS

학생들의 자습서와 학원 교재의 성격을 둘 다 가질 수 있게 만들었다. 그래서 학원에서의 강의는 물론 독학용으로도 사용하도록 준비했다.

1. 상세한 해설을 통해 정답을 공략하는 법과 함께 오답을 피할 수 있는 Skill들을 제시하여 좀 더 높은 점수로의 도약이 가능하게 하였다.

2. TEPS의 4대 영역(독해, 어휘, 청해, 문법)과 기준 점수대별로 학습 목표와 가장 효율적인 방법들을 제시하여 좀 더 전문적이고 체계적인 학습자 맞춤형 학습이 가능하도록 하였다.

3. 애매모호한 이론이나 군더더기 설명을 최대한 배제하여 학습 시간 대비 효율성을 극대화하도록 구성하였다.

TEPS in TEPS

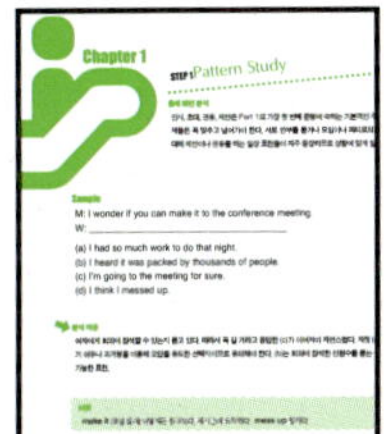

1. TEPS 청해 유형을 완전히 익히는 Sample

기출 변형 문제로 실제 시험의 유형을 익힌다. Sample문제를 통해 확인한 유형은 Clinic과 Actual Test를 통해 연습함으로써 TEPS 청해 유형을 빠르게 정리할 수 있다.

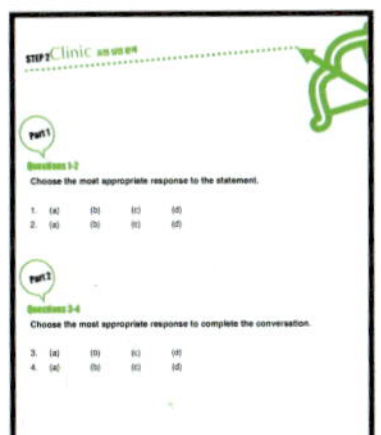

2. TEPS 청해의 해결법을 제시한 Clinic

기출 변형 문제로 실제 시험 문제와 가장 가까운 형태의 지문들을 다룬다. 상세한 해설과 함께 정답 포인트를 집어볼 수 있다.

3. 핵심 단어와 표현을 캐치하는 Dictation

Clinic에 나오는 핵심 단어와 표현을 음성을 들으면서 캐치하는 훈련을 한다.

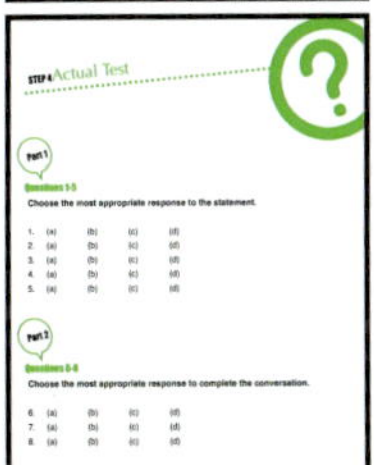

4. 자신만의 해결 노하우를 만들어가는 Actual Test

실전 연습 문제를 통해 실전에 대한 감각을 극대화하도록 한다. 영문 스크립트와 지문의 해석 및 해설은 〈정답 및 해설〉에서 확인하며 충분한 보충학습이 될 수 있도록 하였다.

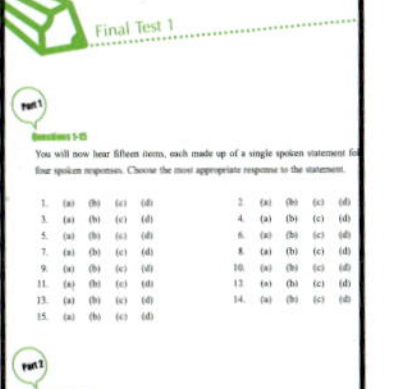

5. 실전보다 더 실전 같은 Final Test

청해 2회분의 모의고사를 실었다. 난이도는 정기시험과 동일하다. 실전 문제를 통해 정확한 자기 실력을 파악할 수 있다.

TEPS in TEPS

TEPS의 구성

TEPS는 청해, 문법, 어휘, 독해 4개 영역에 걸쳐 총 200문항으로 구성되어 있으며 시험 시간은 140분이다. 만점은 문항 반응 이론(IRT)에 따라 채점하기 때문에 전부 맞아도 990점이고 모두 틀려도 10점은 나온다.

영역	PART별 내용	문항 수	시간/배점
청 해 Listening Comprehension	Part Ⅰ : 문장 하나를 듣고 이어질 대화 고르기	15	55분/396점
	Part Ⅱ : 3문장의 대화를 듣고 이어질 대화 고르기	15	
	Part Ⅲ : 6-8문장의 대화를 듣고 질문에 해답하는 답 고르기	15	
	Part Ⅳ : 단문의 내용을 듣고 질문에 해당하는 답 고르기	15	
문 법 Grammar	Part Ⅰ : 대화문의 빈칸에 적절한 표현 고르기	20	25분/99점
	Part Ⅱ : 문장의 빈칸에 적절한 표현 고르기	20	
	Part Ⅲ : 대화에서 어법상 틀리거나 어색한 부분 고르기	5	
	Part Ⅳ : 단문에서 어법상 틀리거나 어색한 부분 고르기	5	
어 휘 Vocabulary	Part Ⅰ : 대화문의 빈칸에 적절한 단어 고르기	25	15분/99점
	Part Ⅱ : 단문의 빈칸에 적절한 단어 고르기	25	
독 해 Reading Comprehension	Part Ⅰ : 지문을 읽고 지문의 빈칸에 들어갈 내용 고르기	16	45분/396점
	Part Ⅱ : 지문을 읽고 질문에 가장 적절한 내용 고르기	21	
	Part Ⅲ : 지문을 읽고 문맥상 어색한 내용 고르기	3	
총계	13개 PART	200	140분/990점

청해(Listening Comprehension) 60문항

정확한 청해 능력을 측정하기 위하여 문제와 보기 문항을 문제지에 인쇄하지 않고 들려줌으로써 자연스러운 의사소통의 인지과정을 최대한 반영하였다. 다양한 의사소통 기능(Communicative Functions)의 대화와 다양한 상황(공고, 방송, 일상 업무 상황, 대학 교양 수준의 강의 등)을 이해하는 데 필요한 전반적인 청해력을 측정하기 위해 대화문(dialogue)과 담화문(monologue)의 소재를 균형 있게 다루었다.

PART 1	15문항

Listen and choose the most appropriate response.

W: How about talking over lunch on Wednesday?
M: ________________________________

(a) Sounds good She'd love it.
(b) Tell me about it.
(c) Sorry. I have an appointment. What about Friday?
(d) Fine. Thanks.

Part 1은 질의응답 문제를 다루며 한 번만 들려준다. 내용 자체는 단순하고 기본적인 수준의 생활 영어 표현으로 구성되어 있지만 교과서적인 지식보다는 재빠른 상황 판단 능력을 요구한다. 따라서 이 파트에서는 속도 적응 능력뿐만 아니라 순발력 있는 상황 판단 능력이 요구된다.

PART 2	15문항

Listen and choose the most appropriate response.

M: How come you know so much about fashion?
W: Actually, my sister is a model.
M: Wow! How long has she been in the industry?
M: ________________________________

(a) She wants to be a fashion designer.
(b) About two years.
(c) Last year she did.
(d) Modeling is a tough job.

Part 2는 짧은 대화 문제로 두 사람이 A-B-A-B 순으로 보통 속도로 대화하는 형식이며 소요 시간은 약 12초 전후로 짧게 구성되어 있다. Part 1과 마찬가지로 한 번만 들려주는 부분이다.

Contents

인사·초대
권유·제안

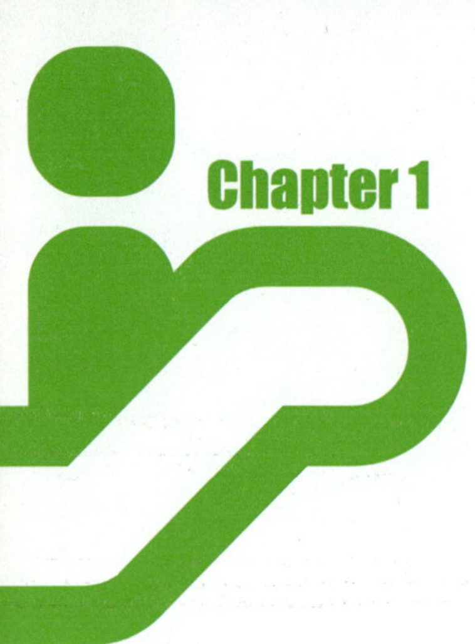

Chapter 1

출제 패턴 분석

인사, 초대, 권유, 제안은 Part 1의 가장 첫 번째 문형에 속하는 기본적인 주제들로, 이 영역의 문제들은 꼭 맞추고 넘어가야 한다. 서로 안부를 묻거나 모임이나 파티로의 초대, 혹은 어떤 일에 대해 제안이나 권유를 하는 일상 표현들이 자주 등장하므로 상황에 맞게 알아 두자.

Sample

M: I wonder if you can make it to the conference meeting.

W: ____

(a) I had so much work to do that night.
(b) I heard it was packed by thousands of people.
(c) I'm going to the meeting for sure.
(d) I think I messed up.

 **분석 적용**

여자에게 회의에 참석할 수 있는지 묻고 있다. 따라서 꼭 갈 거라고 응답한 (c)가 이어져야 자연스럽다. 자칫 (a)를 정답으로 착각하기 쉬우나 과거형을 이용해 오답을 유도한 선택지이므로 유의해야 한다. (b)는 회의에 참석한 인원수를 묻는 질문에 대한 응답으로 가능한 표현.

어휘

make it (모임 등에) 어떻게든 참석하다, 제시간에 도착하다　**mess up** 망치다

Part 1

Questions 1-2

Choose the most appropriate response to the statement.

1. (a)　　(b)　　(c)　　(d)
2. (a)　　(b)　　(c)　　(d)

Part 2

Questions 3-4

Choose the most appropriate response to complete the conversation.

3. (a)　　(b)　　(c)　　(d)
4. (a)　　(b)　　(c)　　(d)

1.

W: What are you up to?

M: _________________________________

(a) I'm currently working for an environmental organization.
(b) I'm sorry, I didn't mean to.
(c) I just got back home.
(d) I will go next summer.

해설

요즘 어떻게 지내는지 근황을 묻고 있으므로 이에 대한 내용이 담긴 **(a)**가 적당하다.

어휘

currently 현재 **environmental organization** 환경단체

2.

M: Are you free on Sunday for Michael's birthday party?

W: _________________________________

(a) I am leaving soon.
(b) I had a great time the other night at his party.
(c) Sorry, I don't want to be tied down.
(d) I will be there for sure.

해설

Are you free ...?는 상대방에게 '~ 시간 있니?'라고 물을 때 쓰는 표현이다. 파티에 올 수 있냐고 묻고 있으므로 '올 수 있다, 없다' 혹은 '잘 모르겠다' 식의 응답이 이어져야 자연스럽다.

어휘

the other night 요전날 밤 **tie down** 구속하다

3.

M: Happy New Year!
W: You too! What did you do on New Year's?
M: I just stayed at home with my family. What about you?
W: ____

(a) I made a wish for my family.
(b) I was stuck at home too.
(c) I haven't seen your family in so long.
(d) I will be home for the next month.

 **해설**

남자 역시 여자에게 뭘 했는지 묻고 있으므로 '나도 하루 종일 집에 있었다'고 응답한 (b)가 자연스럽다.

> **어휘**
>
> **make a wish** 소원을 빌다, 기도하다   **be stuck at home** 집에 처박혀 있다

4.

M: Why don't we work out together now?
W: I am not in a good mood for working out.
M: You need more fresh air to refresh your mind.
W: ____

(a) I have a problem with that.
(b) Okay, it is time to start the work again.
(c) Then let's just walk by the lake a bit.
(d) I thought I told you before.

 **해설**

기분전환을 위해 바람을 쐬야 한다는 남자의 충고에 긍정적으로 응답한 (c)가 정답이다.

> **어휘**
>
> **work out** 운동하다   **be in a good mood** 기분이 좋다

1.

W: What are you up to?

M: ____.

2.

M: Are you free on Sunday for Michael's birthday party?

W: ____.

3.

M: Happy New Year!

W: You too! What did you do on New Year's?

M: I just stayed at home with my family. What about you?

W: ____.

4.

M: Why don't we work out together now?

W: I am not in a good mood for working out.

M: You need more fresh air to refresh your mind.

W: ____.

Part 1

Questions 1-5

Choose the most appropriate response to the statement.

1. (a)   (b)   (c)   (d)
2. (a)   (b)   (c)   (d)
3. (a)   (b)   (c)   (d)
4. (a)   (b)   (c)   (d)
5. (a)   (b)   (c)   (d)

Part 2

Questions 6-8

Choose the most appropriate response to complete the conversation.

6. (a)   (b)   (c)   (d)
7. (a)   (b)   (c)   (d)
8. (a)   (b)   (c)   (d)

초면 인사

Don't I know you from somewhere? 어디서 뵌 적 있지 않나요?
We seem to keep running into each other. 자주 뵙네요.
Yes, I think we've met. 그러게요, 뵌 적이 있는 것 같네요.
Yes, tell me about it. 네, 그러게 말입니다.
No, I don't think so. 아니오, 그런 것 같지 않은데요.
I don't know you either. 저도 당신을 잘 모르겠는데요.
Do I know you? 저 아세요?

소개

Mr. Green, allow me to introduce Mr. Kang. 그린 씨, 강 씨를 소개하게 해주십시오.
I moved there from the company housing only a month ago.
바로 한 달 전에 사택에서 그리로 이사를 했습니다.
What business are you in? 어떤 일에 종사하십니까?

작별

I'm afraid I must be on my way. 죄송하지만 이만 가 봐야겠어요.
Guess I should get going. 이제 가 봐야 할 것 같아요.
Keep me posted. 계속 연락 주세요.
It's an honor for me as well. 당신을 만나서 저 또한 영광입니다.
I'm pleased to make your acquaintance. 만나 뵙게 되어 반갑습니다.
Nice meeting you. 만나서 반가웠어요. *cf.* Nice to meet you. 만나서 반가워요.
Nice talking to you. 얘기 즐거웠어요.
It's the least I could do. 이 정도는 해야죠. → 배웅해 줘 고맙다는 인사에 대한 답례

충고 · 부탁
허락

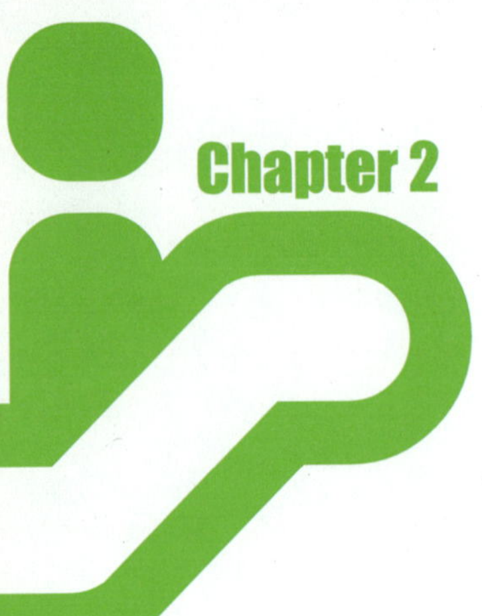

Chapter 2

출제 패턴 분석

충고, 부탁, 허락에 관한 대화인 경우 의문사 없는 문장 형태로 등장하는 경우가 많다. 충고의 경우는 받아들이는 경우의 응답이 많고, 부탁의 경우에는 허락(accept), 또는 거절(refuse)의 두 가지로 구분해서 알아 두도록 하자.

Sample

W: I was wondering if you could put this up on the shelf.

M: _______________________________________

(a) Sure, I will do it.
(b) I already did it.
(c) I made a decision to do that.
(d) Of course I did.

 **분석 적용**

I was wondering if you ...는 상대방에게 뭔가를 아주 공손하게 부탁할 때 쓰는 표현으로, '혹시 ~해 주실 수 있나 모르겠어요' 정도의 의미를 갖는다. 따라서 여자의 부탁에 응하는 **(a)**가 정답이다.

어휘

put up 저장하다, 치우다   **shelf** 선반

STEP 2 Clinic 도전 실전 문제

Part 1

Questions 1-2

Choose the most appropriate response to the statement.

1. (a)　　(b)　　(c)　　(d)
2. (a)　　(b)　　(c)　　(d)

Part 2

Questions 3-4

Choose the most appropriate response to complete the conversation.

3. (a)　　(b)　　(c)　　(d)
4. (a)　　(b)　　(c)　　(d)

1.

M: Could you give me a ride to the convention center?

W: _______________________________________

(a) Why not? Let's meet in front of the office.
(b) Where shall we go tonight?
(c) After the meeting, I'm going to go to the convention center.
(d) Can I have a ride?

 **해설**

차를 태워 주길 부탁하고 있으므로 이에 응하거나 거절하는 선택지를 고르면 된다.

> **어휘**
>
> **give ... a ride** ～를 태워 주다 **convention center** 컨벤션 센터(회의장·숙박 시설이 완비된 종합 빌딩) **have[take] a ride** 한번 타다

2.

M: Can I borrow your laptop to check my email?

W: _______________________________________

(a) Sounds great.
(b) I got an email from the company.
(c) I will keep in touch with you.
(d) Okay, you can use it after I finish my work.

해설

노트북을 빌려도 되는지 허락을 구하고 있으므로 이에 응하는 (d)가 적절하다.

> **어휘**
>
> **laptop** 노트북 **keep in touch with** ～와 연락하고 지내다

3.

W: Could you do me a favor? I need a ride to the post office.

M: For what?

W: I want to send this as priority mail.

M: _______________________________________

(a) These are my favorite things.

(b) I have a lot of baggage.

(c) Get in. I am going the same way.

(d) I will do that for you.

 **해설**

우체국까지 태워다 줄 것을 부탁하고 있으므로 이에 응하는 **(c)**가 정답이다.

어휘

priority mail 우선 취급 우편
→ 미국의 우편 등급은 express mail, priority mail, first-class mail 등으로 나뉘어져 있는데, express mail은 어떤 지역이든 24시간 내에 배달되는 가장 빠른 특급 우편, priority mail은 특급 우편보다는 느리지만 일반 우편보다는 빨리 도착하는 우편, first-class mail은 엽서나 연하장, 그 밖의 서한 형식의 일반 우편물을 보낼 때 이용하는 우편을 말한다.

4.

M: Visitors from overseas are coming today.

W: Today? When do they come?

M: It's around 2 o'clock. Could you show them around the factory?

W: _______________________________________

(a) Sorry, I have an important meeting with my boss.

(b) I agree. What time shall we make it?

(c) Machines in the factory will replace with new ones.

(d) It doesn't make sense to show me.

해설

회사를 방문하는 손님들을 위해 공장 안내를 부탁하는 상황이므로 이를 받아들이거나 거절하는 표현이 담긴 선택지를 고르면 된다.

어휘

visitor 방문객 **show** 안내하다 **factory** 공장

1.

M: Could you give me a ride to the convention center?

W: ___________________________________.

2.

M: Can I borrow your laptop to check my email?

W: ___________________________________.

3.

W: Could you do me a favor? I need a ride to the post office.

M: For what?

W: I want to send this as priority mail.

M: ___________________________________.

4.

M: Visitors from overseas are coming today.

W: Today? When do they come?

M: It's around 2 o'clock. Could you show them around the factory?

W: ___________________________________.

Questions 1-4

Choose the most appropriate response to the statement.

1. (a)   (b)   (c)   (d)
2. (a)   (b)   (c)   (d)
3. (a)   (b)   (c)   (d)
4. (a)   (b)   (c)   (d)

Questions 5-7

Choose the most appropriate response to complete the conversation.

5. (a)   (b)   (c)   (d)
6. (a)   (b)   (c)   (d)
7. (a)   (b)   (c)   (d)

👉 만남

Why, if it isn't Mary! 이거, 메리군!
It's been years since I talked to you! 정말 오랜만이다!
Fancy meeting you here! 여기서 만날 줄이야!
I know. What a coincidence! 그러게요. 정말 우연의 일치네요!

👉 안부

How's life treating you? 어떻게 지내니?
How do you find yourself? 기분이 어때?
How is it going? 잘 지내니?
How're your folks? 가족들은 안녕하신가요?
Give my best regards to your family. 가족들에게 안부 전해 줘.
I'm stuck at home. 집에 콕 박혀 있어.
I'm alive and kicking. 원기왕성합니다.
I'm just surviving. 그럭저럭 지내요.
I can't complain. 잘 지내고 있어.
I'm getting by. 그럭저럭 지내.
I've seen better days./ I've had better days. 그냥 그래.
It couldn't be better. 아주 좋아.
I'm keeping busy. And you? 좀 바빴어. 넌?

칭찬·격려 축하·위로

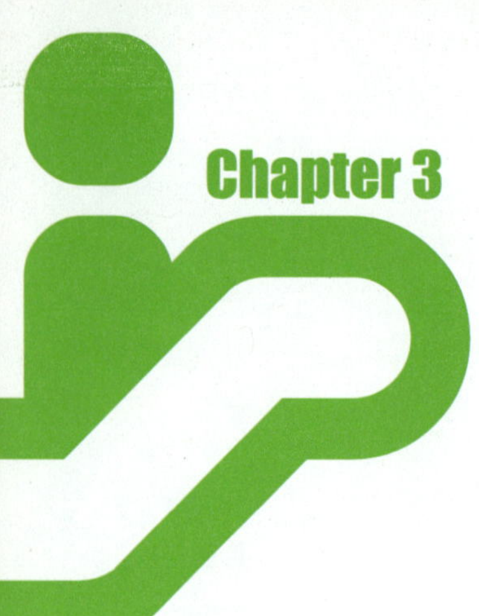

Chapter 3

STEP 1 Pattern Study

출제 패턴 분석

칭찬에 대해서는 감사하다는 응답이 이어지는 반면, 격려나 축하, 위로의 경우엔 다양한 표현의 응답이 가능하므로 각 상황에 맞는 표현들을 잘 알아 두도록 하자.

sample

M: I have butterflies in my stomach.
W: Why are you so nervous?
M: I'm making an opening speech tomorrow.
W: _______________________________________

(a) I think you should prepare it perfectly.
(b) All audiences were impressed by his speech.
(c) Why don't you go to the pharmacy?
(d) You quit your position after all.

 **분석 적용**

(c)는 남자의 첫 대사를 정확히 이해하지 못하는 경우 빠질 수 있는 함정으로, have butterflies in one's stomach은 be nervous와 마찬가지 표현으로 '긴장하다', '안절부절못하다'란 뜻이다. 따라서 내일 개회사를 앞두고 긴장을 하고 있는 남자에게 격려조로 이야기해 주는 (a)가 정답이다.

어휘

opening speech 개회사　**audience** 청중　**impress** 감명을 주다　**pharmacy** 약국　**quit** 그만두다　**position** 직장, 근무처

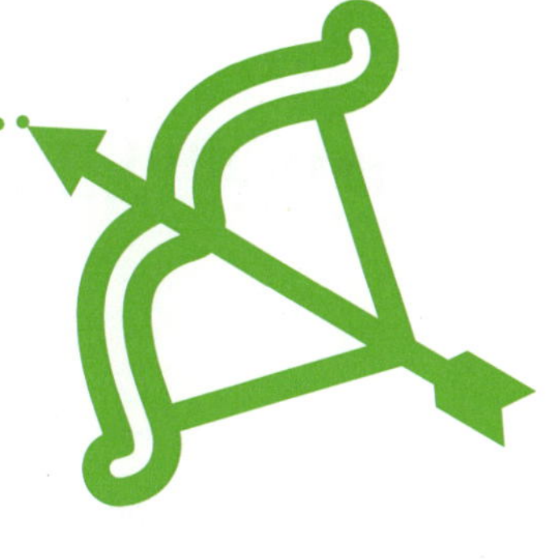

Questions 1-2

Choose the most appropriate response to the statement.

1. (a)   (b)   (c)   (d)
2. (a)   (b)   (c)   (d)

Questions 3-4

Choose the most appropriate response to complete the conversation.

3. (a)   (b)   (c)   (d)
4. (a)   (b)   (c)   (d)

1.

W: What's happening? You've been a little down this week.

M: ______________________________________

(a) I was in downtown with my parents.
(b) Nothing bad, I was just a bit confused.
(c) I will go back home for the next month.
(d) My friends gave me a surprise party two days ago.

 **해설**

What's happening?은 인상을 쓰고 있거나 우울해 보이는 상대방에게 "무슨 일이야?" 하고 물을 때 사용하는 표현이다. What's going on?, What's the matter?, What's wrong? 모두 마찬가지 표현들. 따라서 이에 대한 응답으로 자연스러운 것은 (b)다.

> **어휘**
>
> **down** 기운 없는, 음울한   **confuse** 혼돈하다, 당황하게 하다

2.

W: I heard you're getting married.

M: ______________________________________

(a) Thanks, I'd like to invite you to my wedding.
(b) Who is the lucky girl?
(c) I will be your groomsman.
(d) I am a newlywed.

 **해설**

결혼을 축하하는 의미가 담겨 있으므로 그에 대한 답례가 이어져야 자연스럽다. 따라서 (a)가 정답.

> **어휘**
>
> **groomsman** 신랑 들러리(= bridesman, best man) *cf.* **bridesmaid** 신부 들러리   **newlywed** 신혼자

3.

M: Hey, it is so nice seeing you here!

W: Yeah, what a small world! You guys are still together.

M: Yes, we have been for 2 years.

W: ____

(a) Things are going well for me fortunately.

(b) Wow, you guys get along so well!

(c) I am so pleased to say that.

(d) More than that.

 **해설**

같이 다닌 지 2년 됐다는 말에 감탄의 의미가 담긴 (b)가 이어지는 것이 자연스럽다. (a)의 Things are going well.은 누군가 나에게 어떻게 지내는지, 또는 하는 일이 어떻게 돼 가고 있는지 물었을 때 '만사가 잘 풀리고 있다'란 뜻으로 쓸 수 있는 표현이다.

> **어휘**
> **get along** 잘 어울려 지내다

4.

M: How long did it take you to write it?

W: On and off, three or four years.

M: It's a long time to be writing. That's cool.

W: ____

(a) Yes, I was on purpose.

(b) It won't be that big deal for you.

(c) I always wanted to make my own book.

(d) I love reading as much as writing.

 **해설**

That's cool.은 '멋지다, 끝내주다, 대단하다'라는 뜻의 표현으로, 여자가 오랜 기간에 거쳐 마침내 책을 완성한 것에 대해 감탄 어린 칭찬을 해주고 있다. 따라서 이어질 수 있는 가장 적절한 응답은 늘 자신만의 책을 쓰고 싶었다는 (c)가 된다.

> **어휘**
> **on and off** 때때로, 불규칙하게 **on purpose** 일부러, 고의로(= deliberately) **big deal** 대단한 물건[사람, 일], 큰일

1.

W: What's happening? You've been a little down this week.

M: _______________________________________.

2.

W: I heard you're getting married.

M: _______________________________________.

3.

M: Hey, it is so nice seeing you here!

W: Yeah, what a small world! You guys are still together.

M: Yes, we have been for 2 years.

W: _______________________________________.

4.

M: How long did it take you to write it?

W: On and off, three or four years.

M: It's a long time to be writing. That's cool.

W: _______________________________________.

STEP 4 Actual Test

Questions 1-4

Choose the most appropriate response to the statement.

1. (a)   (b)   (c)   (d)
2. (a)   (b)   (c)   (d)
3. (a)   (b)   (c)   (d)
4. (a)   (b)   (c)   (d)

Questions 5-7

Choose the most appropriate response to complete the conversation.

5. (a)   (b)   (c)   (d)
6. (a)   (b)   (c)   (d)
7. (a)   (b)   (c)   (d)

👉 초대

Why don't you drop in sometime? 한번 들러 주시지 않겠습니까?
Come over to my place for some pizza. 우리 집에 피자 먹으러 와라.
* to one's place ~의 집으로
Can you make it?/ Is it all right with you? 그게 좋겠습니까?
→ 형편을 확인할 때
It's very kind of you to let me come. 초대해 주셔서 감사합니다.
My hands are full. 나 아주 바빠.
I'm tied up. 나 바빠.
I'm booked up. 스케줄이 꽉 차 있어.
I doubt it. 못 갈 것 같아.
I'm not available today. 오늘은 시간이 안 될 것 같아.
I'll have to take a rain check. 다음 기회로 미뤄야겠어요.

👉 제안/ 권유

Let me treat you to dinner. 저녁을 대접하게 해주세요.
I'll treat you to a drink. 제가 한잔 사겠습니다.
Would you care for something to drink? 뭘 좀 마시겠어요?
How would you like your coffee, with sugar and cream?
커피에 설탕과 크림을 넣어 드릴까요?
What do you fancy? 무엇을 드시겠습니까?
With cream and sugar. 크림과 설탕을 넣어 주세요.
No, thank you. I'm on medication. 아니오, 괜찮습니다. 지금 약을 복용하고 있어서요.

감사·사과
항의·불평

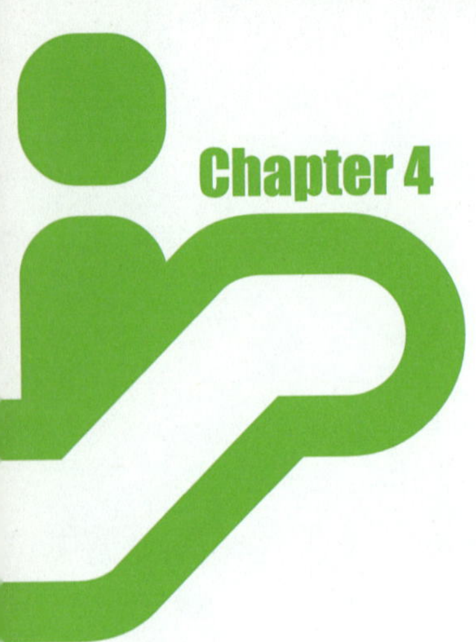

Chapter 4

STEP 1 Pattern Study

감사, 사과, 항의, 불평 관련 표현들은 의문사보다는 평서문 형태를 취하는 경우가 많다. 앞부분에 언급된 화자의 의도를 잘 파악하여 이어질 응답을 짐작할 수 있어야 한다. 한편 대화에 나온 단어를 이용한 응답의 경우 함정일 가능성이 매우 높기 때문에 특히 주의해야 한다.

Sample

M: I'm sorry but you must not take a picture in the museum.

W: ____

(a) Sorry, I clean forgot.
(b) Why did I apologize to him?
(c) You're right. All guests observe a rule.
(d) I used to take a picture on vacation.

분석 적용

잘못을 지적하고 있으므로 사과의 표현이 이어져야 자연스럽다. (d)는 남자의 대사에 나온 take a picture를 이용해 오답을 유도한 함정이다.

어휘

clean forget 깨끗이 잊어버리다(정신이 없어 뭔가 까맣게 잊어버리는 경우에 쓰이는 표현) **apologize** 사과하다 **observe** (규칙 등을) 준수하다, 지키다 **used to** ~하곤 했다

Part 1

Questions 1-2

Choose the most appropriate response to the statement.

1. (a)   (b)   (c)   (d)
2. (a)   (b)   (c)   (d)

Part 2

Questions 3-4

Choose the most appropriate response to complete the conversation.

3. (a)   (b)   (c)   (d)
4. (a)   (b)   (c)   (d)

1.

W: How could you do that to her?

M: ____

(a) Sorry, but it wasn't on purpose.
(b) I'm helping her project.
(c) She did her best.
(d) I'm not sure how you could do that.

해설

그녀에게 어떻게 그럴 수 있는지 따지고 있는 상황이므로 사과의 뜻이 담긴 (a)가 이어지는 것이 자연스럽다.

어휘
do one's best 최선을 다하다

2.

W: It was so much fun. It was much more than I expected.

M: ____

(a) I am sure it will be fun.
(b) I didn't expect that either.
(c) I'm expecting to see you again.
(d) Me, too. It was my pleasure to be with you.

해설

아주 즐거웠다는 여자의 말에 이어질 응답으로 자신도 함께 해서 즐거웠다는 (d)가 적절하다. 이 표현 외에도 '천만에요, 제가 즐거웠습니다'의 뜻으로 You are welcome./ My pleasure./ Don't mention it. 등도 함께 알아 두자.

어휘
expect to ～하길 기대하다

3.

M: Why weren't you there? I would have been there if I could have.

W: I tried to make it but it wasn't possible.

M: Well, you'd better have a good reason for this.

W: ____

(a) I think that's a good reason.

(b) I'll be there soon.

(c) I didn't want to get involved.

(d) I promise I will make it up to you next time.

 **해설**

어떤 장소에 가지 않은 것에 대해 여자에게 불평을 하고 있으므로 다음에는 꼭 가겠다고 약속하는 **(d)**가 적절한 응답이다.

어휘

get involved 연루되다 **make it up** 벌충하다, 만회하다

4.

W: Could you pick up my dogs?

M: Sorry I'm allergic to dogs.

W: Really? I didn't know that.

M: ____

(a) I can't stand them because of my allergies.

(b) Then I will do that for you.

(c) I can't wait to see them.

(d) I will try to do that.

 **해설**

알레르기가 있다는 사실을 미처 몰랐다는 여자의 말에 이어질 응답으로 알레르기 때문에 개가 너무 싫다고 설명하는 **(a)**가 적절하다.

어휘

be allergic to ~에 알레르기가 있다 **I can't wait to** ~하고 싶어 죽겠다

1.

W: How could you do that to her?

M: ____.

2.

W: It was so much fun. It was much more than I expected.

M: ____.

3.

M: Why weren't you there? I would have been there if I could have.

W: I tried to make it but it wasn't possible.

M: Well, you'd better have a good reason for this.

W: ____.

4.

W: Could you pick up my dogs?

M: Sorry I'm allergic to dogs.

W: Really? I didn't know that.

M: ____.

Part 1

Questions 1-4

Choose the most appropriate response to the statement.

1. (a)   (b)   (c)   (d)
2. (a)   (b)   (c)   (d)
3. (a)   (b)   (c)   (d)
4. (a)   (b)   (c)   (d)

Part 2

Questions 5-7

Choose the most appropriate response to complete the conversation.

5. (a)   (b)   (c)   (d)
6. (a)   (b)   (c)   (d)
7. (a)   (b)   (c)   (d)

출제 필수 표현

위로/ 충고

Don't lose heart. 낙담하지 마세요.
Don't be so concerned. 너무 걱정하지 마세요.
Don't forget to lock the door when you leave. 나갈 때 문 잠그는 거 잊지 마세요.

제안

How about taking some time off? 좀 쉬는 게 어때?
I'd like to treat you to lunch. 당신에게 점심을 대접하고 싶은데요.
I'll have to pass this time. 다음 기회에 하자.

전화

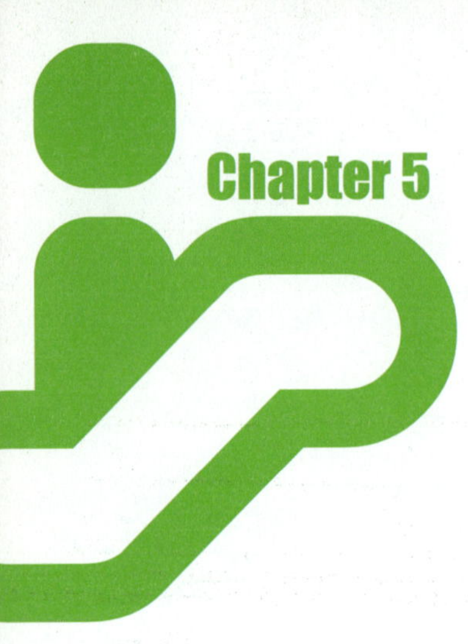

Chapter 5

출제 패턴 분석

전화 내용을 묻는 문제 형태는 꼭 1~2문제씩 출제된다. 따라서 기본적인 전화 표현들을 상황별로 정리해 익혀 두어야 한다.

전화를 받았을 때: ① 본인인 경우(This is ...) ② 당사자가 자리에 없을 경우(I'm sorry, but she is not here.) ③ 당사자를 바꿔 주는 경우(Hold on, I'll put you through.) ④ 잘못 걸려 온 전화인 경우(You have the wrong number.) ⑤ 전화 건 사람이 나중에 다시 걸겠다는 경우(I'll call him later.) ⑥ 전할 메시지가 있으면 남기라고 하는 경우(Would you like to leave a message?)

Sample

M: Did you get any calls while I was at the meeting?

W: _______________________________________

(a) She came to see you.
(b) Someone is waiting for you.
(c) Just a couple of calls from customers.
(d) She is on the phone right now.

 **분석 적용**

자신에게 걸려 온 전화가 있었는지 묻고 있으므로 이에 답하는 선택지를 고르면 된다. (d)는 전화 건 사람이 찾는 당사자가 통화 중이라고 말할 때 사용할 수 있는 표현이다.

어휘
get[receive] a call 전화를 받다

Part 1

Questions 1-2

Choose the most appropriate response to the statement.

1. (a)   (b)   (c)   (d)
2. (a)   (b)   (c)   (d)

Part 2

Questions 3-4

Choose the most appropriate response to complete the conversation.

3. (a)   (b)   (c)   (d)
4. (a)   (b)   (c)   (d)

1.

M: May I use your phone for a second?
W: ___________________________________

(a) I don't have enough time to do that.
(b) Why not? Go ahead.
(c) I will be right back in a second.
(d) The line is busy at the moment.

 **해설**

May[Can] I ...?로 묻는 표현은 허가의 의미가 강하게 담겨 있기 때문에 가능한지 여부에 대해 언급한 선택지를 고르면 된다. 정답은 (b)로, Why not?은 '왜 안 되겠어요?', '그럼요.' 등의 의미로 상대방의 제안에 긍정적인 응답을 할 때 쓰이는 표현이다.

> **어휘**
> **for a second** 잠시 **in a second** 금방, 곧

2.

W: Can I get a message for you?
M: ___________________________________

(a) He is out of town now.
(b) I will call him again later.
(c) I got another message as well.
(d) Maybe he can do it.

 **해설**

전할 메시지가 있는지 묻고 있으므로 전하는 내용이 담겨 있거나 나중에 다시 걸겠다는 식의 표현이 이어져야 자연스럽다.

> **어휘**
> **be out of town** 출장 중이다(be out of town은 최소 2~3일 이상 돌아오지 않을 거라는 의미가 담겨 있는 반면, be away는 장기 출장인지 단기 출장인지 구분이 어렵다. 따라서 일반적으로 He is away for a week.(그는 일주일 동안 여기 없습니다.)처럼 뒤에 기간을 붙여서 말하는 경우가 많다.) **get[take] a message** 메시지를 받다

3.

M: Can I speak to Mr. Brown?
W: I'm sorry he is not available at the moment.
M: Can I ask where he is now?
W: ______________________________________

(a) He is out of town.
(b) I think he will be back soon.
(c) He will be available later tonight.
(d) He is coming soon.

 **해설**

그가 어디 있는지 묻고 있으므로 이에 답하는 선택지를 고르면 된다. (b), (d)는 언제 돌아오는지를 물을 때 나올 수 있는 응답들이다.

> **어휘**
>
> **be not available** 전화를 받을 수 없다(원래 available은 '이용할 수 있는'의 뜻인데, 전화상에서 사람을 주어로 하여 쓰게 되면 '통화 가능한'의 의미로 통한다.)

4.

W: Could I talk to Mrs. Celine?
M: Can I get your name and about what would you like to talk to her?
W: This is Jane and I would like to talk about personal stuff.
M: ______________________________________

(a) OK. Hold on, please.
(b) I don't think that is fair.
(c) I'm not sure if she is coming or not.
(d) I think you are right about that.

해설

셀린 씨와 통화를 하고 싶다고 했으므로 (a)가 정답이다. Hold on, please.는 '잠시만 기다려 주세요'라는 뜻으로, Just a moment, please., Wait a minute, please. 등과 마찬가지 표현이다.

> **어휘**
>
> **personal stuff** 개인적인 일 **hold on** (전화를) 끊지 않고 기다리다 **fair** 공평한, 공정한

1.

M: May I use your phone for a second?

W: ____.

2.

W: Can I get a message for you?

M: ____.

3.

M: Can I speak to Mr. Brown?

W: I'm sorry he is not available at the moment.

M: Can I ask where he is now?

W: ____.

4.

W: Could I talk to Mrs. Celine?

M: Can I get your name and about what would you like to talk to her?

W: This is Jane and I would like to talk about personal stuff.

M: ____.

Part 1

Questions 1-4

Choose the most appropriate response to the statement.

1. (a)   (b)   (c)   (d)
2. (a)   (b)   (c)   (d)
3. (a)   (b)   (c)   (d)
4. (a)   (b)   (c)   (d)

Part 2

Questions 5-6

Choose the most appropriate response to complete the conversation.

5. (a)   (b)   (c)   (d)
6. (a)   (b)   (c)   (d)

출제 필수 표현

부탁 I — 길 찾기 등

I have a big favor to ask of you. 꼭 부탁드릴 게 있어요.

Could you spare some time? 시간 좀 내주시겠어요?

You can't miss it. 바로 찾으실 거예요.

I'm not from around here. 저는 이 동네 사는 사람이 아니에요.

No, thanks. I can find my way around. 아니오, 괜찮습니다. 저 혼자 찾을 수 있습니다.

부탁 II — 사정 봐주기

Give me a rain check, please. 다음 기회를 주십시오.

Could you spare a minute, please? 시간 좀 내주실 수 있습니까?

Could I have a word with you? 말씀 좀 나눌 수 있을까요?

Could you fill me in? 제 대신 일 좀 봐 주시겠어요?

That's enough of that! 이제 제발 그만두게!

Be my guest. 좋을 대로 하세요.

By all means. 물론이죠.

No sweat. 걱정 마세요.

It depends. 상황 봐서요.

I'd rather you didn't. 부탁 안 받은 걸로 하겠습니다.

I wish I could, but I'm swamped with work now.

그러고 싶은데, 지금 일 때문에 바빠서 정신을 못 차리겠어요. * be swamped with ~로 정신을 못 차리다

질의응답

STEP 1 Pattern Study

출제 패턴 분석

질의응답은 질문자의 의견에 대해 동의하거나 반대 의사를 표하는 대화 유형이다. 일정한 패턴
으로 이루어지기 때문에 유형만 잘 익혀 두면 정답을 쉽게 고를 수 있다.

Sample

M: You'd prefer to go to the library rather than stay at home.

W: ____

(a) It's impossible because I feel heavy there.
(b) You're right but I could've read this book yesterday.
(c) Shall we go to my house after lunch?
(d) That's right. I can't concentrate in the library.

분석 적용

집에서 공부하는 것보다 도서관에 가는 게 낫겠다는 남자의 제안에 대해 동의 또는 반대 의사를 표하는 선택지를 고르면 된다. 따라
서 답답해서 갈 수 없다고 응답한 (a)가 정답이다. (d)는 뒷부분이 I can ...이 되면 정답이 될 수 있다.

어휘

concentrate 집중하다

Part 1

Questions 1-2

Choose the most appropriate response to the statement.

1. (a)   (b)   (c)   (d)
2. (a)   (b)   (c)   (d)

Part 2

Questions 3-4

Choose the most appropriate response to complete the conversation.

3. (a)   (b)   (c)   (d)
4. (a)   (b)   (c)   (d)

1.

M: Do you think she is on our side?
W: _________________________________

(a) I don't think she is.
(b) I think she is on the other side of the wall.
(c) I don't think she is on the way.
(d) I think she is in it.

 **해설**

be on our side(우리 편에 있다)의 뜻만 안다면 쉽게 해결할 수 있는 문제다.

> **어휘**
> **be on the way** 오는 중이다

2.

W: How about going to Florida this weekend?
M: _________________________________

(a) I'm leaving later next week.
(b) It is so much fun.
(c) I have so many things to do this week.
(d) It is better to go down there next weekend.

해설

How about ... -ing?는 '~하는 게 어때?'의 뜻으로 상대방에게 어떤 것을 권유 또는 제안할 때 쓰는 표현이다. What about ... -ing?이나 Why don't you ...?도 마찬가지 표현들. 따라서 이를 받아들이거나 거절하는 내용이 담긴 선택지를 고르면 된다.

> **어휘**
> **It is better to ...** ~하는 게 더 낫다

3.

M: Let's get on that bus.
W: Didn't you say that we don't have enough time?
M: Well, I will call Charley from that bus so he can pick us up at the next station.
W: _________________________________

(a) Okay. That way we won't lose any time.
(b) I've never been on these buses.
(c) I will go over it.
(d) Let's take it out.

 **해설**

남자의 의견에 동의나 반대를 하는 내용이 담긴 선택지를 고르면 된다.

> **어휘**
>
> **station** 정류장　**lose time** 시간을 낭비하다　**go over** 검토하다　**take out** (음식 등을) 포장해 가다

4.

M: Do you know how to do this?
W: I am not sure. Maybe Jane knows how to do it.
M: She told me to follow these instructions.
W: _________________________________

(a) I saw that on the other side of the box.
(b) Let's just follow the instructions, then.
(c) It was just a few things to do.
(d) I will take care of it by myself.

 **해설**

사용 설명서대로 하라는 말을 이미 들었다고 했으므로 거기에 나온 대로 해보자는 **(b)**가 자연스럽다.

> **어휘**
>
> **follow** 따르다　**instructions** (제품 등의) 사용 설명서　**by oneself** 혼자서, 혼자 힘으로

1.

M: Do you think she is on our side?

W: _______________________________________.

2.

W: How about going to Florida this weekend?

M: _______________________________________.

3.

M: Let's get on that bus.

W: Didn't you say that we don't have enough time?

M: Well, I will call Charley from that bus so he can pick us up at the next station.

W: _______________________________________.

4.

M: Do you know how to do this?

W: I am not sure. Maybe Jane knows how to do it.

M: She told me to follow these instructions.

W: _______________________________________.

Part 1

Questions 1-3

Choose the most appropriate response to the statement.

1. (a) (b) (c) (d)
2. (a) (b) (c) (d)
3. (a) (b) (c) (d)

Part 2

Questions 4-7

Choose the most appropriate response to complete the conversation.

4. (a) (b) (c) (d)
5. (a) (b) (c) (d)
6. (a) (b) (c) (d)
7. (a) (b) (c) (d)

👉 **위로**

Way to go! 힘내!
Keep your chin up. 힘내세요.

👉 **감사**

Thank you so much for the delicious meal. 맛있는 식사 정말 감사합니다.
Thank you for coming. 와 주셔서 감사해요.
Thanks all the same. 아무튼 고맙습니다.
That's nice of you to say. 그렇게 말해 줘서 고마워요.
How nice of you to say so! 그렇게 말씀해 주시니 정말 고맙습니다.

공공안내 교통

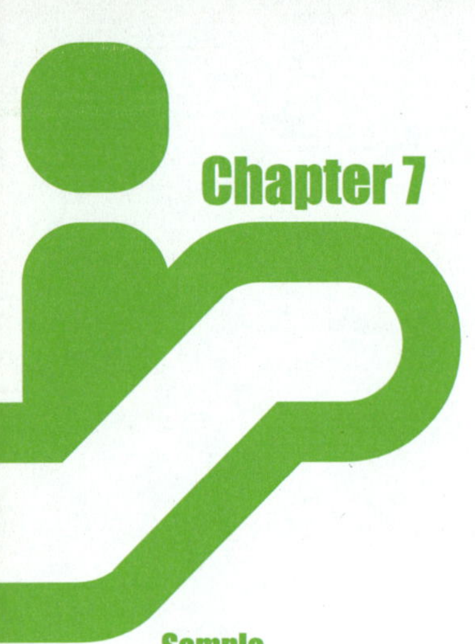

Chapter 7

출제 패턴 분석

공공장소에서의 안내와 길 묻기, 교통에 관련된 문제들은 꼭 1~2문제씩 출제되는 유형이니 주의 깊게 살펴봐야 한다. 한편, 공공안내에 관해서는 의문사로 물어보는 질문에 대한 응답이 거의 90% 이상 출제되기 때문에 그다지 어려운 부분은 아니다. 따라서 각 공공장소마다 일어날 수 있는 대화 내용들을 분류해서 잘 알아 두고, 교통에 관한 기본적인 어휘들을 습득하면 쉽게 해결할 수 있다.

Sample

M: Where can I find the phone booth here?

W: ____

(a) I'm sorry I don't think it is here.

(b) I'm afraid it is out of service.

(c) Right around the corner in this section.

(d) You will see each one of them.

 **분석 적용**

Where로 묻고 있으므로 위치에 대해 알려주는 선택지가 답이 된다. 이런 유형의 문제들은 앞의 의문사를 주의 깊게 듣는 것이 요령이다.

어휘

phone booth 공중전화 박스 **out of service** 사용되지 않는, 고장 난

Part 1

Questions 1-2

Choose the most appropriate response to the statement.

1. (a)   (b)   (c)   (d)
2. (a)   (b)   (c)   (d)

Part 2

Questions 3-4

Choose the most appropriate response to complete the conversation.

3. (a)   (b)   (c)   (d)
4. (a)   (b)   (c)   (d)

1.

M: How did you get back here?

W: ____

(a) I was on the way back.
(b) I was here a long time ago.
(c) I used bicycle to make it back here.
(d) I will get back to you later.

 **해설**

How로 물어봤으므로 교통수단을 묻는 질문임을 알 수 있다. 따라서 자전거를 탔다고 언급한 (c)가 정답이다. 참고로, 다음 표현들도 함께 알아 두자. by taxi 택시로/ by car 차로/ by bike 자전거로/ on foot 걸어서

> **어휘**
>
> **get back** 돌아가다, 돌아오다 **get back to ...** ~에게 다시 전화하다(= call ... back)

2.

M: May I help you? Are you looking for something?

W: ____

(a) I am just looking. Thanks.
(b) I was looking at that part.
(c) I just saw something small here.
(d) I am looking forward to seeing my friend.

해설

점원이 찾고 있는 물건이 있는지 묻고 있으므로 이에 답하는 선택지를 고르면 된다. I am just looking.은 '그냥 둘러보다'의 뜻으로 I am just browsing.이라고 표현하기도 한다. (b)는 과거시제를 이용한 함정.

> **어휘**
>
> **look for** ~을 찾다

3.

W: I don't think I see my bag now.

M: What was the last place right before?

W: I think I was in the furniture section.

M: _______________________________________

(a) Let me ask the saleslady there.

(b) Are you looking for some furniture?

(c) Did you want to buy a new one?

(d) What does he look like?

 해설

마지막으로 갔던 장소가 가구 코너라고 했으므로 그곳 판매 직원에게 물어보겠다는 (a)가 적절하다.

어휘

saleslady (여자) 판매원(= saleswoman)

4.

M: Do you know where she is at the moment?

W: I think she is on the way.

M: Where is she coming from?

W: _______________________________________

(a) She is on the highway.

(b) She was in a business meeting.

(c) She is in a traffic jam.

(d) She is on the way back home.

 해설

어디 있다 오는 길인지 묻고 있으므로 (b)가 정답이다.

어휘

be in a traffic jam 교통체증으로 꼼짝 못하다

1.

M: How did you get back here?

W: _______________________________________.

2.

M: May I help you? Are you looking for something?

W: _______________________________________.

3.

W: I don't think I see my bag now.

M: What was the last place right before?

W: I think I was in the furniture section.

M: _______________________________________.

4.

M: Do you know where she is at the moment?

W: I think she is on the way.

M: Where is she coming from?

W: _______________________________________.

Part 1

Questions 1-4

Choose the most appropriate response to the statement.

1. (a)   (b)   (c)   (d)
2. (a)   (b)   (c)   (d)
3. (a)   (b)   (c)   (d)
4. (a)   (b)   (c)   (d)

Part 2

Questions 5-8

Choose the most appropriate response to complete the conversation.

5. (a)   (b)   (c)   (d)
6. (a)   (b)   (c)   (d)
7. (a)   (b)   (c)   (d)
8. (a)   (b)   (c)   (d)

👉 사과

I didn't mean that. If I offended you, I apologize.
그런 뜻이 아니었어요. 기분 상하셨다면 사과드립니다.

How can I make it up to you? 어떻게 하면 화가 풀리시겠어요?

No offense. 기분 나쁘게 생각지 마라.

Sorry, I didn't mean to let you down. 미안, 실망시키려고 그런 건 아니었는데.

* let ... down ~를 실망시키다

👉 불평/질책

Easier said than done. 말이야 쉽지.

That's easy for you to say. 너야 그렇게 얘기하기 쉽겠지.

I'll let you off this time. 이번은 눈감아 주지. * let ... off ~를 봐주다

여행 · 취미

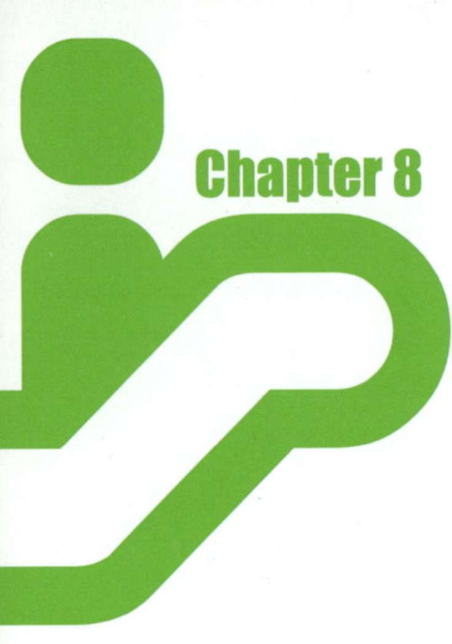

STEP 1 Pattern Study

출제 패턴 분석

여행 관련 대화는 특히 공항에서 이루어지는 경우가 많기 때문에 각 단계별 대화를 구별해서 알아 두는 것이 좋다. 예약(book a flight 비행기표를 예약하다) → 탑승(an aisle/window seat 통로/ 창문 쪽 좌석, weight limit 무게 제한) → 기내에서(remain seated 앉아 있다, will be delayed 지연될 것이다) → 입국 심사(Do you have someone[anyone] here you know? 여기 아는 사람이 있습니까?)

한편, 취미에 관한 대화는 다양하게 이루어지기 때문에 질문의 첫 부분을 주의 깊게 듣는 것이 중요하다.

Sample

M: Have you already arrived to Australia?

W: No, I just landed in Hong Kong. I think I will be here for a week.

M: Then, when are you coming back to Korea?

W: _______________________________________

(a) I don't think I will stay here.

(b) I don't go to Hong Kong around those days.

(c) I think I will be back at the end of this month.

(d) I just got back to Australia.

 **분석 적용**

When으로 물었으므로 날짜나 시기가 언급된 선택지를 고르면 된다.

어휘

land 도착하다   **around those days** 그 즈음에

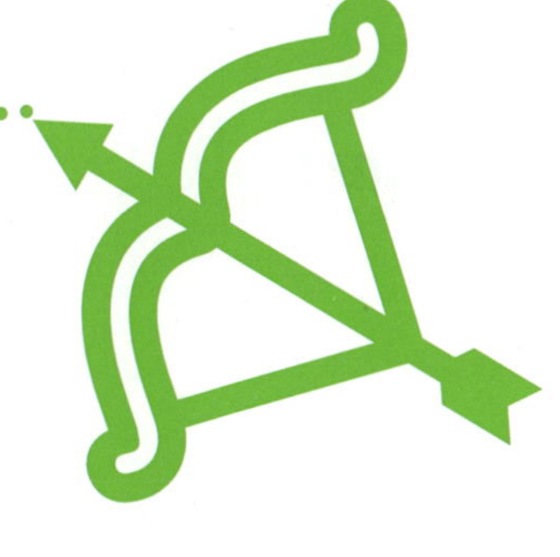

Part 1

Questions 1-2

Choose the most appropriate response to the statement.

1. (a)   (b)   (c)   (d)
2. (a)   (b)   (c)   (d)

Part 2

Questions 3-4

Choose the most appropriate response to complete the conversation.

3. (a)   (b)   (c)   (d)
4. (a)   (b)   (c)   (d)

1.

W: How long were you in Vienna?

M: _______________________________________

(a) It was an awesome place to visit.
(b) A couple of days.
(c) I was on my business trip.
(d) I took a train to travel in Vienna.

 **해설**

How long으로 물었으므로 시간이나 기간으로 응답한 선택지를 고르면 된다.

> **어휘**
> **awesome** 멋진, 굉장한 **business trip** 출장

2.

M: How do you spend your spare time?

W: _______________________________________

(a) I will put that to good use.
(b) I'm doing my laundry at the moment.
(c) I'd rather save this for next time.
(d) I usually go to the movies.

해설

여가 시간을 어떻게 보내는지 묻고 있으므로 이에 관한 내용이 담긴 선택지를 고르면 된다.

> **어휘**
> **put ... to good use** ~을 잘 이용하다 **do the laundry** 빨래하다 **go to the movies** 영화 보러 가다

3.

W: Where did you go on your trip?

M: I went to Japan, Hong Kong and Korea.

W: Three countries for 5 days? You must have been very busy.

M: ____

(a) Yes, so I stopped over in Hong Kong only for a day.

(b) Yes, it was good to see you there.

(c) Yes, I'm so excited about it.

(d) No, it was just enough to see them for a week.

해설

5일 동안 3개국을 돌아다니느라 바빴겠다고 말했으므로 이에 관한 언급이 이어져야 자연스럽다.

어휘

stop over 여행 목적지에서 잠깐 묵다[체류하다]

4.

W: When are you coming back? Bring a souvenir for us.

M: I'm sorry, but I think I won't have much time for shopping.

W: Then, take a lot of pictures to share the memories together!

M: ____

(a) Thanks. I will keep it as a souvenir.

(b) It was good to see them in person.

(c) I'm sure I will.

(d) I'm looking forward to seeing you soon.

해설

기념품 대신 함께 추억을 나눌 사진들을 많이 찍어 오라고 했으므로 이에 응하는 (c)가 적절한 정답이다.

어휘

souvenir 기념품 **in person** 직접, 몸소

1.

W: How long were you in Vienna?

M: ____.

2.

M: How do you spend your spare time?

W: ____.

3.

W: Where did you go on your trip?

M: I went to Japan, Hong Kong and Korea.

W: Three countries for 5 days? You must have been very busy.

M: ____.

4.

W: When are you coming back? Bring a souvenir for us.

M: I'm sorry, but I think I won't have much time for shopping.

W: Then, take a lot of pictures to share the memories together!

M: ____.

Part 1

Questions 1-4

Choose the most appropriate response to the statement.

1. (a)　　(b)　　(c)　　(d)
2. (a)　　(b)　　(c)　　(d)
3. (a)　　(b)　　(c)　　(d)
4. (a)　　(b)　　(c)　　(d)

Part 2

Questions 5-7

Choose the most appropriate response to complete the conversation.

5. (a)　　(b)　　(c)　　(d)
6. (a)　　(b)　　(c)　　(d)
7. (a)　　(b)　　(c)　　(d)

👉 전화 연결 시

Who do you want to speak to?
누구를 바꿔 드릴까요?
May I speak to someone in charge of marketing?
마케팅 담당하시는 분을 바꿔 주시겠습니까?
This is he/she. 전데요.
I think you've dialed the wrong number. 전화를 잘못 거신 것 같습니다.
Who's calling, please? 전화 거시는 분은 누구시죠?
This is Mary. 저는 메리입니다.
He's tied up at the moment. 그는 지금 바빠서 전화를 받을 수 없습니다.
Mr. White, Mr. Brown is on the phone. 화이트 씨, 브라운 씨는 지금 통화 중입니다.
There's no one here by that name. 그런 이름을 가진 사람은 여기 없습니다.

👉 당사자가 없을 때

She just stepped out. 그녀는 방금 나갔는데요.
She's out at the moment. 그녀는 지금 없는데요.
What time is he expected back? 그가 몇 시쯤 돌아올까요?
He's gone for the day. 그는 퇴근했는데요.
He's off today. 그는 오늘 쉽니다.
He's out of town. 그는 출장 중이세요.

👉 당사자에게 연결하기

Will you hold the line a moment, please? 잠시 기다려 주시겠어요?
Hold on./ Hang on. 잠시만 기다려 주십시오.
I'll put you through to the Export Section.
전화를 수출과로 연결해 드리겠습니다.
Mr. White, you are wanted on the phone. 화이트 씨, 전화예요.

비즈니스
학교·직장

Chapter 9

출제 패턴 분석

일에 관한 내용도 자주 출제되는 부분이다. 직장에 관해서는 구직, 면접, 승진이나 퇴직에 관한 내용들이, 학교에 대해서는 숙제, 시험 준비, 수업이나 가르치는 사람에 관한 내용들이 자주 출제 된다.

Sample

W: What was the assignment for Bio class?

M: _______________________________________

(a) I didn't prepare it either.
(b) It was good to do it.
(c) I don't know. I cut last class.
(d) It wasn't easy as pie.

분석 적용

생물 숙제가 뭐였는지 묻고 있으므로 숙제 내용이 언급돼 있거나, 또는 잘 모르겠다는 식의 응답이 담긴 선택지를 고르면 된다. Part 1, 2는 한 번밖에 들려 주지 않기 때문에 기본적인 관용어구나 관련 표현들을 특히 잘 익혀 둘 필요가 있다.

어휘

assignment 숙제   **cut** (수업을) 빼먹다   **be (as) easy as pie** 식은 죽 먹기다

Part 1

Questions 1-2

Choose the most appropriate response to the statement.

1. (a) (b) (c) (d)
2. (a) (b) (c) (d)

Part 2

Questions 3-4

Choose the most appropriate response to complete the conversation.

3. (a) (b) (c) (d)
4. (a) (b) (c) (d)

1.

M: How was the presentation about the agenda?

W: ____

(a) It was an emergency.
(b) It was a well known topic.
(c) It was good to see them in person.
(d) It went very smoothly.

 해설

발표가 어땠는지를 묻고 있으므로 이에 대해 언급한 (d)가 정답이다. (a), (b)는 안건에 관한 질문에 이어질 수 있는 응답들.

> **어휘**
>
> **presentation** 발표 **emergency** 비상사태, 위급 **smoothly** 순조롭게, 원활하게

2.

M: How's the topic on the agenda going?

W: ____

(a) It was going a bit fast.
(b) It's going so quickly.
(c) It will make a difference.
(d) It's going to be the option.

해설

안건의 주제가 어떻게 돼 가고 있는지 진행 상태를 묻고 있으므로 (b)가 정답이다. (a)는 시제를 이용한 오답.

> **어휘**
>
> **make a difference** 변화를 가져오다, 차이를 낳다 **option** 선택사항

3.

W: How are your midterms going so far?

M: I didn't have much time to review them.

W: Me neither. I'm so worried about it.

M: _______________________________________

(a) We need to cram until the very last moment.

(b) Don't worry, you will get over it.

(c) I'm sure you did your best.

(d) We will catch up soon.

 **해설**

둘 다 시험공부를 제대로 못해 걱정하고 있는 상황이므로 마지막 순간까지 공부해야 한다고 다지는 (a)가 적절한 응답이다.

어휘

midterm 중간고사 **review** 복습하다 **cram** 벼락치기하다 **get over** 극복하다

4.

M: I'm going to buy some stocks.

W: It sounds so spontaneous.

M: You should go with me.

W: _______________________________________

(a) I think that's a zero-sum game.

(b) Sorry, I'm not a risk-taker.

(c) That's a high risk, high return.

(d) I'm sorry. I'm busy right now.

해설

go with는 '~와 동행하다'란 뜻으로, 결국 같이 주식을 사자는 얘기다. 따라서 이에 대한 동의 여부가 담긴 선택지를 고르면 된다. (d)는 go with의 의미를 이용해 오답을 유도하려는 함정이므로 유의해야 한다.

어휘

stock 주식 **spontaneous** 충동적인 **zero-sum game** 제로섬 게임(득실의 합계가 항상 0이 되는 게임) **risk-taker** 모험을 즐기는 사람 **return** 수익

1.

M: How was the presentation about the agenda?

W: ____.

2.

M: How's the topic on the agenda going?

W: ____.

3.

W: How are your midterms going so far?

M: I didn't have much time to review them.

W: Me neither. I'm so worried about it.

M: ____.

4.

M: I'm going to buy some stocks.

W: It sounds so spontaneous.

M: You should go with me.

W: ____.

STEP 4 Actual Test

Questions 1-4

Choose the most appropriate response to the statement.

1. (a)   (b)   (c)   (d)
2. (a)   (b)   (c)   (d)
3. (a)   (b)   (c)   (d)
4. (a)   (b)   (c)   (d)

Questions 5-7

Choose the most appropriate response to complete the conversation.

5. (a)   (b)   (c)   (d)
6. (a)   (b)   (c)   (d)
7. (a)   (b)   (c)   (d)

👉 전화 끊기

There's someone on the other line. 다른 전화가 걸려왔어요.
Please hang up and wait till we call you back.
이쪽에서 다시 전화할 때까지 끊고 기다려 주십시오.
I'll get back to you in a while. 잠시 후에 제가 다시 걸게요.

👉 메시지 남기기

I would like to leave a message. 메시지를 남기고 싶습니다.
Could[Can, May] I leave a message (for him)?
(그에게) 메시지를 남겨도 될까요?
Would you like to leave a message for her?
그녀에게 메시지를 남겨 주시겠습니까?
Would you just tell him that I called, please?
그분에게 제가 전화했다고만 전해 주시겠습니까?
That's okay. I'll call him back later. 괜찮아요. 나중에 제가 그에게 전화할게요.
Could you tell him that I called? 제가 전화했다고 전해 주시겠어요?
Could you have him call me? 저한테 전화하라고 전해 주시겠어요?

병원·건강 미용

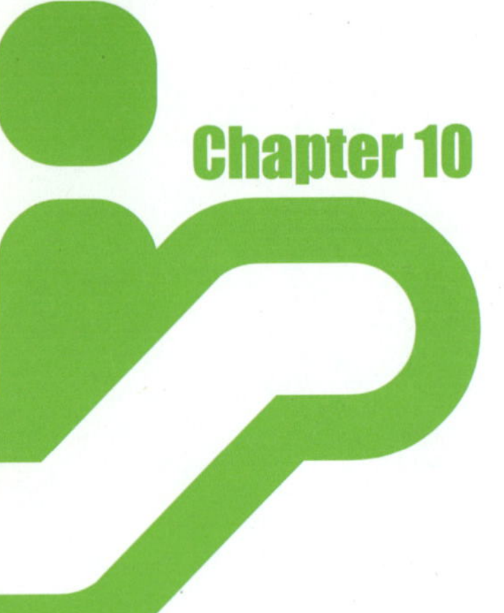

Chapter 10

출제 패턴 분석

병원, 건강, 미용 관련 영역은 자주 출제되진 않지만 어려운 표현들이 많아 놓치기 쉬운 부분이기도 하다. I feel under the weather.(몸이 안 좋아요.), I'll call in sick.(아파서 못 간다고 전화해야겠어요.), I was diagnosed with acute pneumonia.(급성폐렴으로 진단받았어요.) 등 상황별 표현들을 잘 익혀 두도록 하자.

Sample

M: Come in. What are your symptoms?

W: _______________________________________

(a) I have the chills and my head's killing me.
(b) I wrote down the patient registration form.
(c) Have you ever had an adverse reaction to any medicine?
(d) I was inoculated against the bad cold.

분석 적용

병원 관련 내용에서 가장 기본적으로 나오는 대화 유형이다. 증세를 묻고 있으므로 어디가 어떻게 아픈지 언급한 선택지를 고르면 된다.

어휘

symptom 증상　**have the chills** 오한이 나다　**kill** ~를 몹시 괴롭히다[아프게 하다]　**patient registration form** 진료 신청서　**adverse reaction** 부작용(= side effect)　**inoculate** 접종하다

Part 1

Question 1

Choose the most appropriate response to the statement.

1. (a)   (b)   (c)   (d)

Part 2

Questions 2-3

Choose the most appropriate response to complete the conversation.

2. (a)   (b)   (c)   (d)
3. (a)   (b)   (c)   (d)

1.

M: Where should I go to find Dr. Brown?

W: ____.

(a) You have to see him first.
(b) He's on the phone right now.
(c) He's on the second floor.
(d) He's doing his best for you.

해설

브라운 박사가 있는 곳을 묻고 있으므로 그가 있는 위치를 알려주는 선택지를 고르면 된다.

> **어휘**
> **be on the phone** 통화 중이다

2.

M: I'm sorry to hear that you got injured.

W: Thanks. It's getting better.

M: Can you move your left arm?

W: ____

(a) Yes, but I could barely move it last night.
(b) Thanks: I'm sure it will be alright.
(c) I'll move to another room.
(d) I have some surgery left.

해설

왼팔을 움직일 수 있는지 묻고 있으므로 Yes/No가 담긴 선택지를 고르면 된다.

> **어휘**
> **get injured** 상처를[부상을] 입다 **barely** 간신히, 겨우(= scarcely) **surgery** 수술

3.

W: Are you okay? You look a bit pale.

M: I upset my stomach by eating too much last night.

W: Did you throw up?

M: ______________________________________

(a) I have butterflies in my stomach now.

(b) I tried but no use.

(c) I will try not to eat too much anymore.

(d) It will be alright after that.

 **해설**

토했는지 묻고 있으므로 해봤지만 소용없었다는 **(b)**가 적절한 정답이다.

> **어휘**
> **throw up** 토하다 (= vomit)

1.

M: Where should I go to find Dr. Brown?

W: _______________________________.

2.

M: I'm sorry to hear that you got injured.

W: Thanks. It's getting better.

M: Can you move your left arm?

W: _______________________________.

3.

W: Are you okay? You look a bit pale.

M: I upset my stomach by eating too much last night.

W: Did you throw up?

M: _______________________________.

Questions 1-4

Choose the most appropriate response to the statement.

1. (a)   (b)   (c)   (d)
2. (a)   (b)   (c)   (d)
3. (a)   (b)   (c)   (d)
4. (a)   (b)   (c)   (d)

Questions 5-6

Choose the most appropriate response to complete the conversation.

5. (a)   (b)   (c)   (d)
6. (a)   (b)   (c)   (d)

출제 필수 표현

👉 증상/ 길/ 계획 묻기

What seems to be the problem? 뭐가 문제인 거 같아요?

→ 진료실에서 환자에게 어디가 아픈지 물을 때

Am I on the right road for Wall Street? 이 길이 월스트리트로 가는 길 맞죠?

Do you have anything planned for tomorrow?

내일 어떤 계획이라도 있습니까?

👉 이해했는지 물을 때

Do you get the picture? 이제 아시겠어요?

Are you following me? 제 말 이해되세요?

Are you with me so far? 여기까지 이해되시나요?

쇼핑 · 식당

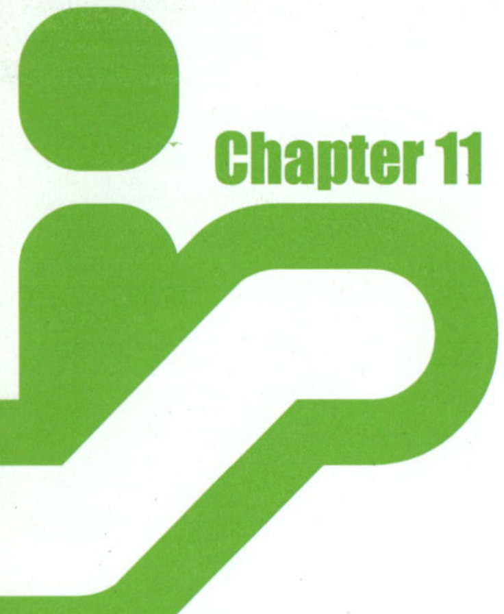

Chapter 11

출제 패턴 분석

쇼핑과 식당에서 일어나는 대화 내용은 자주 출제되는 부분 중 하나이다. 쇼핑의 경우 물건에 대한 의견을 물어보거나, 가격, 서비스에 관한 내용들이, 식당의 경우엔 예약 관련 내용이나 음식, 계산에 관한 내용들이 나오는 경우가 많다.

Sample

M: Your order included coffee. Would you like some now?

W: ____.

(a) Thank you but please without syrup.
(b) I want it. I'm dry as a bone.
(c) I love soluble coffee.
(d) No thanks, it's not enough.

분석 적용

커피를 마실 건지 묻고 있으므로 시럽을 빼고 달라고 응답한 (a)가 정답이다. (c)는 어떤 종류의 커피를 좋아하는지 묻는 질문에 대한 응답으로 가능하다. (d)는 앞뒤 문장의 호응이 맞지 않는다. No thanks, it's enough.(아니, 괜찮아요. 그걸로 충분해요.)가 돼야 옳은 표현.

어휘

be (as) dry as a bone 목이 몹시 마르다　**soluble coffee** 인스턴트 커피

Part 1

Question 1

Choose the most appropriate response to the statement.

1. (a)   (b)   (c)   (d)

Part 2

Questions 2-4

Choose the most appropriate response to complete the conversation.

2. (a)   (b)   (c)   (d)
3. (a)   (b)   (c)   (d)
4. (a)   (b)   (c)   (d)

1.

M: It was great dinner. I enjoyed it a lot.

W: _______________________________________

(a) Me too. Let me check the price.
(b) Me too. I like this place. Nice food, nice atmosphere.
(c) It was a good place to visit, though.
(d) I enjoyed myself at last night's dinner.

 **해설**

저녁 식사가 아주 훌륭했다는 소감을 말하고 있으므로 이에 관한 여자의 소감이 이어지는 것이 자연스럽다.

어휘
atmosphere 분위기

2.

W: What's today's special menu?

M: _______________________________________

(a) We have only two meals today.
(b) It's a turkey with sweet potatoes and cranberry sauce.
(c) It's only for lunch time.
(d) It's available until 6 p.m.

 **해설**

오늘의 특별 메뉴가 뭔지 묻고 있으므로 메뉴가 언급된 선택지를 고르면 된다.

어휘
sweet potato 고구마 **cranberry** 크랜베리 열매

3.

M: May I help you?
W: Thanks. I'm looking for a dress for my sister's wedding.
M: You can see a variety of styles.
W: ______________________________________

(a) I like your style, too.
(b) I think the brown looks well on her.
(c) I like seeing the dress on you.
(d) Can I try the dress in blue over there?

 **해설**

여동생의 결혼식에 입고 갈 드레스를 고르고 있는 상황이므로 (d)가 적절하다.

> **어휘**
>
> **a variety of** 다양한, 갖가지 **look well on** 잘 어울리다

4.

W: Can I get the check please?
M: Sure, here you are.
W: Is the service charge included in the bill already?
M: ______________________________________

(a) The tip is usually part of the bill.
(b) It's on me today.
(c) It's 15 to 20 percent of the bill.
(d) I think it's overpriced.

 **해설**

계산서에 봉사료가 포함돼 있는지 묻고 있으므로 이에 관해 언급한 선택지를 고르면 된다.

> **어휘**
>
> **check** 계산서, 청구서(= bill) **service charge** 봉사료 **overpriced** 너무 비싼

1.

M: It was great dinner. I enjoyed it a lot.

W: ____.

2.

W: What's today's special menu?

M: ____.

3.

M: May I help you?

W: Thanks. I'm looking for a dress for my sister's wedding.

M: You can see a variety of styles.

W: ____?

4.

W: Can I get the check please?

M: Sure, here you are.

W: Is the service charge included in the bill already?

M: ____.

STEP 4 Actual Test

Questions 1-4

Choose the most appropriate response to the statement.

1. (a)   (b)   (c)   (d)
2. (a)   (b)   (c)   (d)
3. (a)   (b)   (c)   (d)
4. (a)   (b)   (c)   (d)

Questions 5-7

Choose the most appropriate response to complete the conversation.

5. (a)   (b)   (c)   (d)
6. (a)   (b)   (c)   (d)
7. (a)   (b)   (c)   (d)

출제 필수 표현

👉 반대/ 부정

No, I don't suppose so. 아니오, 전 그렇게 생각하지 않아요.
It's the other way around. 그 반대예요.
I don't see it that way. 저는 그렇게 보지 않아요.
Over my dead body!/ Not in a million years! 절대 안 돼!

👉 동감

Quite so. 정말 그렇군.
I suppose you're right. 네 말이 맞는 것 같아.
You took the words right out of my mouth. 내 말이 바로 그 말이에요.
I can't agree with you more. 전적으로 동의합니다.
You can say that again. 저도 같은 의견이에요.

👉 확신

I'm for sure. 확신해요.
That'll be all right. 당연하죠.

의문사

Chapter 12

출제 패턴 분석

가장 기본적인 의문사인 What, Where, When, Why, Who, How로 묻는 문제들은 반드시
맞춰야 하는 질문 유형으로, 항상 문장 앞부분을 유심히 들어야 한다. 또한 복합 의문사인 How
come, Why don't you, How long, How often 질문 유형에 대한 응답도 잘 알아 두도록
하자.

Sample

M: When is the best time to visit Seoul?

W: ___________________________________

(a) It's fall season. You will be attracted by autumn colors.

(b) There's around ten minutes left.

(c) Could you mark it on my diary?

(d) I visit with Jenny from time to time.

분석 적용

When은 때를 묻는 의문사로 시간이나 시기가 언급된 선택지를 고르면 된다. 따라서 정답은 (a).

어휘

be attracted by ~에 마음을 빼앗기다, 매료되다 **autumn colors** 단풍, 가을빛 **from time to time** 때때로

Part 1

Question 1

Choose the most appropriate response to the statement.

1. (a)   (b)   (c)   (d)

Part 2

Questions 2-4

Choose the most appropriate response to complete the conversation.

2. (a)   (b)   (c)   (d)
3. (a)   (b)   (c)   (d)
4. (a)   (b)   (c)   (d)

1.

W: What are those for?

M: ___________________________________

(a) Those are five pieces of equipment.
(b) Those are some tools for my father.
(c) They have been together for four years.
(d) Those are my four bags.

 **해설**

물건의 용도를 묻고 있으므로 이에 관해 언급한 선택지를 고르면 된다.

> **어휘**
> **equipment** 장비, 비품 **tool** 도구

2.

W: Are you looking for something?
M: Nothing. I just saw someone passing by.
W: Who was that?
M: ___________________________________

(a) It was something big.
(b) I felt as if he was my acquaintance.
(c) I'm just looking for my friend.
(d) She will be here soon.

 **해설**

본 사람이 누군지 묻고 있으므로 그 사람에 대해 언급한 (b)가 정답이다.

> **어휘**
> **pass by** 지나가다 **feel as if ...** 마치 ~처럼 느끼다 **acquaintance** 아는 사람

3.

M: Haven't you read that one already?
W: The librarian lady wouldn't let me take that one.
M: Why wouldn't she let you take it?
W: _______________________________________

(a) She said it was too boring.
(b) I think she doesn't want me to buy it.
(c) She doesn't allow me to do that.
(d) I think that story of the book is quite complicated.

해설

도서관 사서가 책을 못 빌려가게 한 이유를 묻고 있으므로 이에 관해 언급한 선택지를 고르면 된다.

어휘
librarian 도서관 사서   **complicated** 복잡한

4.

M: Is Mrs. Sandy there? I have a package.
W: That's me. Thank you for delivering.
M: Where do I put this package?
W: _______________________________________

(a) Would you just put it here?
(b) I don't mind. You may choose what you want.
(c) I know it was delivered free.
(d) Don't mention it. It's my job.

해설

소포를 어디에 둘지 묻고 있으므로 장소가 언급된 선택지를 고르면 된다. **(d)**의 경우, 배달해 줘서 고맙다는 말 뒤에 이어질 수 있는 응답 표현이다.

어휘
package 소포   **deliver** 배달하다

1.

W: What are those for?

M: _________________________________.

2.

W: Are you looking for something?

M: Nothing. I just saw someone passing by.

W: Who was that?

M: _________________________________.

3.

M: Haven't you read that one already?

W: The librarian lady wouldn't let me take that one.

M: Why wouldn't she let you take it?

W: _________________________________.

4.

M: Is Mrs. Sandy there? I have a package.

W: That's me. Thank you for delivering.

M: Where do I put this package?

W: _______________________________?

Part 1

Questions 1-5

Choose the most appropriate response to the statement.

1. (a)   (b)   (c)   (d)
2. (a)   (b)   (c)   (d)
3. (a)   (b)   (c)   (d)
4. (a)   (b)   (c)   (d)
5. (a)   (b)   (c)   (d)

Part 2

Questions 6-7

Choose the most appropriate response to complete the conversation.

6. (a)   (b)   (c)   (d)
7. (a)   (b)   (c)   (d)

출제 필수 표현

👉 **운전**

Can I take it for a road test? 도로에서 시험운전 해봐도 되나요?
Can I take it for a test drive? 시험운전 해봐도 되나요?

👉 **교통 – 기차/ 버스/ 택시**

Where's the end of this line? 이 기차의 종착역은 어딥니까?
Take the cross-town bus which goes to 34th Street.
34번가로 가는 시내 횡단 버스를 타십시오.
How much is the fare to Washington D.C.? 워싱턴까지 요금이 얼마죠?
Where is the taxi stand? 택시 타는 곳은 어딥니까?
Will you take me to this address? 이 주소로 데려다 주시겠습니까?

👉 **교통 혼잡**

Cars are bumper-to-bumper on any road on weekdays.
평일에는 어느 도로에든 차가 빽빽하게 밀려 있죠. * bumper-to-bumper 자동차가 꽉 들어찬
Traffic was murder. 교통 체증이 가히 살인적이었어.

대화문 주제 파악하기

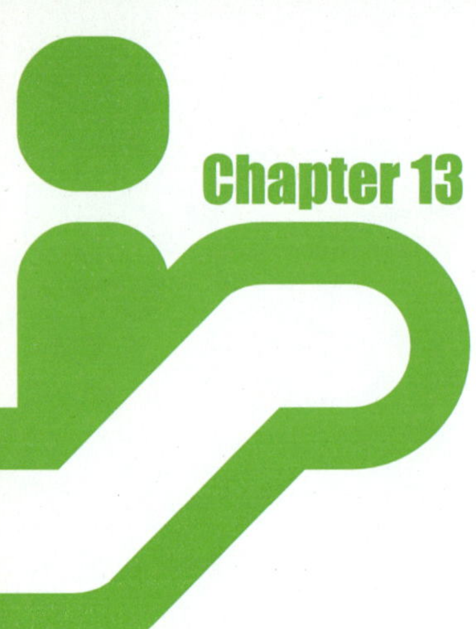

Chapter 13

출제 패턴 분석

대화 주제 파악하기는 Part 3에서 가장 많이 출제되는 문제 유형으로, 대화 내용은 Part 1, 2에서 다뤘던 주제들로 이루어진다. 주로 첫 번째 대사에 핵심 내용이 들어 있기 때문에 이 부분을 주의 깊게 들어야 한다.

Sample

M: I'd like to make a store's membership card.

W: Please fill out this paper.

M: Ok. Then, how could I make an addition to a family membership card?

W: Um... how many families do you have?

M: I have four.

W: If you want it, you should have a copy of the resident registration.

M: Well. Can I submit it later?

W: No problem.

Q. **What is the main topic of the conversation?**

(a) Creating the membership card

(b) Joining the store's new employee

(c) Going to the shopping with family

(d) Submitting the contract

 **분석 적용**

남자의 첫 번째 대사에서 상점 회원카드를 만들고 싶다는 내용이 나오고, 대화 전반에 걸쳐 카드 발급에 관한 질문과 대답이 오가고 있으므로 **(a)**가 정답이다.

어휘

fill out ~를 작성하다　**make an addition** 추가하다　**a copy of the resident registration** 주민등록 등본 1통　**submit** 제출하다

Part 3

Questions 1-2

Choose the option that the best answers the question.

1. (a) (b) (c) (d)
2. (a) (b) (c) (d)

1.

M: Lisa! Why don't you turn the radio off while you are sleeping? Mom agreed, too.

W: Dad, I couldn't sleep without the radio and headphones aren't good for my ears.

M: But I can't sleep well. How about turning down the radio a little bit?

W: All right, then. I'll do it tonight.

M: Good girl. If you keep your word, I'll buy you a new radio.

W: Really? Yes! Thank you dad!

Q. **What is the main focus of the conversation?**

(a) The radio hinders the man from sleeping.

(b) The headphones were broken by the man.

(c) The woman wants to buy a new radio.

(d) The man suffers from insomnia.

 **해설**

대화 첫 부분에 남자가 여자에게 라디오를 꺼 달라고 부탁하는 내용이 나온다. 하지만 여자가 이를 받아들이지 않자 잠을 잘 수 없으니 볼륨이라도 줄여 달라고 다시 부탁하는 것으로 보아 (a)가 정답임을 알 수 있다.

어휘

turn down 볼륨을 줄이다   **keep one's word** 약속을 지키다   **hinder A from B** A가 B하는 것을 방해하다

insomnia 불면증

2.

M: Good afternoon, ma'am.

W: Hi. I've booked a table for three yesterday.

M: OK. What is your name?

W: I'm Kathy.

M: Sorry, your name doesn't exist in the list. Just a moment, please. I'll check again. Oh, your reservation is made tomorrow.

W: Is it? I don't believe it. Then, how long is the wait?

M: Um. Maybe you should wait about 20 minutes.

W: All right. Put me on the waiting list.

Q. What is the main focus of the conversation?

(a) The woman made a wrong reservation.

(b) The woman misunderstood the man's words.

(c) The man is going to be waiting for 20 minutes.

(d) The man serves the woman's table.

 **해설**

대화 초반부를 통해 음식점에서 대화가 이루어지고 있음을 알 수 있다. 미리 예약을 하고 왔는데 확인해 보니 날짜가 내일로 잘못 잡혀 있다는 내용이므로 **(a)**가 정답이다.

어휘
book 예약하다 **exist** 있다, 존재하다

1.

M: Lisa! _________________________________ while you are sleeping? Mom agreed, too.

W: Dad, I couldn't sleep without the radio and headphones aren't good for my ears.

M: But I can't sleep well. ____?

W: All right, then. I'll do it tonight.

M: Good girl. _____________________________________.

W: Really? Yes! Thank you dad!

2.

M: Good afternoon, ma'am.

W: Hi. _________________________________.

M: OK. What is your name?

W: I'm Kathy.

M: Sorry, your name doesn't exist in the list. Just a moment, please. I'll check again. _________________________________.

W: Is it? I don't believe it. Then, how long is the wait?

M: Um. Maybe you should wait about 20 minutes.

W: All right. _____________________________.

Questions 1-6

Choose the option that the best answers the question.

1. (a)   (b)   (c)   (d)
2. (a)   (b)   (c)   (d)
3. (a)   (b)   (c)   (d)
4. (a)   (b)   (c)   (d)
5. (a)   (b)   (c)   (d)
6. (a)   (b)   (c)   (d)

출제 필수 표현

👉 **비행기**

How can I get my seat to recline?
좌석을 눕히려면 어떻게 해야 하나요?
Are you serving a meal on this flight?
기내에서 식사가 제공됩니까?

👉 **환전/ 수화물/ 출입국**

What's a dollar worth in won? 1달러에 얼마입니까?
I would like to cash a traveler's check.
여행자 수표를 현금으로 바꾸고 싶습니다.
Do you want to check that bag in or take it on board?
그 가방을 짐칸에 실으시겠어요, 아니면 기내에 들고 가시겠어요?
What's the purpose of the trip? 여행 목적이 무엇입니까?
Do you have anything to declare? 신고하실 물건이 있습니까?

👉 **호텔**

I'd like a room with a view of the ocean.
바다가 보이는 방을 원합니다.
Could I leave some of my valuables in the hotel safe?
귀중품 몇 개를 호텔 금고에 맡길 수 있겠습니까?
You made 200 dollars deposit, so the total is 600 dollars.
200달러를 예치하셨으므로, 합계 600달러입니다.
What time is check-in? 몇 시에 체크인합니까?
What is the rate for a room per night? 하룻밤 방값이 얼마입니까?

대화문 세부 내용 파악하기

Chapter 14

출제 패턴 분석

대화의 세부 내용을 묻는 문제도 출제 비중이 높은 편이다. 세부적인 내용을 잘 기억해야 하기 때문에 다소 어려울 수도 있지만, 마지막까지 선택지를 소거하는 방식으로 문제를 풀어 나가면 쉽게 해결할 수 있다. 특히 남자와 여자의 대화 내용을 잘 구별해 듣도록 하자.

Sample

M: Hi, Marry. Where are you going now?

W: I'm going to the fair next to the beach. Where are you going?

M: I'm going home.

W: Are you free? Can you come with me?

M: I'd love to go with you but I'm not dressing up now.

W: It doesn't matter. Let's go! There is a big performance today.

M: Really? I should go there.

W: It must be fun!

Q. **Why didn't the man want to go to the fair at first?**

(a) Because of the man's appointment
(b) Because of the man's appearance
(c) Because of the woman's complaints
(d) Because of the woman's urging words

분석 적용

남자의 세 번째 대사를 보면, 같이 가고 싶지만 옷을 제대로 차려입지 않았다는 내용이 나오므로 (b)가 정답임을 알 수 있다.

어휘

fair 박람회 **beach** 바닷가, 해변 **dress up** 차려입다, 꾸미다 **performance** 공연, 행사 **appearance** 외관, 겉모습 **complaint** 불평 **urging** 재촉하는, 성가신

Part 3

Questions 1-2

Choose the option that the best answers the question.

1. (a)　　(b)　　(c)　　(d)
2. (a)　　(b)　　(c)　　(d)

1.

M: Hello. How do you do?

W: Hi, are you Mike, John's friend? John said that you are his best friend.

M: Right. May I come in your house?

W: Sure. Come in. John is taking a shower now. Would you like to drink some coke or juice?

M: Thanks. I'll have juice, please. Are those John's pictures?

W: Yes. He was a junior baseball player.

M: Wow, I've never heard before.

Q. Which is correct according to the conversation?

(a) The man visited his friend's house.

(b) The man became a baseball player.

(c) The woman invited the man.

(d) The woman moved to a new house.

해설

여자의 첫 번째 대사를 통해 남자가 존의 친구임을 알 수 있으며, 바로 이어지는 남자의 대사에서 집에 들어가도 되는지 묻고 있으므로 정답은 (a)다.

어휘
coke 콜라   junior baseball player 청소년 야구 선수

2.

M: Hi. Long time no see, Jenny.

W: Long time no see, Brian. I heard you traveled in Australia.

M: Yes. My grandfather has been living for three years. So I went there with my family.

W: Great. How was Australia? I've never traveled overseas.

M: Haven't you? It was amazing. I saw many koalas. Oh, this is a present for you.

W: Thank you! It's a koala doll. What a cute doll!

M: I'm happy you like it.

Q. Which is correct according to the conversation?

    (a) The woman loves traveling.

    (b) The woman had crush on him.

    (c) The man took a journey.

    (d) The man is going to go abroad.

 **해설**

가족과 함께 호주에 갔었다는 얘기가 나오므로 정답은 (c)다.

> **어휘**
>
> **amazing** 놀랄 만한, 굉장한　**have crush on** ~에게 홀딱 반하다　**take[make] a journey** 여행을 하다　**go abroad** 해외로 가다

1.

M: Hello. How do you do?

W: Hi, are you Mike, John's friend? ___________________________.

M: Right. May I come in your house?

W: Sure. Come in. John is taking a shower now. ___________________________?

M: Thanks. I'll have juice, please. Are those John's picture?

W: Yes. ___________________________.

M: Wow, I've never heard before.

2.

M: Hi. Long time no see, Jenny.

W: Long time no see, Brian. _________________________________.

M: Yes. My grandfather has been living for three years. So I went there with my family.

W: Great. _________________? I've never traveled overseas.

M: Haven't you? It was amazing. I saw many koalas. Oh, this is a present for you.

W: Thank you! It's a koala doll. What a cute doll!

M: I'm happy you like it.

Questions 1-6

Choose the option that the best answers the question.

1. (a)   (b)   (c)   (d)
2. (a)   (b)   (c)   (d)
3. (a)   (b)   (c)   (d)
4. (a)   (b)   (c)   (d)
5. (a)   (b)   (c)   (d)
6. (a)   (b)   (c)   (d)

👉 구직/ 이직/ 취업

I'm self-employed. 자영업을 하고 있습니다.

I'm between jobs. 일자리를 구하고 있는 중이에요.

What line of work are you in? 어떤 종류의 일을 하고 계십니까?

The newcomer will arrive in two weeks.

신입사원은 2주 후에 올 겁니다.

I turned down the offer. 일자리를 거절했어요.

I got a better offer. 더 좋은 자리를 제안받았어요.

Are you willing to relocate? 근무지를 옮겨도 괜찮으시겠습니까?

I'm taking my time as it's a big decision.

중요한 결정이라 천천히 생각 중이에요.

We have a compulsory health insurance system for employees.

종업원들은 의무적으로 의료보험에 가입하게 되어 있습니다.

The amount of paid holidays depends on the length of service.

유급 휴가 일수는 근무 연한에 따라 다릅니다.

대화문 내용 추론하기

Chapter 15

출제 패턴 분석

대화 내용을 추론하는 문제는 난이도가 높은 편이다. 출제 비중은 낮지만 배정된 점수가 높기 때문에 신경 써야 한다. 지문에 직접적인 단서가 바로 나오는 경우가 드물기 때문에 특히 첫 문장과 마지막 문장을 주의 깊게 듣도록 하자.

Sample

W: Hey, Jim! How was your ice hockey game?

M: I lost by a neck. Don't say anything.

W: Oh, I'm so sorry but your team was getting the lead in the match 20 minutes ago.

M: Right. But we had a swollen head. Finally, we suffered a reversal.

W: Your team is always doing well, so you'll win next time. I'll go to cheer you.

M: Thank you very much.

Q.   What can be inferred from the conversation?

(a) The woman is a hockey player.
(b) There is another match this afternoon.
(c) The man got an injured head in the middle of the game.
(d) The woman will go to the next game.

 **분석 적용**

여자의 마지막 대사에 응원하러 가겠다는 내용이 나오므로 다음번 시합을 보러 갈 것임을 알 수 있다.

어휘

lose by a neck 아깝게 지다   **get the lead** ~에 앞서다   **have a swollen head** 자만하다   **suffer a reversal** 패배하다

Questions 1-2

Choose the option that the best answers the question.

1. (a)   (b)   (c)   (d)
2. (a)   (b)   (c)   (d)

1.

M: Kate! You said that there is a Hot pizza place downtown. Could you give me directions in detail?

W: Of course. You know the R&E building, don't you?

M: Ah, is that on the Main street?

W: Right. Turn right in front of the building, then go straight two blocks and it's next to the drug store. Probably many people are in line.

M: Thank you. I'm looking forward to having a pizza.

W: I'm sure you'll be a patron like me.

M: So will I. Go with me next time.

Q. **What can be inferred from the conversation?**

(a) The woman goes to the pizza store frequently.
(b) The building is next to the pizza store.
(c) The woman is going to take a walk.
(d) The man refused the woman's proposal.

해설

여자의 마지막 대사에서, 자기처럼 단골(patron)이 될 거라고 말하는 것으로 보아 (a)가 정답임을 알 수 있다.

> **어휘**
> **in detail** 상세히 **be in line** 줄 서다 **patron** 단골손님(= regular) **take a walk** 산책하다

2.

M: Hello. Could you help me?

W: Sure. What can I do for you?

M: My name is Jake. I heard that your hospital is looking for Dr. White's assistant. I want to apply.

W: Do you have your resume?

M: Yes. here.

W: Ok. If you pass the document, I'll call you for an interview date.

M: I'm sorry, but do you know when he will decide the date exactly?

W: Maybe we'll notice it to you before this Friday.

Q.　What can be inferred from the conversation?

(a) The woman is working in the hospital.
(b) The woman helped the man's inconvenience.
(c) The man is going to an interview this Friday.
(d) The woman promised to call the man.

 **해설**

남자의 두 번째 대사 중 I hear that your hospital is looking for ... 부분을 통해 여자가 이 병원에 근무하고 있음을 짐작할 수 있다. 따라서 정답은 (a)가 된다.

어휘
assistant 조수, 보조자　**pass the document** 서류전형에 합격하다　**inconvenience** 불편함

1.

M: Kate! ____. Could you give
  me directions in detail?

W: Of course. You know the R&E building, don't you?

M: Ah, is that on the Main street?

W: Right. ____.
  Probably many people are in line.

M: Thank you. I'm looking forward to having a pizza.

W: I'm sure you'll be a patron like me.

M: So will I. Go with me next time.

2.

M: Hello. Could you help me?

W: Sure. What can I do for you?

M: My name is Jake. ____.
  I want to apply.

W: Do you have your resume?

M: Yes. here.

W: Ok. If you pass the document, I'll call you for an interview date.

M: ____?

W: Maybe we'll notice it to you before this Friday.

Questions 1-5

Choose the option that the best answers the question.

1. (a) (b) (c) (d)
2. (a) (b) (c) (d)
3. (a) (b) (c) (d)
4. (a) (b) (c) (d)
5. (a) (b) (c) (d)

출제 필수 표현

👉 학교

What year[grade] are you in? 몇 학년이에요?
I have to stay up late to cram for my midterm.
중간고사 벼락치기 공부를 해야 해서 밤늦게까지 못 자.
I messed up my final. 기말고사를 망쳤어.
I blew the math exam today. 오늘 수학시험을 망쳤어.
I flunked math. 수학에서 낙제했어.

👉 우체국/ 은행

Please send this by parcel post. 이것을 소포로 보내 주십시오.
A regular savings account, please. 보통예금 계좌로 해주세요.
I want a savings account, please. 예금 계좌를 원합니다.
What's the remittance charge? 송금 수수료는 얼마입니까?

담화문 요지 파악하기

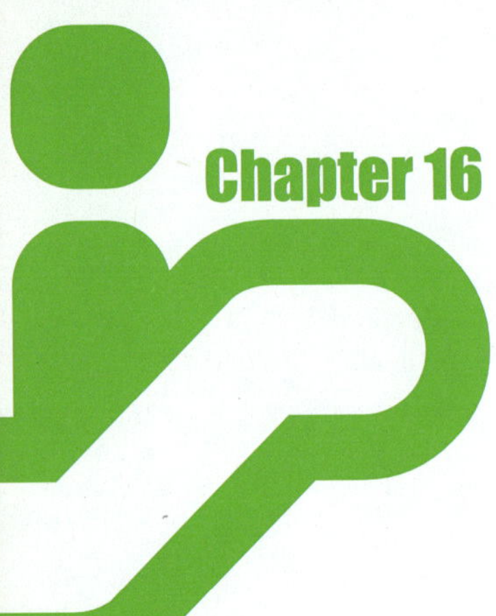

Chapter 16

출제 패턴 분석

Part 4에서 가장 많이 출제되는 유형으로, 첫 문장이나 마지막 문장에서 단서를 얻을 수 있기 때문에 그 두 부분을 특히 주의 깊게 들어야 한다.

Sample

Is there a way to get some additional protection from a tornado? Is it practical to build a bomb-shelter type structure on our property? When the weather is calm it seems foolish to think this way. But when the wind was howling we couldn't help thinking that all the money in the world wouldn't save us if a tornado hits our house — especially now that the weather patterns seem to bring more violent storms.

Q. **What is the main point of the talk?**

(a) How to protect from a tornado
(b) How to keep your money from a misfortune
(c) How to repair the way after the tornado
(d) How to predict a tornado

분석 적용

폭풍으로부터 보호받을 수 있는 방법이 있는지, 그리고 공습대피소 같은 건물을 짓는 것이 실용적인지 질문을 던짐으로써 글을 시작하고 있다. 또 마지막 부분에서 맹렬한 바람이 불어대는 날씨엔 그 같은 대피 건물에 대한 생각을 더욱더 하게 된다고 했으므로 정답은 (a)가 된다.

어휘

additional 추가적인 **tornado** 토네이도, 폭풍 **practical** 실용적인 **bomb-shelter** 공습대피소 **structure** 건물 **property** 토지, 자산, 소유물 **calm** 고요한, 잔잔한 **howl** (바람 등이) 세차게 불다 **can't help -ing** ~할 수밖에 없다 **violent storm** 맹렬한[심한] 폭풍우 **misfortune** 재난, 불운 **predict** 예측하다

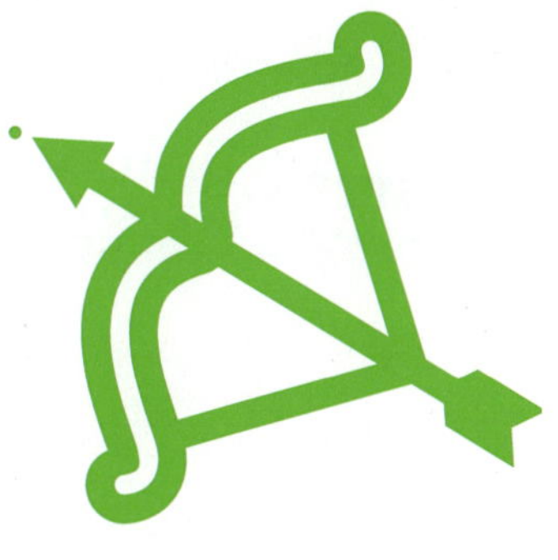

Questions 1-2

Choose the option that the best answers the question.

1. (a)   (b)   (c)   (d)
2. (a)   (b)   (c)   (d)

1.

We live in this country. There is no gas service on our street, so everything in our house runs on electricity. Our bills are absolutely killing us! $312 in July; $283 in August. We don't even have air conditioning. We have an in-ground pool, a freezer, an electric water heater, and have to run a dehumidifier in the basement. But other than that, we're not at home during the day and turn off lights whenever we leave rooms at night. So where is all the electricity going?

Q. **What is the main idea of the talk?**

(a) The speaker doesn't know why the electricity bill is too expensive.
(b) The speaker should pay a lot of electricity bill due to an air conditioning.
(c) The speaker is trying to economize in electricity.
(d) The government is going to raise the electricity charge.

해설

화자는 집에서 전기 기구를 많이 사용하지 않음에도 지나치게 많은 전기세가 청구되는 것에 의문을 갖고 있다. 마지막 문장이 의문형으로 끝났으므로 이는 그 이유를 모르겠다는 의미를 나타내며, 이것이 곧 이 글의 요지가 된다.

어휘

electricity 전기　**kill** (사람에게) 격심한 고통을 주다　**in-ground pool** 땅을 파서 설치한 수영장　**freezer** 냉동고
electric water heater 전기 온수기　**dehumidifier** 제습기　**basement** 지하실　**other than that** 그것 말고는
during the day 낮 동안, 낮 시간에　**economize** 절약하다　**raise** 올리다

2.

The most important way to take care of your skin is to protect it from the sun. Ultraviolet light — the invisible but intense rays from the sun — damages your skin, causing deep wrinkles, dry, rough skin, liver spots, and more serious disorders, such as noncancerous and cancerous skin tumors. In fact, most of the changes seen in aging skin are actually caused by a lifetime of sun exposure.

Q. **What is the main point of the talk?**

(a) Sunlight is harmful to your health.
(b) Basking in the sun is the best way to protect your skin.
(c) It is true that whoever doesn't want to grow old.
(d) The aging process of skin is caused by sunlight.

해설

자외선이 피부에 미치는 악영향에 대해 열거한 글이다. 이 글의 요지 역시 맨 마지막 문장에 나와 있다. In fact라는 표현을 사용하여 피부 노화의 변화는 태양에 노출된 수명에 의해 발생한다는 사실을 강조하고 있다.

어휘

ultraviolet light 자외선 **invisible** 눈에 보이지 않는 **intense** 강렬한 **rays** 광선, 빛 **damage** 손상시키다 **wrinkle** 주름 **rough** 거친 **liver spots** 기미 **disorder** (심신 기능의) 장애, (가벼운) 병 **noncancerous skin tumor** 양성 피부 종양 **cancerous skin tumor** 악성 피부 종양 **aging skin** 노화 피부 **be caused by** ~에 기인하다, ~이 원인이다 **lifetime** 수명 **exposure** 노출 **be harmful to** ~에 해롭다 **bask in the sun** 햇볕을 쬐다

1.

We live in this country. ______________________________________, so everything in our house runs on electricity. Our bills are absolutely killing us! $312 in July; $283 in August. We don't even have air conditioning. We have an in-ground pool, a freezer, an electric water heater, and have to run a dehumidifier in the basement. But other than that, we're not at home during the day and ____________________________. ______________________________________?

2.

______________________________________ is to protect it from the sun. Ultraviolet light — the invisible but intense rays from the sun — damages your skin, causing deep wrinkles, dry, rough skin, liver spots, and more serious disorders, such as noncancerous and cancerous skin tumors. In fact, ____________________________ ______________________________________.

Questions 1-6

Choose the option that the best answers the question.

1. (a)   (b)   (c)   (d)
2. (a)   (b)   (c)   (d)
3. (a)   (b)   (c)   (d)
4. (a)   (b)   (c)   (d)
5. (a)   (b)   (c)   (d)
6. (a)   (b)   (c)   (d)

👉 감기/ 두통

I have a nose cold. 코감기에 걸렸습니다.
I have a headache/migraine. 두통/편두통이 있어요.
I have a running nose. 콧물이 흘러요.
I have a stuffy nose. 코가 막혀요.
I have a sore throat. 목이 아파요.
I have swollen tonsils. 편도선이 부었습니다.
I feel chilly. 오한이 납니다.
I have a splitting headache. 머리가 깨질 듯이 아파요.

👉 변비/ 복통/ 숙취

I suffer from chronic constipation. 만성 변비로 고생하고 있어요.
I have an upset stomach. 배탈이 났습니다.
I feel like vomiting[throwing up]. 토할 것 같아요.
I have diarrhea. 설사를 해요.
I have an acute[sharp] stomachache. 배가 심하게 아파요.
I have a hangover. 숙취가 있어요.

👉 어깨 결림/ 요통

I've got a stiff shoulder./ My shoulders are stiff. 어깨가 결립니다.
I have a stiff shoulder. 어깨가 뻐근해요.
I have a backache. 등이 아파요.
I'm in pains all around the waist. 허리 주변이 다 아파요.

담화문 내용 파악하기

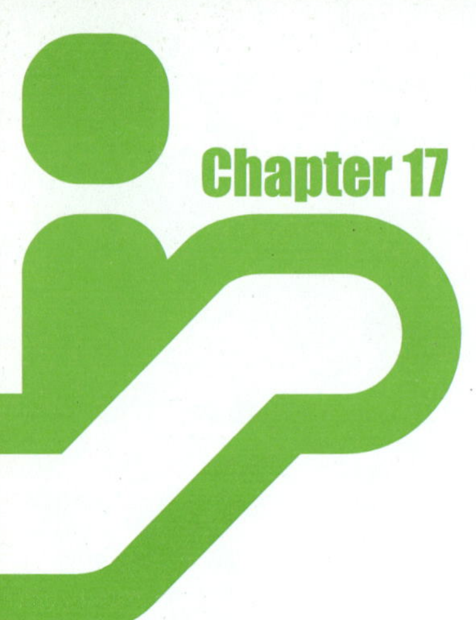

STEP 1 Pattern Study

출제 패턴 분석

Part 4에서 담화문의 요지를 파악하는 문제 다음으로 출제 비중이 높은 영역으로, 질문 유형이 다양하게 나올 수 있다. 담화문의 특정 부분만을 듣고는 질문에 대한 답을 찾기가 쉽지 않기 때문에 담화문의 내용을 전체적으로 주의 깊게 잘 듣고 질문의 내용을 들은 다음, 하나하나씩 선택지를 소거하는 방식으로 문제를 해결해 나가야 한다.

Sample

A Vancouver boy was injured today when he rode his bicycle through a stop sign and collided with a Tran bus, police said. Matthew, a seventh-grader at Vancouver School of Arts and Academics, was in serious condition at Legacy Emanuel Children's Hospital after the 9:24 a.m. collision.

Q. **Which of the following is true according to the report?**

(a) The boy was taken to the hospital.
(b) The police discovered the accident first.
(c) The bus drove through a red light.
(d) There were two witnesses at the road.

분석 적용

글 마지막 부분을 통해 병원에 있음을 알 수 있으므로 정답은 (a)다. (b), (d)는 알 수 없는 내용이며, (c)는 소년이 정지 신호를 무시하고 가다가 버스와 충돌한 것이므로 내용에 어긋난다.

어휘

injured 부상당한   **through a stop sign** 정지 신호를 무시하고   **collide with** ~와 충돌하다   **be in serious condition** 중태이다   **witness** 목격자

Questions 1-2

Choose the option that the best answers the question.

1. (a)   (b)   (c)   (d)
2. (a)   (b)   (c)   (d)

1.

A fast-paced, growing importer is looking for an energetic accounting assistant to join our team. Candidates should have at least 3 years of experience in accounts payable and accounts receivable. Candidates should have a positive attitude, be multi-task oriented and possess a sense of urgency. Please submit resume with salary requirements to denny@brain.com.

Q. **Which of the following is NOT true according to the advertisement?**

(a) The firm wants a staff to have good computer skills.
(b) Applicants should have experiences in the same market.
(c) Candidates who are interested in this ad can send a resume by e-mail.
(d) The company is looking for an accounting assistant.

해설

이 회사는 회계 보조를 찾고 있으며 그 분야에서 3년 이상의 유경험자를 원하고 있다. 또 메일 주소를 알려주면서 이력서를 제출하라고 했으므로 정답은 (a)다. 컴퓨터 능력에 대해선 언급돼 있지 않으므로 글 내용에 어긋난다.

어휘
fast-paced 속도가 빠른, 빨리 진행되는 **growing** 성장하는 **importer** 수입자, 수입업체 **energetic** 열정적인, 활기에 찬 **accounting assistant** 회계 보조 **accounts payable** 지급 계정 **accounts receivable** 수취 계정 **candidate** 후보자, 지원자 **multi-task oriented** 다중 업무 처리 능력을 지향하는 **possess** 소유하다, 지니다 **a sense of urgency** 위기 의식, 절박감 **salary requirements** 희망 연봉

2.

Now, anyone can book a tee time — and lodging, if desired — on the golf page on the Michigan.org site, found under the outdoors link. We improved our site recently. Once there, you can search by region, course or date. Say you've suddenly got a Friday morning opening and a hankering to drive north. The site will tell you what tee times are open and where, and then let you book from there. Incredibly, the state has 850 golf courses to choose from.

Q. **Which of the following is correct according to the advertisement?**

(a) This company's types of business is travel.
(b) Customers can make a reservation on the internet web site.
(c) The web site will be improved in a month.
(d) If you want a Friday course, you should book it soon as possible.

 **해설**

골프 관련 웹사이트를 광고하는 글로, 최근에 사이트를 향상시켰으며 다양한 방식으로 검색해서 찾을 수 있다는 내용이 나오고 있다. 금요일에 원하면 예약 가능하다고 했지 가능한 빨리 예약해야 한다고는 하지 않았으므로 (d)는 내용에 어긋난다. 또 골프 코스를 소개해 주는 회사이지 여행사는 아니므로 (a) 역시 맞지 않다. 따라서 정답은 (b)가 된다.

어휘
tee time 골프 시작 시간 **lodging** 숙박 **hanker** 동경, 갈망 **incredibly** 믿기 어려울 만큼

1.

A fast-paced, growing importer is looking for an energetic accounting assistant to join our team. ____, accounts payable and accounts receivable. Candidates should have a positive attitude, be multi-task oriented and possess a sense of urgency. _____________________ _________________ to denny@brain.com.

2.

Now, anyone can book a tee time — and lodging, if desired — on the golf page on the Michigan.org site, found under the outdoors link. ________________________________ ____. Say you've suddenly got a Friday morning opening and a hankering to drive north. ____, and then let you book from there. Incredibly, the state has 850 golf courses to choose from.

Part 4

Questions 1-7

Choose the option that the best answers the question.

1. (a) (b) (c) (d)
2. (a) (b) (c) (d)
3. (a) (b) (c) (d)
4. (a) (b) (c) (d)
5. (a) (b) (c) (d)
6. (a) (b) (c) (d)
7. (a) (b) (c) (d)

구경

No thanks. Just looking. 아니, 괜찮습니다. 그냥 구경하는 거예요.
I'm just browsing. 그냥 둘러보는 거예요.

가격 묻기

How much do I owe you? 얼마입니까?
What's your rate?/ What's the charge?/ How much is the fare?
요금이 얼마입니까?

가격이 비쌀 때

I can't spend that much. 그렇게 많은 돈이 없습니다.
That's over my budget. 제 예산 밖입니다.

할인/ 재고

Can you cut the price by 20 percent? 20퍼센트 할인해 주실 수 있습니까?
That item is already marked down. 그 품목은 이미 가격이 인하되었습니다.
We're having a clearance sale. 점포 세일 중입니다.
We are out of stock now. 지금은 재고가 없습니다.

담화문 추론하기

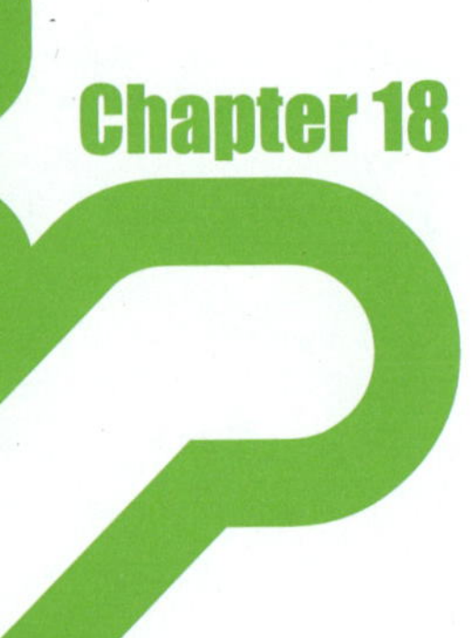

Chapter 18

출제 패턴 분석

Part 4의 담화문 추론 문제는 마지막에 2~3문제 정도 출제된다. 상당히 난이도 있는 문제 유형으로, 전체 내용을 주의 깊게 듣고 질문과 선택지를 잘 들으면서 소거법을 사용하여 문제를 풀어 나가야 한다.

Sample

Woody Karel of Kenya won the 100 meters Thursday night, set a world record, and did it so easily she was mugging for the camera before she crossed the finish line. Karel finished in 10.9 seconds, despite dropping her hands and losing her form about 20 meters from the finish line. She appeared to glance at the video screen overhead and to her left, then lowered her hands and slowed as she neared the finish line. But she lost the 400 meters this morning.

Q. **What can be mentioned from the report?**

(a) She is the only person who won the gold medal in Kenya.
(b) Nobody expected her to win the game.
(c) She will win the 400 meters next morning.
(d) She was awarded a gold medal.

분석 적용

첫 부분에서 우디 카렐이 목요일 밤 100미터에서 이기고 세계 기록을 수립했다는 내용이 나오므로 (d)가 정답이다. (b)는 글의 내용으로 알 수 없다.

어휘

set a record 기록을 세우다 **mug for camera** 카메라를 향해 포즈를 취하다 **cross the finish line** 결승점에 골인하다 **form** 몸 컨디션 **glance at** ~을 힐끗 보다

Part 4

Questions 1-2

Choose the option that the best answers the question.

1. (a)   (b)   (c)   (d)
2. (a)   (b)   (c)   (d)

1.

When we went down to the basement, where the rabbit had been banished, we found no sign of our furry friend. Mom said that it must have hopped out when she accidentally left the door open. But don't be too hard on Mom. She never had a chance to attend the Rabbit Advocates' presentation on how to care for a rabbit, what it's like to have a rabbit as a pet so we decided to buy the book written about animals and to raise the rabbit.

Q.   **What can be inferred from the talk?**

(a) The family discovered the bunny in their house.
(b) The mother has the various animals of knowledge.
(c) The rabbit has been sick due to the car accident.
(d) The family doesn't want to keep any animals.

해설

토끼가 지하실로 내쫓겼었다는 사실을 통해 집에서 발견됐음을 짐작해 볼 수 있다. (b)는 글의 내용에 비추어 상반되는 내용이며, (c)는 전혀 알 수 없는 내용이다. 또 글 마지막 부분에서 토끼를 기르기로 결정했다고 했으므로 (d) 역시 정답이 될 수 없다.

어휘

banish 추방하다, 내쫓다   **furry** 부드러운 털의   **hop out** 깡충 뛰어나가다   **accidentally** 잘못하여, 뜻하지 않게
be hard on ~에게 심하게 대하다   **advocate** 옹호[지지]자   **care for** ~를 돌보다   **raise** 기르다, 사육하다
bunny 어린 토끼

2.

The amount of caffeine in two cups of coffee a day is not harmful. However, the amount of caffeine in more than three cups of coffee can raise the systolic and diastolic pressure in people without high blood pressure. Some researchers believe that caffeine narrows blood vessels by blocking the effects of adenosine.

Q. What can be inferred from the talk?

(a) Caffeine is one of the most dangerous things for human heath.
(b) Caffeine isn't harmful.
(c) The amount of caffeine in 2~3 cups of coffee is helpful to people with diabetes.
(d) The effects of adenosine help keep blood vessels widened.

해설

마지막 부분에 언급된, 카페인이 아데노신의 효과를 막음으로써 혈관을 좁힌다는 내용으로 보아 아데노신의 효과가 혈관 확장을 돕는다는 사실을 짐작할 수 있다.

어휘

harmful 해로운 **systolic pressure** 최고 혈압 **diastolic pressure** 최저 혈압 **high blood pressure** 고혈압 **narrow** 좁히다 **blood vessel** 혈관 **block** 막다, 방해하다 **adenosine** 아데노신 **widen** 넓히다 **diabetes** 당뇨병

1.

____, we found no sign of our furry friend. ____ __________________________. But don't be too hard on Mom. She never had a chance to attend the Rabbit Advocates' presentation on how to care for a rabbit, what it's like to have a rabbit as a pet so we decided to buy the book written about animals and to raise the rabbit.

2.

The amount of caffeine in ____. However, the amount of caffeine in more than three cups of coffee can raise the systolic and diastolic pressure ____. Some researchers believe that caffeine narrows blood vessels by blocking the effects of adenosine.

Part 4

Questions 1-4

Choose the option that the best answers the question.

1. (a)   (b)   (c)   (d)
2. (a)   (b)   (c)   (d)
3. (a)   (b)   (c)   (d)
4. (a)   (b)   (c)   (d)

출제 필수 표현

👉 **음식점**

Are you being served? 주문하셨나요?
Can I take your order? 주문하시겠습니까?
On the rocks, please. 얼음 좀 넣어 주세요.
Are you serving lunch now? 지금 점심 식사를 할 수 있나요?
Would you care for dessert? 디저트 드시겠어요?
I'll have my usual. 늘 먹던 걸로 하겠습니다.
I'd prefer it lightly simmered. 살짝 데쳐 주세요.
For here or to go? 여기서 드실 건가요, 아님 가져가실 건가요?
What about something to nibble on? 뭐 잡수실 거 드릴까요?

* nibble 조금씩 먹다, 뜯어먹다

👉 **계산**

It's my treat. 내가 낼게.
This dinner is on me. 이번 저녁은 내가 살게.
I'll pick up the tab this time. 이번엔 내가 낼게.
Let's split the bill. 각자 내자.
Let's go fifty-fifty on the bill. 반반씩 내자.

Final Test

Final Test 1

Questions 1-15

You will now hear fifteen items, each made up of a single spoken statement followed by four spoken responses. Choose the most appropriate response to the statement.

1.	(a)	(b)	(c)	(d)		2.	(a)	(b)	(c)	(d)
3.	(a)	(b)	(c)	(d)		4.	(a)	(b)	(c)	(d)
5.	(a)	(b)	(c)	(d)		6.	(a)	(b)	(c)	(d)
7.	(a)	(b)	(c)	(d)		8.	(a)	(b)	(c)	(d)
9.	(a)	(b)	(c)	(d)		10.	(a)	(b)	(c)	(d)
11.	(a)	(b)	(c)	(d)		12.	(a)	(b)	(c)	(d)
13.	(a)	(b)	(c)	(d)		14.	(a)	(b)	(c)	(d)
15.	(a)	(b)	(c)	(d)						

Questions 16-30

You will now hear fifteen conversation fragments, each made up of a three spoken statements followed by four spoken responses. Choose the most appropriate response to the statement.

16.	(a)	(b)	(c)	(d)		17.	(a)	(b)	(c)	(d)
18.	(a)	(b)	(c)	(d)		19.	(a)	(b)	(c)	(d)
20.	(a)	(b)	(c)	(d)		21.	(a)	(b)	(c)	(d)
22.	(a)	(b)	(c)	(d)		23.	(a)	(b)	(c)	(d)
24.	(a)	(b)	(c)	(d)		25.	(a)	(b)	(c)	(d)
26.	(a)	(b)	(c)	(d)		27.	(a)	(b)	(c)	(d)
28.	(a)	(b)	(c)	(d)		29.	(a)	(b)	(c)	(d)
30.	(a)	(b)	(c)	(d)						

Part 3

Questions 31-45

You will now hear fifteen complete conversations. For each item, you will hear a conversation and its corresponding question which will be read twice. Then you will hear four options which will be read only once. Choose the most appropriate response to the statement.

31.	(a)	(b)	(c)	(d)	32.	(a)	(b)	(c)	(d)
33.	(a)	(b)	(c)	(d)	34.	(a)	(b)	(c)	(d)
35.	(a)	(b)	(c)	(d)	36.	(a)	(b)	(c)	(d)
37.	(a)	(b)	(c)	(d)	38.	(a)	(b)	(c)	(d)
39.	(a)	(b)	(c)	(d)	40.	(a)	(b)	(c)	(d)
41.	(a)	(b)	(c)	(d)	42.	(a)	(b)	(c)	(d)
43.	(a)	(b)	(c)	(d)	44.	(a)	(b)	(c)	(d)
45.	(a)	(b)	(c)	(d)					

Part 4

Questions 46-60

You will now hear fifteen spoken monologuess. For each item, you will hear a monologues and its corresponding question which will be read twice. Then you will hear four options which will be read only once. Choose the most appropriate response to the statement.

46.	(a)	(b)	(c)	(d)	47.	(a)	(b)	(c)	(d)
48.	(a)	(b)	(c)	(d)	49.	(a)	(b)	(c)	(d)
50.	(a)	(b)	(c)	(d)	51.	(a)	(b)	(c)	(d)
52.	(a)	(b)	(c)	(d)	53.	(a)	(b)	(c)	(d)
54.	(a)	(b)	(c)	(d)	55.	(a)	(b)	(c)	(d)
56.	(a)	(b)	(c)	(d)	57.	(a)	(b)	(c)	(d)
58.	(a)	(b)	(c)	(d)	59.	(a)	(b)	(c)	(d)
60.	(a)	(b)	(c)	(d)					

Final Test 2

Questions 1-15

You will now hear fifteen items, each made up of a single spoken statement followed by four spoken responses. Choose the most appropriate response to the statement.

1.	(a)	(b)	(c)	(d)		2.	(a)	(b)	(c)	(d)
3.	(a)	(b)	(c)	(d)		4.	(a)	(b)	(c)	(d)
5.	(a)	(b)	(c)	(d)		6.	(a)	(b)	(c)	(d)
7.	(a)	(b)	(c)	(d)		8.	(a)	(b)	(c)	(d)
9.	(a)	(b)	(c)	(d)		10.	(a)	(b)	(c)	(d)
11.	(a)	(b)	(c)	(d)		12.	(a)	(b)	(c)	(d)
13.	(a)	(b)	(c)	(d)		14.	(a)	(b)	(c)	(d)
15.	(a)	(b)	(c)	(d)						

Questions 16-30

You will now hear fifteen conversation fragments, each made up of a three spoken statements followed by four spoken responses. Choose the most appropriate response to the statement.

16.	(a)	(b)	(c)	(d)		17.	(a)	(b)	(c)	(d)
18.	(a)	(b)	(c)	(d)		19.	(a)	(b)	(c)	(d)
20.	(a)	(b)	(c)	(d)		21.	(a)	(b)	(c)	(d)
22.	(a)	(b)	(c)	(d)		23.	(a)	(b)	(c)	(d)
24.	(a)	(b)	(c)	(d)		25.	(a)	(b)	(c)	(d)
26.	(a)	(b)	(c)	(d)		27.	(a)	(b)	(c)	(d)
28.	(a)	(b)	(c)	(d)		29.	(a)	(b)	(c)	(d)
30.	(a)	(b)	(c)	(d)						

Questions 31-45

You will now hear fifteen complete conversations. For each item, you will hear a conversation and its corresponding question which will be read twice. Then you will hear four options which will be read only once. Choose the most appropriate response to the statement.

31.	(a)	(b)	(c)	(d)		32.	(a)	(b)	(c)	(d)
33.	(a)	(b)	(c)	(d)		34.	(a)	(b)	(c)	(d)
35.	(a)	(b)	(c)	(d)		36.	(a)	(b)	(c)	(d)
37.	(a)	(b)	(c)	(d)		38.	(a)	(b)	(c)	(d)
39.	(a)	(b)	(c)	(d)		40.	(a)	(b)	(c)	(d)
41.	(a)	(b)	(c)	(d)		42.	(a)	(b)	(c)	(d)
43.	(a)	(b)	(c)	(d)		44.	(a)	(b)	(c)	(d)
45.	(a)	(b)	(c)	(d)						

Questions 46-60

You will now hear fifteen spoken monologuess. For each item, you will hear a monologues and its corresponding question which will be read twice. Then you will hear four options which will be read only once. Choose the most appropriate response to the statement.

46.	(a)	(b)	(c)	(d)		47.	(a)	(b)	(c)	(d)
48.	(a)	(b)	(c)	(d)		49.	(a)	(b)	(c)	(d)
50.	(a)	(b)	(c)	(d)		51.	(a)	(b)	(c)	(d)
52.	(a)	(b)	(c)	(d)		53.	(a)	(b)	(c)	(d)
54.	(a)	(b)	(c)	(d)		55.	(a)	(b)	(c)	(d)
56.	(a)	(b)	(c)	(d)		57.	(a)	(b)	(c)	(d)
58.	(a)	(b)	(c)	(d)		59.	(a)	(b)	(c)	(d)
60.	(a)	(b)	(c)	(d)						

정답 및
해설

Chapter 1 인사·초대·권유

STEP 1 Pattern Study

Sample

해석_ M: 당신이 회의 모임에 갈 수 있을지 모르겠어요.

W: _______________________________

(a) 그날 밤 할 일이 너무 많았어요.

(b) 수천 명의 사람들로 꽉 찼다고 들었어요.

(c) 모임에 확실히 참석할 거예요.

(d) 내가 망친 것 같아요.

정답_ (c)

STEP 2 Clinic

Part 1

1.

해석_ W: 요즘 어떻게 지내니?

M: _______________________________

(a) 나 현재 환경단체에서 일하고 있어.

(b) 미안해, 그런 뜻은 아니었는데.

(c) 지금 막 집에 돌아왔어.

(d) 내년 여름에 갈 거야.

정답_ (a)

2.

해석_ M: 일요일 마이클 생일파티에 올 수 있니?

W: _______________________________

(a) 곧 나갈 거야.

(b) 요전날 밤 그의 파티에서 아주 멋진 시간을 보냈어.

(c) 미안, 난 구속받고 싶지 않아.

(d) 확실히 갈 거야.

정답_ (d)

Part 2

3.

해석_ M: 새해 복 많이 받으세요!

W: 당신도요! 설날 뭐 했어요?

M: 그냥 식구들하고 집에 있었어요. 당신은요?

W: _______________________________

(a) 가족을 위해서 기도했어요.

(b) 저도 집에 하루 종일 있었어요.

(c) 당신 가족 못 본 지가 꽤 됐네요.

(d) 다음 달에는 집에 있을 거예요.

정답_ (b)

4.

해석_ M: 지금 같이 운동하지 않을래?

W: 운동할 기분 아니야.

M: 기분전환을 위해 바람 좀 쐬야 해.

W: _______________________________

(a) 그것에 문제가 있어.

(b) 그래, 다시 일 시작할 시간이다.

(c) 그럼 호숫가를 좀 걷자.

(d) 전에 너한테 얘기했던 것 같은데.

정답_ (c)

STEP 3 Dictation

정답_ 1. I'm currently working for an environmental organization
2. I will be there for sure
3. I was stuck at home too
4. Then let's just walk by the lake a bit

STEP 4 Actual Test

Part 1

1.

M: Don't you need rest? Do you smoke?

W: _______________________________

(a) Oh, I'm sorry. I am a nonsmoker.

(b) I can't stand it when people who smoke
walk down the street.

(c) Could you smoke outside of my office?

(d) I think I'll quit smoking.

해석_ M: 휴식이 필요하지 않으세요? 담배 피우시나요?

W: _______________________________

(a) 아, 죄송해요. 전 담배 안 피웁니다.

(b) 담배 피우는 사람들이 거리를 걸어가면 참을 수가 없어요.

(c) 사무실 밖에서 피워 주시겠습니까?

(d) 담배를 끊을 생각이에요.

해설_ 담배를 피우는지 묻고 있으므로 이에 답하는 선택지를 고르면
된다.

어휘_ nonsmoker 비흡연가 **stand** 참다, 견디다

정답_ (a)

2.

M: Why don't you join my social party?

W: ＿＿＿＿＿＿＿＿＿＿＿＿＿＿＿＿＿＿＿

(a) The manager gets ready for the party.

(b) The party wasn't a total disaster.

(c) I'd love to, but as you know I am bashful in
company.

(d) Didn't you go to the family party last
Sunday?

해석_ M: 우리 사교 모임에 함께 가지 않을래요?

W: ＿＿＿＿＿＿＿＿＿＿＿＿＿＿＿＿＿

(a) 매니저가 파티 준비를 해요.

(b) 파티가 완전 엉망은 아니었어요.

(c) 그러고 싶지만, 당신도 알다시피 제가 사람들 앞에서 수줍음
이 많아서요.

(d) 지난 일요일에 가족 모임에 가지 않았나요?

해설_ 사교 모임에 함께 가자고 제안하고 있으므로 갈지 여부에 대해
응답한 선택지를 고르면 된다.

어휘_ a total disaster 엉망진창, 큰 실패 **bashful** 수줍어하는,
부끄럼 타는(shy) **in company** 사람들 앞에서

정답_ (c)

3.

M: I heard that you moved to a new house.
Aren't you going to give a housewarming?

W: ＿＿＿＿＿＿＿＿＿＿＿＿＿＿＿＿＿＿＿

(a) I'll talk about it with my husband.

(b) I have to take care of household affairs.

(c) Oh, I didn't know you are a family person!

(d) Do you think they will come to the party?

해석_ M : 너 새집으로 이사했다는 소식 들었어. 집들이 안 할 거니?

W: ＿＿＿＿＿＿＿＿＿＿＿＿＿＿＿

(a) 신랑하고 상의해 볼게.

(b) 집안일을 해야 해.

(c) 오, 네가 가정적인 사람인 줄 몰랐는걸!

(d) 그들이 파티에 올 거라고 생각해?

해설_ 집들이를 안 할 건지 묻고 있으므로 이에 관해 언급한 (a)가 이
어지는 것이 자연스럽다.

어휘_ housewarming 집들이(단어 뜻 그대로 하면 집을 따뜻이 한다는
의미인데, 미국에서는 새집에 사람들이 가서 생기를 넣어 준다는 뜻으로 집
들이를 이렇게 표현한다.) **household affairs** 집안일
family person 가정적인 사람

정답_ (a)

4.

W: We're having a charity party. Will you join
us?

M: ＿＿＿＿＿＿＿＿＿＿＿＿＿＿＿＿＿＿＿

(a) When is the party going to start?

(b) That foundation was built in 1991.

(c) I'm making a donation for homeless people.

(d) I can't decide now. Let's enjoy the party
anyway.

해석_ W: 우리는 자선 파티를 열 예정이야. 같이 할래?

M: ＿＿＿＿＿＿＿＿＿＿＿＿＿＿＿＿＿

(a) 파티가 언제 시작되는데?

(b) 그 재단은 1991년에 설립됐어.

(c) 노숙자들을 위해 기부할 거야.

(d) 지금 결정 못하겠어. 어쨌든 파티나 즐기자.

해설_ 자선 파티를 같이 하자는 제안에 이어질 응답으로, 파티가 언제
시작되는지 묻는 (a)가 가장 자연스럽다.

어휘_ charity party 자선 파티 **foundation** 재단 **make a
donation** 기부하다 **homeless people** 노숙자

정답_ (a)

5.

M: Have you ever seen him before?

W: ＿＿＿＿＿＿＿＿＿＿＿＿＿＿＿＿＿＿＿

(a) I thought this would last a while.

(b) It was my first time seeing him.

(c) I always wanted to see her.

(d) He is doing great.

해석_ M: 전에 그를 본 적이 있니?

W: _____________________________

(a) 내 생각엔 이게 잠시 지속될 것 같아.

(b) 처음 봤어.

(c) 늘 그녀를 만나고 싶었어.

(d) 그는 잘 지내고 있어.

해설 전에 그를 본 적이 있는지 묻고 있으므로 이에 답하는 선택지를 고르면 된다.

어휘 **(for) a while** 잠시

정답 (b)

Part 2

6.

M: I can't believe you are here!

W: I've lived here in Paris since I got back from the job.

M: Great. How was it going so far here?

W: _____________________________

(a) I don't speak French either.

(b) So far so good.

(c) I am going home now.

(d) It has been a while though.

해석 M: 네가 여기 있다니 믿을 수가 없어!

W: 은퇴한 이후로 이곳 파리에서 살았어.

M: 그렇구나. 여기서 지금껏 어떻게 지냈니?

W: _______________________

(a) 나도 프랑스어 못해.

(b) 그럭저럭 지냈어.

(c) 나 지금 집에 가고 있어.

(d) 오랜만이다.

해설 안부를 묻고 있으므로 (b)가 적절한 응답이다.

어휘 **get back from the job** 은퇴하다 **so far** 지금까지

정답 (b)

7.

M: Hey, Ann. I haven't spoken to you for a long time. How are things?

W: I am doing pretty well reading some books recently.

M: What kinds of books?

W: _____________________________

(a) They are all my favorites.

(b) The author is just fantastic.

(c) Mostly, crime fiction.

(d) About twelve books.

해석 M: 안녕, 앤. 오랫동안 얘기 못 나눠 봤구나. 어떻게 지내니?

W: 요즘 책 몇 권 읽으면서 아주 잘 지내고 있어.

M: 어떤 종류의 책들인데?

W: _______________________

(a) 모두 내가 좋아하는 것들이야.

(b) 작가가 굉장해.

(c) 대부분 범죄 소설이야.

(d) 한 12권 정도.

해설 책의 종류를 묻고 있으므로 이에 관해 언급한 선택지를 고르면 된다.

어휘 **author** 저자, 작가 **fantastic** 굉장한, 멋진 **crime** 범죄 **fiction** 소설

정답 (c)

8.

M: Excuse me, do I know you? You are shooting a glance at me.

W: Haven't we met before at Sarah's wedding party?

M: Who is Sarah? I don't know her.

W: _____________________________

(a) No, I don't think so.

(b) I think I know you.

(c) Sorry, I am busy.

(d) Sorry, I mistook you for someone I knew.

해석 M: 죄송하지만, 저를 아시나요? 저를 계속 쳐다보셔서요.

W: 지난번 사라의 웨딩파티에서 뵌 적 있지 않나요?

M: 사라가 누군가요? 전 그녀를 모르는데요.

W: _______________________

(a) 아뇨, 전 그렇게 생각지 않아요.

(b) 제가 아는 분 같은데요.

(c) 죄송해요, 제가 바빠서요.

(d) 죄송해요, 제가 아는 분으로 착각했어요.

해설 여자는 사라의 웨딩파티에서 본 남자라고 생각했는데 남자는 사라를 모르는 상황이므로 착각했다는 (d)가 적절하다.

어휘 **shoot a glance at** ~를 힐끗 보다 **mistake** 착각하다

정답 (d)

Chapter 2 충고·부탁·허락

STEP 1 Pattern Study

Sample

해석_ W: 이것 좀 선반 위에 놓아 주실 수 있을까요?

M: _______________________________

(a) 네, 그럴게요.

(b) 벌써 그렇게 했어요.

(c) 그렇게 하려고 맘먹었어요.

(d) 물론 했죠.

정답_ (a)

STEP 2 Clinic

Part 1

1.

해석_ M: 컨벤션 센터까지 저 좀 태워 주실 수 있을까요?

W: _______________________________

(a) 그럼요. 사무실 앞에서 만나요.

(b) 오늘 밤 어디 갈까요?

(c) 회의 끝나고 컨벤션 센터에 갈 거예요.

(d) 한번 탈 수 있어요?

정답_ (a)

2.

해석_ M: 이메일 확인하게 네 노트북 좀 빌릴 수 있을까?

W: _______________________________

(a) 대단한데.

(b) 그 회사로부터 이메일을 받았어.

(c) 연락할게.

(d) 그래, 내 작업이 끝나면 사용해.

정답_ (d)

Part 2

3.

해석_ W: 부탁 하나 해도 될까? 우체국까지 차를 타고 가야 해.

M: 뭐 때문에?

W: 이걸 빠른 우편으로 보내려고.

M: _______________________________

(a) 이것들은 내가 가장 좋아하는 거야.

(b) 짐이 많아.

(c) 타. 나도 같은 방향이야.

(d) 널 위해 그렇게 할게.

정답_ (c)

4.

해석_ M: 오늘 해외에서 손님들이 오세요.

W: 오늘요? 언제 오시는데요?

M: 한 2시쯤요. 당신이 공장 주변을 안내해 줄 수 있을까요?

W: _______________________________

(a) 죄송해요, 사장님과 중요한 회의가 있어요.

(b) 저도 같은 생각이에요. 몇 시에 만날까요?

(c) 공장의 기계들은 새것으로 교체될 거예요.

(d) 저에게 보여 주다니 말도 안 돼요.

정답_ (a)

STEP 3 Dictation

정답_ 1. Why not? Let's meet in front of the office.
2. Okay, you can use it after I finish my work.
3. Get in. I am going the same way.
4. Sorry, I have an important meeting with my boss.

STEP 4 Actual Test

Part 1

1.

M: Excuse me, would you do me a favor?

W: _______________________________

(a) My choice depends on what it is.

(b) Sure. I'd like to give the poor orphan a hand.

(c) Oh, I love it. It's my favorite.

(d) I'm sorry, but it isn't a big deal.

해석_ M: 죄송하지만, 부탁 좀 드려도 될까요?

W: _______________________________

(a) 뭔지 들어 보고요.

(b) 그럼요. 불쌍한 고아들에게 도움을 주고 싶어요.

(c) 아, 저 그거 좋아해요. 제가 정말 좋아하는 일이에요.

(d) 죄송한데, 저한테 부담이 되네요.

해설 뭔가 부탁을 해도 괜찮은지 허락을 구하고 있으므로 (a)가 정답
이다. (b), (c), (d)는 부탁의 종류에 대해 듣고 나서 이어질 수 있
는 응답들이다.

어휘 **depend on** ~에 달려 있다 **give ... a hand** ~를 돕다
orphan 고아

정답 (a)

2.

M: I recommend you go out early.
W: ____

(a) I am almost ready to go out.
(b) I recognized him immediately.
(c) Don't push me. I finished my work.
(d) Please stop. It's ridiculous.

해석 M: 너 일찍 나가는 게 좋을 거야.
W: ________________________________

(a) 나갈 준비 거의 다 됐어.
(b) 그를 즉시 알아봤어.
(c) 조르지 마. 일 다 끝냈어.
(d) 제발 그만 해. 어리석은 일이야.

해설 서두르는 게 좋겠다는 남자의 충고에 이어질 응답으로, 나갈 준
비가 거의 다 됐다는 (a)가 가장 자연스럽다.

어휘 **be ready to ...** ~할 준비가 되다 **push** 강요하다, 조르다

정답 (a)

3.

M: I wish to ask you a favor.
W: ____

(a) Yes, it is my favorite, too.
(b) Sure, let me know how I can help you.
(c) I would love to be a famous actor.
(d) Yes, my class starts next week.

해석 M: 부탁 드릴 게 하나 있는데요.
W: ________________________________

(a) 네, 저도 그게 제일 좋아요.
(b) 그러세요. 어떻게 도와 드릴까요?

(c) 전 유명한 배우가 되고 싶어요.

(d) 네, 제 수업은 다음주에 시작해요.

해설 부탁하고 싶은 게 있다고 했으므로 이를 받아들이거나 거절하는
표현이 담긴 선택지를 고르면 된다.

어휘 **would love to ...** ~하고 싶다

정답 (b)

4.

M: Could you give me a ride to the station?
W: ____

(a) I want to ride a train.
(b) I will make a note.
(c) Nothing is going to change.
(d) I think you'd better take a taxi.

해석 M: 역까지 태워다 주실래요?
W: ________________________________

(a) 기차를 타고 싶어요.
(b) 필기할게요.
(c) 아무것도 변하지 않아요.
(d) 택시를 타는 게 나을 것 같은데요.

해설 역까지 태워 줄 수 있겠냐는 부탁에 이어질 응답으로, 그보다는
택시를 타는 게 더 좋겠다고 제안한 (d)가 자연스럽다.

어휘 **ride a train** 기차를 타다 **make a note** 노트에 적다, 필
기하다

정답 (d)

Part 2

5.

W: Sean, do you have some time for helping
me out with this project?
M: Of course, what are you up to?
W: Just a little problem with this.
M: ____

(a) Let me see the details on it.
(b) I will be back in thirty minutes.
(c) I don't have any problems.
(d) I will clean it up now.

해석 W: 션, 이 프로젝트 도와줄 시간 좀 있니?
M: 물론이지, 무슨 일인데?
W: 그냥 문제가 좀 있어서.

M: ___________________________

(a) 어디 자세히 한번 보자.

(b) 30분 후에 다시 올게.

(c) 난 아무 문제 없어.

(d) 지금 깨끗이 치울게.

해설_ 문제가 좀 있다고 했으므로 어떤 문제인지 자세히 보겠다는 (a)

가 이어져야 자연스럽다.

어휘_ clean up 깨끗이 청소하다, 치우다

정답_ (a)

6.

W: Could you fix my radio?

M: What's wrong with it?

W: I have no idea.

M: _______________________________

(a) Okay, bring it tomorrow.

(b) I will take care of it.

(c) I don't have any problems.

(d) You should take care of them.

해석_ W: 제 라디오 좀 고쳐 주시겠어요?

M: 뭐가 문제죠?

W: 잘 모르겠어요.

M: _____________________

(a) 좋아요, 내일 가져오세요.

(b) 제가 맡겠습니다.

(c) 전 아무 문제 없어요.

(d) 당신이 그들을 돌봐 주는 게 좋겠어요.

해설_ 라디오 수리를 부탁하고 있으므로 내일 가져와 보라는 (a)가 적

절하다.

어휘_ fix 고치다, 수리하다 **take care of** ~을 돌보다, 처리하다

정답_ (a)

7.

W: Did you catch a cold? Everybody's catching
colds.

M: I slept with the window open at night.

W: You should go to the doctor, before it gets
worse.

M: _______________________________

(a) I know, but I hate shots all around the
world.

(b) Thank you. I see what you say.

(c) But I confuse worse with better.

(d) How can I make an agreement?

해석_ W: 너 감기 걸렸니? 요즘 감기가 유행이구나.

M: 밤에 창문을 열어 놓고 잤어.

W: 더 나빠지기 전에 병원에 가 보는 게 좋겠다.

M: _____________________

(a) 나도 알지만, 난 세상에서 주사가 제일 싫어.

(b) 고마워. 무슨 말인지 알겠어.

(c) 하지만 뭐가 좋고 뭐나 나쁜지 모르겠어.

(d) 어떻게 합의를 하지?

해설_ 병원에 가 보라는 충고에 이어질 응답으로, 그러는 게 좋겠다는

건 알지만 주사 맞는 게 싫다고 응답한 (a)가 적절하다.

어휘_ shot 주사 **make an agreement** 합의하다

정답_ (a)

Chapter 3 칭찬·격려·축하·위로

STEP 1 Pattern Study

Sample

해석_ M: 마음이 조마조마해.

W: 왜 그렇게 초조한데?

M: 내일 개막 연설을 할 거야.

W: ________________________________

(a) 완벽히 준비해야 할 것 같다.

(b) 모든 청중들이 그의 연설에 감동받았어.

(c) 약국 가 보는 게 어때?

(d) 결국 일을 관뒀구나.

정답_ (a)

STEP 2 Clinic

Part 1

1.

해석_ W: 무슨 일 있어? 너 이번주 내내 기분이 안 좋다.

M: ________________________________

(a) 부모님이랑 시내에 있었어.

(b) 나쁜 거 없어. 그냥 좀 혼란스러웠어.

(c) 다음 달에 집으로 돌아갈 거야.

(d) 이틀 전에 내 친구들이 깜짝 파티를 열어 줬어.

정답_ (b)

2.

해석_ W: 너 결혼한단 소식 들었어.

M: ________________________________

(a) 고마워, 결혼식에 널 초대하고 싶어.

(b) 그 행운의 소녀는 누구야?

(c) 내가 들러리 서 줄게.

(d) 나 신혼이야.

정답_ (a)

Part 2

3.

해석_ M: 이야, 여기서 널 보다니!

W: 그래, 세상 참 좁다! 너희들 여전히 함께 다니는구나.

M: 응, 2년째 됐어.

W: ________________________________

(a) 다행히도 일들이 잘돼 가고 있어.

(b) 와, 너희들 아주 잘 지내는구나.

(c) 그런 말 들어서 너무 기쁘다.

(d) 그보다 더 됐어.

정답_ (b)

4.

해석_ M: 너 그거 쓰는 데 얼마나 걸렸어?

W: 불규칙적으로 해서, 3~4년 정도.

M: 쓰는 데 오래 걸리는구나. 대단하다.

W: ________________________________

(a) 응, 일부러 그랬어.

(b) 너한테 그렇게 대단한 일은 아닐 거야.

(c) 난 항상 나만의 책을 쓰고 싶었어.

(d) 난 쓰는 것만큼이나 읽는 것도 너무 좋아해.

정답_ (c)

STEP 3 Dictation

정답_ 1. Nothing bad, I was just a bit confused

2. Thanks, I'd like to invite you to my wedding

3. Wow, you guys get along so well!

4. I always wanted to make my own book

STEP 4 Actual Test

Part 1

1.

W: Oh, I've lost my purse. I left it in the restaurant.

M: ________________________________

(a) I'm sorry about that. You should report a lost card.

(b) May I have your order?

(c) I'm just about brain dead anyway.

(d) You shouldn't worry. I ordered another one.

해석_ W: 어머나, 나 지갑 잃어버렸어. 식당에 두고 왔나 봐.

M: ___________________________

(a) 그거 안됐구나. 카드 분실 신고해야겠다.

(b) 주문하실래요?

(c) 어쨌든 지금은 아무 생각도 할 수가 없어.

(d) 걱정 마. 내가 다른 거 주문했어.

해설 여자가 지갑을 잃어버렸으므로 해결책에 대한 조언이나 충고가 담긴 응답 표현이 이어져야 자연스럽다. (c)는 직역하면 '나 지금 막 뇌사 상태에(brain dead) 있다'로, 즉 '지금은 아무 생각도 할 수 없다'란 뜻으로 쓰이는 표현이다.

어휘 report a lost card 카드 분실 신고를 하다

정답 (a)

2.

M: Finally we lost the game.

W: ___________________________

(a) Don't be disappointed. You did your best.

(b) I'll cheer your team all the time.

(c) Don't worry. You'll be a winner.

(d) You've become addicted to computer games.

해석 M: 결국 우리가 시합에서 졌어.

W: ___________________________

(a) 실망하지 마. 너희는 최선을 다했어.

(b) 내가 항상 너희 팀을 응원할게.

(c) 걱정 마. 너희는 이길 거야.

(d) 너 컴퓨터 게임에 빠졌구나.

해설 시합에 졌다고 했으므로 그에 대해 위로해 주는 말이 이어져야 자연스럽다.

어휘 disappointed 낙심한 addicted to ~에 중독된

정답 (a)

3.

M: I was transferred to a Singapore branch office.

W: ___________________________

(a) You are? Great, congratulations!

(b) No way! If I were you, I wouldn't refuse it.

(c) How much does it cost for moving?

(d) You may go to travel alone.

해석 M: 싱가폴 지사로 발령받았어요.

W: ___________________________

(a) 네가? 잘됐다, 축하해!

(b) 안 돼! 내가 너라면, 거절 안 할 거야.

(c) 이사하는 데 비용이 얼마야?

(d) 너 혼자 여행가도 돼.

해설 상대방의 발령 소식에 대해 축하해 주는 응답이 이어져야 자연스럽다. (b)의 No way!는 '안 돼!'의 의미로, 상대방의 주장이나 제의 등을 강하게 부정할 때 쓰는 표현이다.

어휘 be transferred to 발령받다 branch office 지사

정답 (a)

4.

W: You play the drum very well!

M: ___________________________

(a) I was in a marching band in highschool.

(b) Thanks for playing the music.

(c) It was all her fault.

(d) Sure, let me know when you are free.

해석 W: 너 드럼을 정말 잘 치는구나!

M: ___________________________

(a) 고등학교 때 고적대에 있었어.

(b) 음악 연주 고마워.

(c) 그건 전부 그녀 잘못이었어.

(d) 그래, 언제 한가한지 알려 줘.

해설 드럼을 잘 친다는 칭찬에 이어질 응답으로 고등학교 때 고적대 멤버였다고 설명하는 (a)가 적절하다.

어휘 marching band 고적대 fault 실수, 잘못

정답 (a)

Part 2

5.

W: It smells good. What is in it?

M: It is soup with mushrooms.

W: Wow! Can I have some?

M: ___________________________

(a) There are no more mushrooms.

(b) I think it is too big for that.

(c) No problem.

(d) I want to have some mushrooms, too.

해석 W: 냄새 좋은데. 그 속에 든 거 뭐야?

M: 버섯 수프야.

W: 왜! 좀 먹어 봐도 돼?

M: _______________________

(a) 버섯이 더 없는데.

(b) 그거 너무 큰 것 같다.

(c) 물론이지.

(d) 나도 버섯 먹고 싶다.

해설_ 버섯 수프 냄새가 좋다며 한번 먹어 봐도 되는지 허락을 구하고 있으므로 '물론이지.' 하고 흔쾌히 응하는 (c)가 적절하다.

어휘_ **It smells ...** ~한 냄새가 나다 **mushroom** 버섯

정답_ (c)

6.

M: I failed chemistry. I must study again.

W: Come on. Look on the bright side.

M: Do you really think I can?

W: _______________________

(a) Don't give up. It's up to you.

(b) I think you should study instead of going out.

(c) You may study chemistry as a minor.

(d) It could be professor James.

해석_ M: 나 화학 낙제했어. 다시 공부해야 해.

W: 힘내. 긍정적으로 생각해.

M: 정말 내가 할 수 있을 거라고 생각해?

W: _______________________

(a) 포기하지 마. 그건 너한테 달렸어.

(b) 내 생각에 넌 외출하지 말고 공부를 해야 할 것 같다.

(c) 부전공으로 화학을 공부해도 돼.

(d) 제임스 교수님일 가능성이 있어.

해설_ 남자가 낙심해 있으므로 위로나 격려의 내용이 담긴 선택지를 고르면 된다. (a)의 It's up to you.는 '너한테 달렸다', '너 하기 나름이다'라는 뜻으로, 즉 마음만 먹으면 잘해 낼 수 있을 거라는 격려의 의미가 담겨 있다.

어휘_ **fail** 낙제하다 **look on the bright side** 긍정적으로 생각하다 **minor** 부전공 과목

정답_ (a)

7.

M: Congratulations! I heard you've got a wedding ring.

W: Thank you. I love my ring.

M: Where are you going on your honeymoon after you get married?

W: _______________________

(a) I hope we'll have a grand rest at the Maldives.

(b) We decided the date on Saturday July 16th.

(c) My wedding is coming up next month.

(d) I haven't gotten the wedding invitation yet.

해석_ M: 축하해! 결혼 반지 받았단 소식 들었어.

W: 고마워. 반지가 너무 맘에 들어.

M: 결혼식 끝나고 신혼여행은 어디로 갈 거야?

W: _______________________

(a) 몰디브에서 푹 쉬었으면 좋겠어.

(b) 7월 16일 토요일로 정했어.

(c) 다음 달이면 내 결혼식이야.

(d) 난 아직 청첩장 못 받았어.

해설_ 신혼여행을 어디로 가는지 묻고 있으므로 여행지를 언급한 선택지를 고르면 된다.

어휘_ **go on one's honeymoon** 신혼여행 가다 **have a grand rest** 충분히 쉬다 **come up** 다가오다 **wedding invitation** 청첩장

정답_ (a)

Chapter 4 감사·사과·항의·불평

STEP 1 Pattern Study

Sample

해석_ M: 죄송하지만, 박물관 내에서 사진촬영은 금지입니다.

W: _______________________________

(a) 죄송해요. 깜빡 했어요.

(b) 내가 왜 그 사람한테 사과했지?

(c) 당신 말이 맞아요. 모든 손님들은 규칙을 따르죠.

(d) 전 휴가 때 사진을 찍곤 했어요.

정답_ (a)

STEP 2 Clinic

Part 1

1.

해석_ W: 너 그녀한테 어떻게 그럴 수 있어?

M: _______________________________

(a) 미안, 하지만 고의는 아니었어.

(b) 난 그녀의 프로젝트를 돕고 있어.

(c) 그녀는 최선을 다했어.

(d) 난 네가 어떻게 그럴 수 있는지 잘 모르겠다.

정답_ (a)

2.

해석_ W: 정말 재밌었어. 기대 이상이었어.

M: _______________________________

(a) 정말 재밌을 거라고 확신해.

(b) 나도 기대하지 않았어.

(c) 널 다시 만나길 기대할게.

(d) 나도 너와 함께 해서 즐거웠어.

정답_ (d)

Part 2

3.

해석_ M: 너 왜 거기에 안 갔어? 할 수만 있었다면, 난 거기 갔었을 텐데.

W: 가려고 했는데 그럴 수가 없었어.

M: 음, 그럴 만한 합당한 이유가 있겠지.

W: _______________________________

(a) 그게 합당한 이유인 것 같다.

(b) 곧 그리로 갈게.

(c) 연루되고 싶지 않았어.

(d) 다음번엔 가겠다고 약속할게.

정답_ (d)

4.

해석_ W: 우리 개들 좀 태워 줄 수 있니?

M: 미안, 나 개 알레르기가 있어.

W: 정말? 그걸 몰랐네.

M: _______________________________

(a) 알레르기 때문에 개가 너무 싫어.

(b) 그럼 널 위해 그렇게 해줄게.

(c) 그들을 빨리 만나 보고 싶다.

(d) 그렇게 하도록 노력해 볼게.

정답_ (a)

STEP 3 Dictation

정답_ 1. Sorry, but it wasn't on purpose

2. Me, too. It was my pleasure to be with you

3. I promise I will make it up to you next time

4. I can't stand them because of my allergies

STEP 4 Actual Test

Part 1

1.

M: Sorry, I'm late. Have you been waiting long?

W: _______________________________

(a) No, not that long.

(b) I had been waiting for 2 hours.

(c) I'm great. How are you doing?

(d) Jason is waiting in the meeting room.

해석_ M: 죄송해요, 늦었습니다. 오래 기다리셨죠?

W: _______________________________

(a) 아뇨, 별로요.

(b) 2시간 동안 기다리고 있었어요.

(c) 전 좋아요. 당신은 어떻게 지냈어요?

(d) 제이슨이 회의실에서 기다리고 있어요.

해설_ 늦은 것에 대해 미안해하며 오래 기다렸는지 묻고 있으므로 이에 답하는 (a)가 정답이다. (b)는 How long have you been waiting?(얼마나 오래 기다리셨어요?)에 대한 응답에 해당된다.

정답_ (a)

2.

M: I'm sorry but I didn't mean to say that.

W: _______________________________________

(a) I didn't expect to say that.

(b) It means a lot to me.

(c) It is okay, I won't care about it.

(d) I hope to hear from you soon.

해석_ M: 미안하지만, 그렇게 말하려고 했던 건 아니었어.

W: _______________________________

(a) 그렇게 말하리라 예상하지 않았어.

(b) 그건 내게 큰 의미가 있어.

(c) 괜찮아, 신경 안 써.

(d) 곧 너한테 소식 듣게 되길 바랄게.

해설_ 남자의 사과에 대해 괜찮다고 응답하는 (c)가 정답이다.

어휘_ **care about** ~에 신경을 쓰다, ~에 관심을 가지다

정답_ (c)

3.

M: We've been waiting for our order about 40 minutes.

W: _______________________________________

(a) We are so sorry, we got the wrong order.

(b) I apologize for coming late.

(c) As soon as we bring it, I'll contact you.

(d) You never keep at it.

해석_ M: 주문한 거 기다린 지가 40분 정도 됐어요.

W: _______________________________

(a) 정말 죄송합니다. 저희가 주문을 잘못 받았네요.

(b) 늦게 와서 죄송합니다.

(c) 우리가 그걸 받자마자 당신한테 연락할게요.

(d) 그걸 계속하면 절대 안 돼요.

해설_ 주문한 음식을 기다린 지 한참 됐으므로 사과의 표현이 이어져야 자연스럽다.

어휘_ **keep at** ~을 계속해서 하다

정답_ (a)

4.

W: I was so pissed off when he didn't allow me to go to the party that night.

M: _______________________________________

(a) So was I. I am so peaceful inside.

(b) It is good to see you at the party.

(c) I had so much fun the other night.

(d) I am sorry to hear that.

해석_ W: 그가 그날 밤 파티에 못 가게 했을 때 정말 화가 났었어.

M: _______________________________

(a) 나도 그랬어. 정말 마음이 편안하다.

(b) 파티에서 널 만나서 기뻐.

(c) 요전날 밤 정말 재밌었어.

(d) 그거 유감이다.

해설_ 화가 나 있는 여자에게 위로의 뜻을 전하는 (d)가 적절한 응답이다.

어휘_ **be pissed off** 화나다(angry보다 화난 정도가 더 강한 표현)

정답_ (d)

Part 2

5.

M: What happened to you? You look so upset.

W: I have some problems with my professor.

M: What's wrong? Tell me about it.

W: _______________________________________

(a) I think he is so stressed out.

(b) I think they are so strict about the rules.

(c) We discussed my project and found out some misunderstandings between us.

(d) It is all about his idea.

해석_ M: 무슨 일 있었어? 무지 화나 보인다.

W: 교수님이랑 문제가 좀 있어서.

M: 뭔데? 나한테 말해 봐.

W: _______________________________

(a) 내 생각엔 그가 스트레스를 너무 받아 지친 것 같아.

(b) 내 생각엔 그들이 규칙에 너무 엄격한 것 같아.

(c) 내 프로젝트에 대해 논의하면서 우리 사이에 약간의 오해를 발견했어.

(d) 그건 전적으로 그의 생각이야.

해설_ 교수와 어떤 문제가 있었는지 얘기해 보라고 했으므로 그 내용이 언급된 선택지를 고르면 된다.

어휘_ **be stressed out** 스트레스로 지치다 **strict** 엄격한 **misunderstanding** 오해

정답_ (c)

6.

W: Excuse me, sir. The first and second lines are all reserved seats.

M: I can't see if I sit at the back.

W: We're sorry. It's already arranged.

M: ___________________________________

(a) Why didn't you mark reserved seats here?

(b) I'm going to arrange my room on the weekend.

(c) I'd rather sit in the aisle seat than the window seat.

(d) Please fasten your seat belt.

해석_ W: 죄송합니다, 손님. 첫 번째와 두 번째 줄은 모두 예약석입니다.

M: 뒤에 앉으면 안 보인단 말이에요.

W: 죄송합니다. 이미 자리 배정이 끝난 상태라서요.

M: _______________________

(a) 왜 여기엔 예약석 표시를 안 했나요?

(b) 난 주말에 방 정리를 할 거예요.

(c) 창가 쪽에 앉느니 차라리 통로 쪽에 앉는 게 나아요.

(d) 안전벨트를 매 주십시오.

해설_ 이미 자리 배정이 끝났다는 말을 들었으므로 미리 예약석 표시를 해놓지 않은 것에 항의하는 (a)가 적절하다. (a) 대신 You could have marked reserved seats here.(여기에 예약석이라고 표시를 해놨어야죠.)와 같은 표현도 가능하다.

어휘_ **reserved seat** 예약석 **arrange** 배치하다

정답_ (a)

7.

M: Jina! What's eating you today?

W: I can't understand what you mean.

M: You seem to have the blues.

W: ___________________________________

(a) It wasn't my day. I've had a traffic accident.

(b) I can't understand what the writer meant at all.

(c) Don't lose any sleep over it.

(d) Your blue skirt really caught my eye!

해석_ M: 지나! 오늘 무슨 걱정 있니?

W: 무슨 말인지 모르겠어.

M: 우울해 보인다구.

W: _______________________

(a) 오늘 일진이 안 좋았어. 교통사고를 당했어.

(b) 작가가 의미한 바를 전혀 이해 못하겠어.

(c) 너무 걱정하지 마.

(d) 네 파란 치마가 내 눈을 사로잡는걸!

해설_ 무슨 안 좋은 일이 있는지 묻고 있으므로 이에 관해 언급한 선택지를 고르면 된다. (d)는 대화 중에 나온 have the blues를 사용해 오답을 유도한 함정이다.

어휘_ **What's eating you?** 무슨 일 있니?, 뭐가 고민이야? **have the blues** 마음이 울적하다, 우울하다 **lose sleep over** ~ 때문에 잠 못 이루고 걱정하다 **catch** (마음 · 눈길 등을) 끌다

정답_ (a)

Chapter 5 전화

STEP 1 Pattern Study

Sample

해석_ M: 회의하는 동안에 전화받은 거 있어요?

W: ________________________________

(a) 그녀가 당신을 만나러 왔어요.

(b) 어떤 분이 당신을 기다리고 계세요.

(c) 고객분들한테 2~3통 정도 왔었어요.

(d) 그녀는 지금 통화 중입니다.

정답_ (c)

STEP 2 Clinic

Part 1

1.

해석_ M: 잠시 전화 좀 쓸 수 있을까요?

W: ________________________________

(a) 그렇게 할 시간이 별로 없어요.

(b) 그럼요. 쓰세요.

(c) 잠시 후에 바로 올게요.

(d) 지금 통화 중입니다.

정답_ (b)

2.

해석_ W: 메시지를 받아 드릴까요?

M: ________________________________

(a) 그는 지금 출장 중이십니다.

(b) 나중에 그에게 다시 전화할게요.

(c) 그 밖에 다른 메시지도 받았어요.

(d) 아마 그가 할 수 있을 거예요.

정답_ (b)

Part 2

3.

해석_ M: 브라운 씨와 통화 가능할까요?

W: 죄송하지만, 지금 통화하실 수 없습니다.

M: 지금 어디 계신지 여쭤 봐도 될까요?

W: ________________________________

(a) 출장 가셨어요.

(b) 곧 돌아오실 것 같아요.

(c) 오늘 밤 늦게 통화 가능하실 거예요.

(d) 곧 돌아오실 거예요.

정답_ (a)

4.

해설_ W: 셀린 씨와 통화할 수 있을까요?

M: 성함과 무슨 일로 통화하고 싶으신지 말씀해 주시겠어요?

W: 저는 제인이고요, 개인적인 일로 통화하고 싶습니다.

M: ________________________________

(a) 알겠습니다. 잠시만 기다리세요.

(b) 전 그게 공평하다고 생각지 않아요.

(c) 그녀가 올지 안 올지 잘 모르겠어요.

(d) 전 그 점에 대해 당신이 옳다고 생각해요.

정답_ (a)

STEP 3 Dictation

정답_ 1. Why not? Go ahead

2. I will call him again later

3. He is out of town

4. OK, hold on, please

STEP 4 Actual Test

Part 1

1.

M: I haven't spoken to you for a long time. I have been through a lot.

W: ________________________________

(a) We need to catch up soon.

(b) I like talking with you.

(c) I am waiting for the speech.

(d) I have another interview.

해석_ M: 오랫동안 얘기 못 나눠 봤구나. 그동안 많은 일이 있었어.

W: ________________________________

(a) 빨리 만나서 그동안 밀린 얘기 하자.

(b) 너랑 얘기하는 게 좋아.

(c) 그 연설을 기다리고 있어.

(d) 또 다른 인터뷰가 있어.

해설_ 그동안 많은 일이 있었다고 했으므로 (a)가 자연스러운 응답이
다. catch up은 마지막 만난 시점부터 지금까지의 소식을 따라
잡는다는 의미로 '그동안 밀린 얘기를 하다', '만나다' 등으로
해석된다.

어휘_ be through a lot 많은 일들을 겪다

정답_ (a)

2.

M: Hello, I am calling regarding the agenda.
W: ＿＿＿＿＿＿＿＿＿＿＿＿＿＿＿＿＿＿＿

(a) She is in a meeting now.
(b) Regardless of the weather, I will call her.
(c) I don't think Amanda is available now.
(d) Could I have your name please?

해석_ M: 여보세요, 안건에 관해 전화드렸습니다.
　　　　W: ＿＿＿＿＿＿＿＿＿＿＿＿＿＿＿

　　　　(a) 그녀는 지금 회의 중이신데요.
　　　　(b) 날씨와 상관없이 난 그녀에게 전화할 거예요.
　　　　(c) 아만다는 지금 전화받기 곤란할 것 같은데요.
　　　　(d) 성함이 어떻게 되시죠?

해설_ 누군가가 어떤 일에 관해 전화를 했을 때 일단 그 사람의 이름부
터 확인하는 게 순서일 것이다. 따라서 정답은 (d).

어휘_ regarding ~에 관하여　**agenda** 안건　**regardless of**
　　　~와 상관없이

정답_ (d)

3.

M: Could you take a message for Mr. Kim?
W: ＿＿＿＿＿＿＿＿＿＿＿＿＿＿＿＿＿＿

(a) You can send an invoice mail for the
　　contract.
(b) Sure, go ahead.
(c) Of course, you can send a voice mail or
　　message.
(d) I will take a message and get back to you
　　soon.

해석_ M: 김 선생님께 메시지를 전해 주시겠습니까?
　　　　W: ＿＿＿＿＿＿＿＿＿＿＿＿＿＿＿

　　　　(a) 그 계약에 대한 송장 메일을 보내 주시면 돼요.

(b) 물론이죠, 그렇게 하세요.
(c) 네, 음성 메일이나 메시지를 보내 주시면 돼요.
(d) 메시지 받고 곧 연락드릴게요.

해설_ 메시지를 전해 달라고 부탁하고 있으므로 이에 응하는 (b)가 정
답이다.

어휘_ invoice mail 송장 메일　**contract** 계약　**voice mail**
　　　음성 메시지

정답_ (b)

4.

M: This is Kates Company. How may I help
　　you?
W: ＿＿＿＿＿＿＿＿＿＿＿＿＿＿＿＿＿＿＿

(a) I'd like to speak to a repairman.
(b) Do you know the receptionist?
(c) Please, press No. 2.
(d) Pardon me? What's his name?

해석_ M: 케이츠 회사입니다. 어떻게 도와 드릴까요?
　　　　W: ＿＿＿＿＿＿＿＿＿＿＿＿＿＿＿

　　　　(a) 수리공과 통화하고 싶은데요.
　　　　(b) 그 접수원 아세요?
　　　　(c) 2번을 눌러 주십시오
　　　　(d) 다시 말씀해 주실래요? 그 사람 이름이 뭐라고요?

해설_ 어떤 도움을 원하는지 묻고 있으므로 그 내용이 담긴 선택지를
고르면 된다.

어휘_ repairman 수리공　**receptionist** 접수원

정답_ (a)

Part 2
5.

W: Do you know how to make the international
　　calls?
M: Of course. Where do you want to make a
　　call?
W: Australia. My sister lives there.
M: ＿＿＿＿＿＿＿＿＿＿＿＿＿＿＿＿＿＿

(a) You must put the country code in front of
　　the number.
(b) Where does your brother live?
(c) I didn't get a dial tone.
(d) My parents have been traveling in Australia.

해석_ W: 국제 전화 어떻게 사용하는지 아니?

M: 물론이지. 어디에 전화하고 싶은데?

W: 호주. 내 여동생이 거기 살고 있어.

M: _______________________

(a) 전화번호 앞에 국가 번호를 붙여야 해.

(b) 네 남동생은 어디 사는데?

(c) 전화가 먹통이야.

(d) 우리 부모님은 호주 여행 중이셔.

해설_ 국제 전화 사용법을 묻고 있으므로 이에 관한 설명이 담긴 선택지를 고르면 된다.

어휘_ **make a call** 전화하다(= phone, call) **country code** 국가 번호 **dial tone** 발신음 *cf.* 영국식 영어로는 dialling tone

정답_ (a)

6.

M: Hello. May I speak to Jack?

W: Jack is taking a shower. Would you like to call back again?

M: Please ask him to check his e-mail.

W: _______________________

(a) I'll convey what you said.

(b) Yes. You've been thoughtful anytime.

(c) Jack has told me about you.

(d) Great. Let us introduce ourselves.

해석_ M: 여보세요. 잭과 통화할 수 있을까요?

W: 잭은 지금 샤워 중이야. 다시 할래?

M: 이메일 확인하라고 좀 전해 주세요.

W: _______________________

(a) 네가 말한 대로 전할게.

(b) 그래. 넌 언제나 사려 깊어.

(c) 잭이 너에 대해서 얘기했었어.

(d) 좋아. 우리 소개할게.

해설_ 전화를 받은 여자에게 메시지 전달을 부탁하고 있는 상황이므로 이에 응하는 선택지를 고르면 된다.

어휘_ **take a shower** 샤워하다 **convey** 전달하다, 알리다 **thoughtful** 사려 깊은

정답_ (a)

Chapter 6 질의응답

STEP 1 Pattern Study

Sample

해석_ M: 넌 집에 있는 것보다 도서관에 가는 게 낫겠다.

W: _______________________

(a) 거긴 답답해서 도저히 견딜 수가 없어.

(b) 맞는 말이지만 난 어제 이 책을 읽을 수 있었어.

(c) 점심 먹고 우리 집에 같이 갈까?

(d) 맞아. 도서관에서는 집중할 수가 없어.

정답_ (a)

STEP 2 Clinic

Part 1

1.

해석_ M: 넌 그녀가 우리 편이라고 생각해?

W: _______________________

(a) 우리 편이라고 생각지 않아.

(b) 그녀가 벽 반대쪽에 있는 것 같아.

(c) 그녀가 오는 중인 것 같지 않아.

(d) 그녀가 그 안에 있다고 생각해.

정답_ (a)

2.

해석_ W: 이번 주말에 플로리다 가는 거 어때?

M: _______________________

(a) 다음주 늦게 떠날 거야.

(b) 그거 정말 재미있어.

(c) 이번주에 할 일이 너무 많아.

(d) 다음 주말에 가는 게 더 나아.

정답_ (d)

Part 2

3.

해석_ M: 저 버스 타자.

W: 우리 시간 별로 없다고 그러지 않았어?

M: 음, 버스 안에서 찰리한테 전화해 다음 정류장에서 우릴 태워 가라고 할 거야.

W: _______________________________

(a) 좋아. 그게 시간 낭비 않는 방법이겠다.

(b) 난 이런 버스들을 타 본 적이 한 번도 없어.

(c) 검토해 볼게.

(d) 그거 싸 가자.

정답_ (a)

4.

해석_ M: 이거 하는 방법 알아?

W: 잘 몰라. 아마 제인은 알고 있을 거야.

M: 걔가 여기 사용 설명서대로 하라고 말해 줬어.

W: _______________________________

(a) 나 그거 상자 반대편에 있는 거 봤어.

(b) 그럼 그 사용 설명서대로 해보자.

(c) 몇 가지만 하면 됐어.

(d) 나 혼자서 처리할게.

정답_ (b)

STEP 3 Dictation

정답_ 1. I don't think she is

2. It is better to go down there next weekend

3. Okay. That way we won't lose any time

4. Let's just follow the instructions, then

STEP 4 Actual Test

Part 1

1.

M: Do you have any preferred seats in the airplane?

W: _______________________________

(a) Yes, I'd like to stay in the hotel.

(b) No, I don't care that much.

(c) I think it is going to be closed.

(d) I felt full in the morning.

해석_ M: 특별히 선호하는 기내 좌석이 있나요?

W: _______________________________

(a) 네, 호텔에 머물고 싶어요.

(b) 아뇨, 별로 개의치 않아요.

(c) 문 닫을 것 같은데요.

(d) 아침을 많이 먹었어요.

해설_ 선호하는 좌석이 있는지 묻고 있으므로 이에 관한 응답이 담긴 선택지를 고르면 된다. 참고로, 비행기 좌석은 위치에 따라서 window seat(창가 쪽 좌석), aisle seat(통로 쪽 좌석), middle seat(중간 좌석)이 있으며, 등급에 따라 first class(1등석), business class(비즈니스석), coach(= economy class, 3등석)로 나뉜다.

어휘_ **preferred** 선호하는, 우선의

정답_ (b)

2.

W: Sometimes I need to spend my free time alone.

M: _______________________________

(a) Of course. Everybody thinks like you.

(b) I don't think you need to spend a lot of money.

(c) It's a good idea. When will you be free?

(d) I spend my spare time climbing a mountain.

해석_ W: 가끔은 혼자 여가 시간을 보내는 게 필요해.

M: _______________________________

(a) 물론이지. 누구든지 너처럼 생각해.

(b) 네가 많은 돈을 쓸 필요는 없다고 생각해.

(c) 좋은 생각이야. 언제 시간 돼?

(d) 난 등산하면서 여가 시간을 보내.

해설_ 혼자 여가 시간을 보내는 것의 필요성을 얘기했으므로 그에 대한 남자의 의견이 이어지는 것이 자연스럽다. (d)는 여가 시간에 뭘 하는지 물었을 때의 응답 표현.

어휘_ **climb a mountain** 등산하다

정답_ (a)

3.

W: Are you putting cinnamon in this pie? It's the same as my way.

M: _______________________________

(a) Do you know how much sugar is in the cake?

(b) Cinnamon smells too strong to me.

(c) What a delicious pie!

(d) It's perfect! You are the only one who can read my mind.

해석_ W: 이 파이에 계피 넣을 거니? 나랑 만드는 방식이 똑같다.

M: _______________________________

(a) 케이크에 설탕이 얼마나 들어가는지 아니?

(b) 시나몬 향기는 내게 너무 강해.

(c) 파이가 정말 맛있다!

(d) 완벽해! 넌 내 마음을 아는 유일한 사람이야.

해설_ 자신과 케이크 만드는 방식이 똑같다는 말을 들었으므로 (d)가 가장 적절하다.

어휘_ **cinnamon** 계피 **read one's mind** 속마음을 알아채다

정답_ (d)

Part 2

4.

M: Did you hear the new policy?

W: I haven't heard it yet. What is it?

M: All employees must wear uniforms beginning next month.

W: _______________________________

(a) Sure. I can't stand men who wear short pants.

(b) I never consent to it. What do you think of it?

(c) Yes, I saw it. It's quite good.

(d) No. Who authorized her to do this project?

해석_ M: 새로운 방침 들었니?

W: 아직 못 들었는데. 그게 뭐니?

M: 모든 직원은 다음 달 초부터 유니폼을 입어야 해.

W: _______________________________

(a) 물론이지. 난 반바지 입는 남자 딱 질색이야.

(b) 절대 동의 못해. 넌 어떻게 생각해?

(c) 그래, 봤어. 꽤 좋더라.

(d) 아니. 누가 그녀에게 이 프로젝트 하라고 한 거야?

해설_ 다음 달 초부터 유니폼을 입어야 한다는 회사 방침에 대해 동의나 반대의 의견이 담긴 응답이 이어져야 자연스럽다.

어휘_ **employee** 직원 **consent** 동의하다 **authorize** 권한을 [권리를] 부여하다

정답_ (b)

5.

W: Have you ever seen my newspaper?

M: No. Do you subscribe to a paper? Many people read the paper on the internet these days.

W: Yes. But every time I read it on the internet I have a headache.

M: _______________________________

(a) That's right. It's because of electromagnetic waves.

(b) I'll subscribe to a magazine next month.

(c) Right. I always read the newspaper in the morning.

(d) Do you? I have had a headache since Monday.

해석_ W: 내 신문 본 적 있니?

M: 아니. 너 신문 구독하니? 요즘엔 많은 사람들이 인터넷으로 신문 보던데.

W: 그래. 근데 인터넷으로 보면 난 머리가 아파.

M: _______________________________

(a) 맞아. 전자파 때문이지.

(b) 다음 달부터 잡지 정기 구독할 거야.

(c) 맞아. 난 항상 아침에 신문을 읽어.

(d) 그래? 난 월요일부터 머리가 아팠어.

해설_ 인터넷으로 신문을 보면 머리가 아프다는 남자의 말에 공감하거나 반대 의견을 말하는 선택지를 고르면 된다.

어휘_ **subscribe to** ~을 구독하다 **have a headache** 두통이 있다, 머리가 아프다 **electromagnetic wave** 전자파

정답_ (a)

6.

M: No way! The government will make landfill in our town.

W: Is it true? Where did you get it?

M: I just watched the news. Do you agree?

W: _______________________________

(a) Whatever you want, I'll agree with you.

(b) No, I agreed. It doesn't matter.

(c) That's ridiculous! Nobody discussed it with residents.

(d) Oh, my god. You weren't against it.

해석_ M: 말도 안 돼! 정부에서 우리 동네에 쓰레기 매립지를 만들 거래.

W: 그게 사실이야? 어디서 들었어?

M: 방금 뉴스 봤어. 넌 동의하니?

W: ______________________________

(a) 네가 원하는 것은 무엇이든 난 네 의견에 동의할 거야.

(b) 아니, 난 동의했어. 신경 안 써.

(c) 말도 안 돼! 아무도 주민들과 상의하지 않았는걸.

(d) 이런. 넌 반대하지 않았구나.

해설_ 정부의 쓰레기 매립지 조성에 대해 동의하는지 묻고 있으므로 이에 관한 의견이 담긴 선택지를 고르면 된다.

어휘_ **landfill** 쓰레기 매립지 **resident** 거주자, 주민

정답_ (c)

7.

W: Do you think she is going to follow my idea?

M: I don't think she is concerned with it.

W: But it seems like she is always against me.

M: ______________________________

(a) I think it is out of control.

(b) She thinks it is interesting.

(c) Honestly, she is not that into it.

(d) It is considerably important.

해석_ W: 그녀가 내 아이디어에 따를 거라고 생각해?

M: 그녀는 관심이 없는 것 같은데.

W: 하지만 그녀는 항상 내 의견에 반대하는 것 같단 말이야.

M: ______________________________

(a) 그건 통제할 수 없는 것 같아.

(b) 그녀는 그게 흥미롭다고 생각해.

(c) 솔직히 그녀가 아주 좋아하진 않아.

(d) 그건 상당히 중요해.

해설_ 그녀가 항상 자신의 의견에 반대하는 것 같다는 여자의 생각에 대해 동의 또는 반대의 의미가 담긴 선택지를 고르면 된다. 남자의 첫 대사에서 그녀가 여자의 아이디어에 관심이 없는 것 같다고 했으므로 (b)는 틀리다.

어휘_ **be concerned with** ~에 관심이 있다 **out of control** 통제할 수 없는 **be into ...** ~에 푹 빠지다, ~을 무척 좋아하다 **considerably** 상당히

정답_ (c)

Chapter 7 공공안내 · 교통

STEP 1 Pattern Study

Sample

해석_ M: 여기 공중전화 박스는 어디 있어요?

W: ______________________________

(a) 미안하지만, 여기가 아닌 것 같아요.

(b) 유감스럽게도 고장 났어요.

(c) 이 구역 모퉁이 돌면 바로 있어요.

(d) 그것들을 각각 보게 될 거예요.

정답_ (c)

STEP 2 Clinic

Part 1

1.

해석_ M: 여기 어떻게 돌아왔어?

W: ______________________________

(a) 다시 돌아오는 길이었어.

(b) 예전에 여기 있었어.

(c) 자전거 타고 다시 왔어.

(d) 나중에 다시 연락할게.

정답_ (c)

2.

해석_ M: 도와 드릴까요? 뭐 찾으시는 거 있으세요?

W: ______________________________

(a) 그냥 둘러보는 거예요. 고맙습니다.

(b) 저 부분을 들여다보고 있었어요.

(c) 그냥 여기 작은 것을 봤어요.

(d) 친구와 만나기를 고대하고 있어요.

정답_ (a)

Part 2

3.

해석_ W: 지금 내 가방이 안 보이는 것 같다.

M: 바로 전에 마지막으로 갔던 장소가 어디였지?

W: 가구 코너에 있었던 것 같아.

M: ______________________________

(a) 거기 판매 직원한테 물어볼게.

(b) 가구 찾으세요?

(c) 새거 사고 싶었어?

(d) 그 사람 어떻게 생겼어?

정답_ (a)

4.

해석_ M: 그녀가 지금 어디 있는지 알아?

W: 오는 중인 것 같은데.

M: 어디서 오는 길인데?

W: _______________________________

(a) 고속도로에 있어.

(b) 회의에 참석했었어.

(c) 길이 막혀 꼼짝 못하고 있어.

(d) 집으로 돌아오는 중이야.

정답_ (b)

STEP 3 Dictation

정답_ 1. I used bicycle to make it back here

2. I am just looking. Thanks

3. Let me ask the saleslady there

4. She was in a business meeting

STEP 4 Actual Test

Part 1

1.

W: Help me! I don't know where my son is.

M: _______________________________

(a) Calm down. I suppose he will have been taken to the lost children center.

(b) Sure. I am willing to help you.

(c) I believe he bought this book for a song.

(d) He seemed to be a little bit tired.

해석_ W: 도와주세요! 우리 아들을 잃어버렸어요.

M: _______________________________

(a) 진정하세요. 아드님은 미아 보호소에 있을 겁니다.

(b) 물론이죠. 기꺼이 도와드리겠습니다.

(c) 그가 이 노래 책을 샀다고 생각해요.

(d) 그는 좀 피곤해 보였어요.

해설_ 아이가 없어져 당황해하는 아이 엄마를 안심시키는 내용이 이어져야 자연스럽다. (b)는 Can you help me with this luggage?(짐 옮기는 것 좀 도와줄래요?)와 같이 일상적인 도움 요청에 어울리는 응답으로, 여기서처럼 다급하게 도움을 구하는 상황에서는 부자연스럽다.

어휘_ **calm down** 진정하다 **lost children center** 미아 보호소 **be willing to** 기꺼이 ~하다

정답_ (a)

2.

M: Could you please change this fifty-dollar bill?

W: _______________________________

(a) OK, how do you want to change it?

(b) It's changed a lot before I lived there.

(c) Sure. I need some cash.

(d) Please give me the bill.

해석_ M: 이 50달러 지폐 좀 바꿔 주시겠어요?

W: _______________________________

(a) 네, 어떻게 바꿔 드릴까요?

(b) 예전에 살았을 때보다 많이 변했어요.

(c) 물론이죠. 전 현금이 좀 필요해요.

(d) 계산서 좀 갖다 주세요.

해설_ 남자가 지폐를 바꿔 달라고 했으므로 어떻게 바꿔 주길 원하는지 묻는 질문이 이어져야 자연스럽다.

어휘_ **bill** 지폐 **cash** 현금

정답_ (a)

3.

M: My neighbor just had a traffic accident at an intersection.

W: _______________________________

(a) Keep me informed.

(b) Turn left at the crossroads.

(c) That place is bad for accidents.

(d) Oh, no. What happened to you?

해석_ M: 우리 이웃이 교차로에서 막 교통사고가 났대요.

W: _______________________________

(a) 나한테 계속 알려줘요.

(b) 횡단보도에서 좌회전하세요.

(c) 그곳은 사고 다발 지역이에요.

(d) 저런. 무슨 일이에요?

해설_ 남자의 이웃이 교차로에서 교통사고를 당했다는 소식을 들었으므로 그 사고나 사고 장소와 관련된 응답을 한 선택지를 고르면 된다.

어휘_ **intersection = crossroads** 교차로 **keep ... informed** ∼에게 계속해서 알려주다

정답_ (c)

4.

W: I need to buy a round-trip ticket to New York. What time is the earliest flight?

M: ___________________________________

(a) The flight has been delayed about half an hour.

(b) I've never been to New York all my life.

(c) Go straight. You can see an inquiry office.

(d) The next flight to New York leaves this Friday at 7:00 AM.

해석_ W: 뉴욕행 왕복 티켓을 사려고 하는데요. 가장 빠른 비행기 시간이 몇 시죠?

M: ___________________________________

(a) 그 비행기는 약 30분 정도 지연됐어요.

(b) 난 평생 뉴욕에 가 본 적이 없어요.

(c) 곧장 가세요. 안내소가 보일 거예요.

(d) 다음 뉴욕행 비행기는 이번주 금요일 오전 7시 정각에 출발합니다.

해설_ 다음 비행기 시간을 묻고 있으므로 (d)가 정답이다.

어휘_ **round-trip ticket** 왕복 티켓 cf. one way ticket 편도 **inquiry office** 안내소

정답_ (d)

Part 2

5.

W: Excuse me, sir. Where is the departure platform?

M: Could you show me the ticket?

W: Here. Did I take the wrong road?

M: ___________________________________

(a) No, you are right. The road is being repaired.

(b) You can go upstairs and check the train.

(c) No, you were able to buy it at the ticket office.

(d) You might postpone your departure time.

해석_ W: 실례합니다. 출발 승강장이 어디죠?

M: 티켓을 보여 주시겠습니까?

W: 여기요. 제가 길을 잘못 왔나요?

M: ___________________________________

(a) 아뇨, 맞아요. 길이 보수 공사 중이에요.

(b) 위층에 올라가셔서 열차 확인하세요.

(c) 아뇨, 당신은 매표소에서 그걸 살 수 있었어요.

(d) 출발 시간을 연기해도 좋아요.

해설_ 길을 잘못 들었는지 묻고 있으므로 이에 답하는 선택지를 고르면 된다.

어휘_ **departure platform** 출발 승강장 **ticket office** 매표소 **postphone** 연기하다(= put off, delay)

정답_ (a)

6.

W: Excuse me. Can I ask you a question?

M: Sure. How can I help you?

W: I'm a stranger. How far is it to the 63 building from here?

M: ___________________________________

(a) It is the fastest way to take a taxi.

(b) All passengers get off at the last stop.

(c) I think it takes 10 minutes if you walk along this street.

(d) The building will be far different before it changes.

해석_ W: 실례합니다. 뭐 좀 여쭤봐도 될까요?

M: 물론이죠. 어떻게 도와 드릴까요?

W: 이곳이 처음이라서요. 여기서 63빌딩이 얼마나 먼가요?

M: ___________________________________

(a) 택시 타는 게 제일 빨라요.

(b) 모든 승객이 종점에서 내립니다.

(c) 제 생각에 이 길을 따라 걸으시면 10분 걸릴 거예요.

(d) 그 건물은 바뀌기 전과 상당히 다를 거예요.

해설_ 63빌딩까지 가는 데 걸리는 시간을 묻고 있으므로 (c)가 정답이다.

어휘_ **passenger** 승객   **stop** 정거장
정답_ (c)

7.

M: Could I open up a joint account?
W: OK. Do you have any account with this bank?
M: No, I don't.
W: ___________________________

(a) First, just fill this request form and come again please.
(b) You ought to know your daughter's social security number.
(c) Unfortunately, it's our policy.
(d) Wasn't the bank open at 9 o'clock?

해석_ M: 공동 예금 계좌를 만들 수 있을까요?
　　　 W: 네. 이 은행 계좌를 갖고 계신가요?
　　　 M: 아니오, 없습니다.
　　　 W: ___________________________
　　　 (a) 우선, 이 신청서 기입하시고 다시 와 주세요.
　　　 (b) 따님의 주민등록번호를 아셔야 합니다.
　　　 (c) 유감스럽게도, 그건 저희 방침입니다.
　　　 (d) 은행은 9시에 열지 않나요?
해설_ 남자가 은행 계좌가 없다고 했으므로 계좌 신청서 작성을 요구하는 (a)가 적절하다.
어휘_ **joint account** 공동 예금 계좌   **fill** 기입하다   **request form** 신청서   **social security number** 사회보장번호, 주민등록번호   **policy** 방침, 정책
정답_ (a)

8.

W: Excuse me. Do you know how I can get to the Main Hotel?
M: I think you should walk rather than take a vehicle.
W: Please, tell me why. Because I'm late.
M: ___________________________

(a) I'm afraid I couldn't find your reservation.
(b) Because there were two subway lines.
(c) The front of the hotel is under construction.
(d) I don't know why. Let me ask the staff.

해석_ W: 실례합니다. 메인 호텔까지 어떻게 가는지 아십니까?
　　　 M: 차를 타는 것보다 걸어가시는 게 나을 것 같아요.
　　　 W: 이유를 말씀해 주세요. 제가 늦어서요.
　　　 M: ___________________________
　　　 (a) 죄송합니다만, 예약하신 내용을 확인할 수 없군요.
　　　 (b) 왜냐하면 지하철 노선이 두 개 있었거든요.
　　　 (c) 호텔 앞쪽이 공사 중이에요.
　　　 (d) 이유는 잘 모르겠네요. 직원한테 물어볼게요.
해설_ 차를 타는 것보다 걸어가는 게 나은 이유를 묻고 있으므로 이에 대해 언급한 선택지를 고르면 된다. 걸어가는 게 낫다고 말한 건 그 이유를 알고 있다는 얘기이므로 (d)는 앞뒤가 맞지 않는다.
어휘_ **reservation** 예약   **subway line** 지하철 노선   **under construction** 공사 중인
정답_ (c)

Chapter 8 여행·취미

STEP 1 Pattern Study

Sample

해석_ M: 벌써 호주에 도착했어?

W: 아니, 지금 막 홍콩에 도착했어. 일주일간 여기 있을 것 같아.

M: 그럼 한국에 언제 다시 오는데?

W: ___________________________

(a) 여기 머무를 것 같지 않아.

(b) 그 즈음에 홍콩에 가지 않아.

(c) 이달 말에 돌아갈 것 같아.

(d) 방금 호주로 돌아왔어.

정답_ (c)

STEP 2 Clinic

Part 1

1.

해석_ W: 비엔나에 얼마나 오래 있었죠?

M: ___________________________

(a) 그곳은 방문하기에 멋진 곳이었어요.

(b) 이틀 정도요.

(c) 출장 갔었어요.

(d) 비엔나행 열차를 탔어요.

정답_ (b)

2.

해석_ M: 여가 시간을 어떻게 보내요?

W: ___________________________

(a) 잘 쓸게요.

(b) 지금 빨래하고 있어요.

(c) 다음을 위해 아껴두는 게 낫겠어요.

(d) 보통 영화 보러 가요.

정답_ (d)

Part 2

3.

해석_ W: 어디로 여행 다녀왔니?

M: 일본, 홍콩, 한국에 갔었어.

W: 5일 동안 3개국을? 무척 바빴겠구나.

M: ___________________________

(a) 응, 그래서 홍콩에 딱 하루만 머물렀어.

(b) 그래, 거기서 만나서 좋았어.

(c) 응, 무척 흥분돼.

(d) 아니, 일주일 동안 보는 데 충분했어.

정답_ (a)

4.

해석_ W: 너 언제 돌아오니? 우리 기념품 사와.

M: 미안하지만, 쇼핑할 시간이 별로 없을 것 같아.

W: 그럼, 함께 추억을 나눌 사진들이나 많이 찍어 와!

M: ___________________________

(a) 고마워. 기념품으로 잘 간직할게.

(b) 그들을 직접 만나서 좋았어.

(c) 꼭 그럴게.

(d) 곧 다시 만나길 기대할게.

정답_ (c)

STEP 3 Dictation

정답_ 1. A couple of days

2. I usually go to the movies

3. Yes, so I stopped over in Hong Kong only for a day

4. I'm sure I will

STEP 4 Actual Test

Part 1

1.

M: What time are you leaving for Sydney?

W: ___________________________

(a) I was in Sydney when I was eleven.

(b) I used to go to the swimming pool.

(c) I think I might be going to Sydney on Sunday.

(d) In 30 minutes from now.

해석_ M: 시드니로 몇 시에 떠나니?

W: ______________________________

(a) 11살 때 시드니에 있었어.

(b) 수영장에 가곤 했지.

(c) 일요일에 시드니 갈 것 같아.

(d) 지금부터 30분 후에.

해설_ 몇 시에 떠날 건지 묻고 있으므로 시간이 언급된 선택지를 고르면 된다.

어휘_ leave for ~로 떠나다 **swimming pool** 수영장

정답_ (d)

2.

W: What did you think of the movie?

M: ______________________________

(a) Okay, I will try to make it tonight.

(b) It was alright but a bit ridiculous.

(c) I don't understand what you are talking about.

(d) I don't think I can make it tonight.

해석_ W: 그 영화 어땠니?

　　M: ______________________________

　　(a) 그래 좋아, 오늘 밤엔 가 보도록 해볼게.

　　(b) 괜찮긴 했는데 좀 엉뚱했어.

　　(c) 네가 무슨 말을 하고 있는지 잘 모르겠어.

　　(d) 오늘 밤엔 못 갈 것 같아.

해설_ 영화를 본 소감을 묻고 있으므로 이에 대해 언급한 선택지를 고르면 된다.

어휘_ ridiculous 터무니없는, 우스꽝스러운

정답_ (b)

3.

M: How long are you going to stay in the States?

W: ______________________________

(a) It is only for 5 days for a business trip.

(b) I think I will go to America next year.

(c) I didn't go to the Empire State Building.

(d) She is staying with her daughter.

해석_ M: 미국에 얼마나 오래 머물 거야?

　　W: ______________________________

　　(a) 출장으로 5일만.

(b) 내년에 미국에 갈 것 같아.

(c) 엠파이어 스테이트 빌딩에 가지 않았어.

(d) 그녀는 딸과 함께 머물고 있어.

해설_ 얼마나 오래 머물 건지 묻고 있으므로 기간이 언급된 선택지를 고르면 된다.

어휘_ the Empire State Building 뉴욕시 맨해튼에 소재한 102층짜리 초고층 빌딩

정답_ (a)

4.

M: Isn't your hobby listening to music? What kind of music do you like?

W: ______________________________

(a) I usually listen to rock music on my spare time.

(b) I'm into jazz music.

(c) My MP3 player was broken.

(d) Why don't we go to a pop concert?

해석_ M: 음악 듣기가 네 취미 아니니? 어떤 음악 좋아해?

　　W: ______________________________

　　(a) 난 시간 날 때 보통 록 음악을 들어.

　　(b) 난 재즈 음악을 무지 좋아해.

　　(c) 내 MP3 플레이어가 고장 났어.

　　(d) 팝 콘서트 보러 갈까?

해설_ 좋아하는 음악 장르를 묻고 있으므로 (b)가 정답이다.

어휘_ break 고장 나다 **pop concert** 팝 콘서트

정답_ (b)

Part 2

5.

W: Honey! DVDs are overdue, aren't they?

M: Oh, they were due the day before yesterday.

W: It slipped my mind again.

M: ______________________________

(a) You're right. They split in two.

(b) My son paid a small fine of $3.50.

(c) We need to leave a note for lending.

(d) Can I borrow a novel this week?

해석_ W: 자기야! DVD 대여 기간 지나지 않았어?

　　M: 앗, 그저께까지였는데.

W: 또 깜박 잊었네.

M: ＿＿＿＿＿＿＿＿＿＿＿＿＿＿＿＿＿＿

(a) 당신 말이 맞아. 그것들은 두 개로 쪼개졌어.

(b) 우리 아들이 3달러 50센트의 소액 벌금을 물었어.

(c) 대여한 것에 대해 메모를 해둬야겠어.

(d) 이번주에 소설책 한 권 빌릴 수 있을까?

해설_ DVD 반납하는 걸 또 깜박 잊었다고 했으므로 이에 대한 해결
책이 언급된 (c)가 연결 응답으로 적절하다.

어휘_ **overdue** 기한이 지난　　**slip one's mind** 깜박 잊다
split 쪼개다　**fine** 벌금　**lend** 대여하다

정답_ (c)

6.

M: This spray is prohibited to be brought in the
airplane.

W: I didn't know. Should I throw it away?

M: It's possible to explode and you should do
it under the regulations.

W: ＿＿＿＿＿＿＿＿＿＿＿＿＿＿＿＿＿＿＿＿

(a) Sure, I will.

(b) Do you know the weight limit?

(c) How can I check in my luggage?

(d) I see. I have another one.

해석_ M: 이 스프레이는 기내 반입이 금지돼 있습니다.

W: 몰랐어요. 버려야 하나요?

M: 폭발 가능성이 있어서 규정상 버리셔야 합니다.

W: ＿＿＿＿＿＿＿＿＿＿＿＿＿＿＿

(a) 좋아요, 그럴게요.

(b) 제한 중량을 아십니까?

(c) 제 짐을 어떻게 부칠 수 있죠?

(d) 알겠습니다. 저는 하나가 더 있어요.

해설_ 남자의 첫 번째 대사를 통해 공항에서 이루어지고 있는 대화
임을 알 수 있다. 규정상 스프레이를 버려야 한다고 했으므로
이에 응하는 (a)가 정답이다.

어휘_ **prohibit** 금지하다　**explode** 폭발하다　**under the**
regulations 규정상　**weight limit** 제한 중량

정답_ (a)

7.

W: What a great painting! Did you paint it by
yourself?

M: Sure. Will you come to my exhibition next
week?

W: Wow! Your hobby isn't a hobby anymore.

M: ＿＿＿＿＿＿＿＿＿＿＿＿＿＿＿＿＿＿＿＿＿＿

(a) I painted my own house.

(b) Well begun, half done.

(c) Don't bother me!

(d) Thank you. You praise me too much.

해석_ W: 정말 멋진 그림이다! 너 혼자 그린 거야?

M: 물론. 다음주 내 전시회에 올래?

W: 와! 네 취미는 이제 취미 이상이구나.

M: ＿＿＿＿＿＿＿＿＿＿＿＿＿＿＿＿＿

(a) 내가 우리 집 페인트칠 했어.

(b) 시작이 반이야.

(c) 날 귀찮게 하지 마!

(d) 고마워. 너무 과분한 칭찬인데.

해설_ 그림 솜씨에 대해 칭찬을 받았으므로 이에 대한 답례가 담긴
선택지를 고르면 된다.

어휘_ **exhibition** 전시회　**Well begun, half done.** 〈속담〉
시작이 반이다.　**praise** 칭찬하다

정답_ (d)

Chapter 9 비즈니스·학교·직장

STEP 1 Pattern Study

Sample
해석_ W: 생물 수업 숙제가 뭐였니?

M: ___________________________

(a) 나도 준비 못했어.

(b) 그걸 해서 좋았어.

(c) 나도 몰라. 지난 수업 빼먹었어.

(d) 아주 쉽진 않았어.

정답_ (c)

STEP 2 Clinic

Part 1
1.

해석_ M: 그 안건에 대한 발표는 어땠어?

W: ___________________________

(a) 긴급한 거였어.

(b) 잘 알려진 주제였어.

(c) 그들을 직접 만나서 좋았어.

(d) 아주 순조로웠어.

정답_ (d)

2.

해석_ M: 안건에 대한 주제는 어떻게 진행되고 있니?

W: ___________________________

(a) 약간 빠르게 진행되고 있었어.

(b) 아주 신속하게 진행 중이야.

(c) 그건 변화를 가져올 거야.

(d) 그건 선택사항이 될 거야.

정답_ (b)

Part 2
3.

해석_ W: 지금까지 중간고사 준비는 잘돼 가니?

M: 복습할 시간이 많이 없었어.

W: 나도 그래. 무지 걱정된다.

M: ___________________________

(a) 우린 마지막 순간까지 벼락치기해야 해.

(b) 걱정 마, 넌 이겨낼 거야.

(c) 난 네가 최선을 다했다고 확신해.

(d) 우린 곧 만날 거야.

정답_ (a)

4.

해석_ M: 나 주식을 좀 살 거야.

W: 너무 충동적으로 들린다.

M: 너도 같이 사야 해.

W: ___________________________

(a) 난 그게 제로섬 게임이라고 생각해.

(b) 미안, 난 모험을 즐기는 사람이 아니야.

(c) 그건 고위험 고수익 상품이야.

(d) 미안해. 난 지금 바빠.

정답_ (b)

STEP 3 Dictation

정답_ 1. It went very smoothly

2. It's going so quickly

3. We need to cram until the very last moment

4. Sorry, I'm not a risk-taker

STEP 4 Actual Test

Part 1
1.

M: I sent you an e-mail this morning. Did you check the details?

W: ___________________________

(a) I'm sorry. I've just come from a business trip.

(b) Do you know when the deadline is?

(c) I've been waiting for the mail all day.

(d) Please send us the mail right away.

해석_ M: 오늘 아침에 이메일을 보냈는데요. 자세한 사항을 보셨나요?

W: ___________________________

(a) 죄송해요. 지금 막 출장에서 돌아왔어요.

(b) 마감 시간이 언제인지 아세요?

(c) 하루 종일 메일을 기다리고 있었어요.

(d) 저희에게 바로 메일 보내 주세요.

해설_ 보낸 메일을 읽어 봤는지 묻고 있으므로 이에 관한 응답이 담긴 선택지를 고르면 된다.

어휘_ deadline 마감 시간

정답_ (a)

2.

W: Wait, let me give you my business card if you want.

M: ________________________________

(a) No thanks, I'll give you my card.

(b) I appreciate it and I'll contact you Tuesday afternoon.

(c) What do you want to do in this business contract?

(d) I have my hands full at the moment.

해석_ W: 잠깐만요, 원하신다면 제 명함을 드릴게요.

　　　 M: ________________________________

　　　 (a) 아니, 괜찮습니다. 제 명함을 드릴게요.

　　　 (b) 감사합니다. 화요일 오후에 연락드릴게요.

　　　 (c) 이 사업 계약에서 뭘 원하시나요?

　　　 (d) 지금은 너무 바쁘네요.

해설_ 원하면 명함을 주겠다는 여자의 말에 이어질 응답으로, 공손히 사양하며 자기 명함을 주겠다는 (a)가 적절하다.

어휘_ business card 명함(= card)　**have one's hands full** 매우 바쁘다

정답_ (a)

3.

M: Who is in charge of this project?

W: ________________________________

(a) That would be the head of the sales division.

(b) You don't need any charge for admission.

(c) Did you make an appointment?

(d) Mrs. Park has almost finished her third quarter project.

해석_ M: 이 프로젝트 담당자가 누굽니까?

W: ________________________________

(a) 판매부 부장님일 거예요.

(b) 입장료는 낼 필요 없어요.

(c) 약속하셨나요?

(d) 파크 씨는 그녀의 3분기 프로젝트를 거의 끝냈어요.

해설_ 프로젝트 담당자를 묻고 있으므로 정답은 (a)다. (b)는 대화 중에 나온 charge를 이용해 오답을 유도하려는 함정이므로 유의하자.

어휘_ in charge of ~을 맡고 있는, 담당의　**sales division** 판매부　**charge** 요금　**admission** 입장　**make an appointment** 약속을 하다　**quarter** 분기

정답_ (a)

4.

W: What do you expect for your graduation gift?

M: ________________________________

(a) I think the white one is better.

(b) My brother gave me some flowers a few days ago.

(c) Yes, I am pretty close to my grandmother.

(d) Actually I have never thought about it seriously.

해석_ W: 졸업 선물로 뭘 받았으면 좋겠니?

　　　 M: ________________________________

　　　 (a) 제 생각엔 흰 것이 더 나은 것 같아요.

　　　 (b) 오빠가 며칠 전에 꽃을 줬어요.

　　　 (c) 네, 전 할머니와 아주 친해요.

　　　 (d) 사실 그것에 대해 진지하게 생각해 본 적이 없어요.

해설_ 졸업 선물로 받고 싶은 것을 묻고 있으므로 이에 관해 언급한 선택지를 고르면 된다.

어휘_ graduation 졸업　**close to** ~와 친한　**seriously** 진지하게

정답_ (d)

Part 2

5.

M: You had an interview yesterday. How was it?

W: I think I didn't pass the interview.

M: Why? You were full of confidence before.

W: ___________________________________

(a) The questions were more difficult than I
expected.
(b) I have three years of experience in this
market.
(c) Those are my strong points.
(d) I don't know why I didn't pass the exam.

해석_ M: 너 어제 면접 봤잖아. 어땠어?

W: 면접에서 떨어졌을 거야.

M: 왜? 가기 전엔 자신감이 넘쳤었잖아.

W: _______________________________

(a) 질문이 생각보다 어려웠어.

(b) 난 이 시장에서 3년 경험이 있어.

(c) 그것들이 나의 장점이야.

(d) 내가 왜 시험에 떨어졌는지 모르겠어.

해설_ 면접에서 떨어졌을 거라고 생각하는 이유를 묻고 있으므로 이
에 관한 내용이 담긴 (a)가 정답이다.

어휘_ **resume** 이력서 *cf.* 영국식 영어로는 C.V.(= Curriculum
Vitae) **strong point** 강점, 장점

정답_ (a)

6.

M: Did Mark's big meeting begin?
W: No, it's a little delayed.
M: Good. I've got the copy of Mark's proposal.
W: ___________________________________

(a) The proposal will be accepted.
(b) You can't get in without your identification.
(c) He desires you come out here.
(d) We are all in the same boat.

해석_ M: 마크의 중요 회의 시작 했나요?

W: 아니요, 약간 늦춰졌어요.

M: 잘됐군요. 마크의 제안서 사본을 가지고 있거든요.

W: _______________________________

(a) 그 제안은 받아들여질 겁니다.

(b) 신분증 없이 들어갈 수 없습니다.

(c) 그가 당신을 몹시 기다렸어요.

(d) 우리 모두 같은 처지예요.

해설_ 마크의 제안서 사본을 갖고 있다고 했으므로 (c)가 가장 적절
한 응답이다.

어휘_ **copy** 사본 **identification** 신분증 **desire** 몹시 바라다
come out 나타나다, 출현하다 **in the same boat** 같
은 처지의

정답_ (c)

7.

W: Great job! You will be promoted from next
month.
M: Thank you. I'm happy that I concluded the
contract with the ER company.
W: You are lucky. Let's have a drink.
M: ___________________________________

(a) It'll save them money.
(b) Absolutely! I'll treat you.
(c) It serves you right!
(d) You shouldn't twist my arm.

해석_ W: 잘했어요! 다음 달에 승진할 거예요.

M: 감사합니다. ER사와 계약을 마무리해서 기뻐요.

W: 운이 좋군요. 술 한잔 해요.

M: _______________________________

(a) 그것이 그들에게 돈을 절약해 줄 거예요.

(b) 물론이죠! 제가 살게요.

(c) 그거 쌤통이군요!

(d) 강요하지 않아도 돼요.

해설_ 술 한잔 하자고 했으므로 이에 응하는 (b)가 자연스럽다.

어휘_ **be promoted** 승진하다 **conclude** 끝내다, 결론짓다
It serves you right. 자업자득이다, 쌤통이다(= you
deserve it.) **twist one's arm** ~에게 강요[협박]하다

정답_ (b)

Chapter 10 병원·건강·미용

STEP 1 Pattern Study

Sample
해석_M: 들어오세요. 증상이 어떻게 되세요?

W: ________________________

(a) 몸이 오싹하고 머리가 몹시 아파요.

(b) 진료 신청서를 작성했어요.

(c) 약에 대한 부작용을 겪은 적이 있나요?

(d) 독감 주사를 맞았어요.

정답_(a)

STEP 2 Clinic

Part 1
1.

해석_M: 브라운 박사님을 찾으려면 어디로 가야 하죠?

W: ________________________

(a) 당신은 먼저 그를 만나야 합니다.

(b) 그는 지금 통화 중입니다.

(c) 그는 2층에 있어요.

(d) 그는 당신을 위해 최선을 다하고 있어요.

정답_(c)

Part 2
2.

해석_M: 다쳤다는 얘기 들어서 유감이야.

W: 고마워. 점점 나아지고 있어.

M: 왼팔을 움직일 수 있니?

W: ________________________

(a) 응, 하지만 지난밤에는 간신히 움직였어.

(b) 고마워. 꼭 괜찮아질 거야.

(c) 다른 방으로 옮길 거야.

(d) 수술 받아야 해.

정답_(a)

3.

해석_W: 괜찮니? 약간 창백해 보인다.

M: 지난밤에 너무 많이 먹어서 배탈이 났어.

W: 토했니?

M: ________________________

(a) 지금 너무 긴장 돼.

(b) 해봤는데 소용없었어.

(c) 더 이상 과식하지 않도록 노력할 거야.

(d) 그 후에는 괜찮을 거야.

정답_(b)

STEP 3 Dictation

정답_1. He's on the second floor

2. Yes, but I could barely move it last night

3. I tried but no use

STEP 4 Actual Test

Part 1
1.

M: What kind of hair cut do you want this time?

W: ________________________

(a) Please make my hair like the person in this picture.

(b) Look. This is the newest style.

(c) Please trim my nails.

(d) I got a cut on my hand with paper.

해석_M: 이번엔 머리를 어떻게 잘라 드릴까요?

W: ________________________

(a) 이 사진에 나온 사람처럼 해주세요.

(b) 보세요. 이건 최신 유행이라고요.

(c) 손톱 손질해 주세요.

(d) 종이에 손을 베었어요.

해설_ 원하는 헤어스타일을 묻고 있으므로 파마를 하고 싶다는 (a)가 정답이다.

어휘_the newest style 최신 유행   trim 손질하다   nail 손톱

정답_(a)

2.

W: I was wondering if I was on the waiting list for surgery.

M: ________________________

(a) Let me see. You are on the top of it now.
(b) I was walking around that.
(c) I think it is possible.
(d) I was too busy to make a list.

해석_ W: 제가 수술 대기자 명단에 있는지 알고 싶은데요.

M: ______________________________

(a) 어디 한번 볼게요. 현재 명단 맨 위에 있습니다.

(b) 그 주변을 걷고 있었어요.

(c) 그게 가능하다고 생각해요.

(d) 너무 바빠서 명단을 만들지 못했어요.

해설_ 수술 대기자 명단에 있는지 묻고 있으므로 이를 확인해 주는
내용이 담긴 선택지를 고르면 된다.

어휘_ **waiting list** 대기자 명단

정답_ (a)

3.

M: Who is the newest hair dresser in the hair
   salon?

W: ______________________________

(a) It is located on South Hill Avenue.
(b) It is a newly renovated hair salon.
(c) James is the new one here.
(d) I often go to there for my hair style.

해석_ M: 미용실에 가장 최근에 온 미용사가 누구예요?

W: ______________________________

(a) 사우스 힐 가에 있어요.

(b) 거긴 새로 단장한 미용실이에요.

(c) 제임스가 여기 새로 온 사람이에요.

(d) 저는 머리하러 거기 자주 가요.

해설_ Who로 물었으므로 사람을 언급한 선택지를 고르면 된다.

어휘_ **hair salon** 미용실 **be located on[in]** ~에 위치해 있
다 **renovate** 새롭게 하다, 개조하다

정답_ (c)

4.

W: I think your son can be leaving the hospital
   sometime next week.

M: ______________________________

(a) That's nice. He will be out of hospital earlier
    than I have expected.

(b) I had left the hospital late this morning.
(c) Why don't you go to the hospital with me?
(d) It's a national holiday next Wednesday.

해석_ W: 아드님이 다음주 중에 퇴원할 수 있을 것 같아요.

M: ______________________________

(a) 좋네요. 예상했던 것보다 빨리 퇴원하는군요.

(b) 저는 오늘 아침 늦게 병원에서 퇴원했어요.

(c) 나랑 병원에 같이 갈래요?

(d) 다음주 수요일은 국경일이에요.

해설_ 아들이 다음주 중에 퇴원할 수 있을 거라는 얘기를 들었으므
로 이에 기뻐하는 내용의 응답이 이어지는 것이 적절하다.

어휘_ **leave the hospital = be out of hospital** 퇴원하다
national holiday 국경일

정답_ (a)

Part 2

5.

W: Have you gotten my test results?
M: Yes. I recommend you be hospitalized. Do
   you have any medical insurance?
W: Yes. Is there a benefit from insurance?
M: ______________________________

(a) I think, your insurance will cover 70%.
(b) I guarantee it for one year.
(c) What kind of benefits do you have for your
    employees?
(d) I purchased life insurance.

해석_ W: 제 검사 결과 받으셨나요?

M: 네. 입원하시는 게 좋겠습니다. 의료보험 있으세요?

W: 네. 의료보험 혜택이 있나요?

M: ______________________________

(a) 제 생각엔 보험이 70% 적용될 것 같네요.

(b) 1년간 보증합니다.

(c) 직원에게는 어떤 종류의 혜택이 있나요?

(d) 전 생명보험에 가입했어요.

해설_ 의료보험이 적용되는지를 묻고 있으므로 이에 관한 내용이 담
긴 선택지를 고르면 된다.

어휘_ **be hospitalized** 입원하다 **medical insurance** 의료
보험 **benefit** 혜택 **cover** 적용되다 **guarantee** 보증
하다

정답_ (a)

6.

M: The doctor has sewn up my wound.

W: Gee. It seems quite painful.

M: I didn't notice a pain due to anesthesia but after about an hour I would die.

W: ________________________________

(a) Listen to what I'm telling you.

(b) I'm afraid that your grandmother passed away.

(c) Don't worry. She sewed my socks.

(d) I think you should be careful anytime and anywhere.

해석_ M: 의사가 내 상처를 꿰매 줬어.

W: 이런. 아주 고통스러워 보여.

M: 마취 때문에 고통을 못 느꼈는데, 한 시간쯤 지나면 아파 죽을 거야.

W: ________________________________

(a) 내가 말하는 거 잘 들어.

(b) 할머니가 돌아가셔서 유감이다.

(c) 걱정 마. 그녀가 내 양말을 꿰매 줬어.

(d) 난 네가 언제 어느 곳에서든 조심해야 한다고 생각해.

해설_ 상처를 바늘로 꿰매 고통스러워하는 남자에게 다시는 다치지 않도록 주의를 주는 (d)가 자연스럽다.

어휘_ **sew up** (상처 등을) 꿰매다, 봉합하다 **wound** 상처 **painful** 고통스러운, 아픈 **notice** 알아채다, 인지하다 **due to** ~ 때문에 **anesthesia** 마취 **pass away** 돌아가시다

정답_ (d)

Chapter 11 쇼핑 · 식당

STEP 1 Pattern Study

Sample

해석_ M: 주문에 커피가 포함되었습니다. 지금 드시겠습니까?

W: ________________________________

(a) 고마워요, 그런데 시럽은 빼주세요.

(b) 난 그걸로 할게요. 목말라 죽겠어요.

(c) 난 인스턴트 커피가 좋아요.

(d) 아니, 괜찮아요. 그것으론 부족해요.

정답_ (a)

STEP 2 Clinic

Part 1

1.

해석_ M: 훌륭한 저녁 식사였어요. 정말 맛있게 먹었어요.

W: ________________________________

(a) 저도요. 가격을 알아 볼게요.

(b) 저도요. 이곳이 맘에 들어요. 멋진 음식, 근사한 분위기.

(c) 하지만 방문하기 좋은 장소였어요.

(d) 어젯밤 저녁 식사 즐거웠어요.

정답_ (b)

Part 2

2.

해석_ W: 오늘의 특별 메뉴는 뭐죠?

M: ________________________________

(a) 오늘은 두 끼 식사만 됩니다.

(b) 고구마와 크랜베리 소스를 곁들인 칠면조입니다.

(c) 그것은 점심 시간만을 위한 것입니다.

(d) 오후 6시까지 이용 가능합니다.

정답_ (b)

3.

해석_ M: 도와 드릴까요?

W: 고마워요. 제 여동생 결혼식에 입고 갈 드레스를 찾고 있는 중이에요.

M: 다양한 스타일을 보실 수 있습니다.

W: _______________________________

(a) 나도 당신 스타일이 맘에 들어요.

(b) 갈색이 그녀에게 잘 어울릴 것 같네요.

(c) 당신이 입은 드레스를 보는 게 좋아요.

(d) 저쪽에 있는 파란 드레스를 입어 볼 수 있나요?

정답_ (d)

4.

해석_ W: 계산서 좀 갖다 주시겠어요?

M: 네. 여기 있습니다.

W: 계산서에 이미 봉사료가 포함돼 있나요?

M: _______________________________

(a) 팁이 보통 청구돼 있습니다.

(b) 오늘은 내가 낼게요.

(c) 청구액의 15~20%입니다.

(d) 너무 비싼 것 같아요.

정답_ (a)

STEP 3 Dictation

정답_ 1. Me, too. I like this place. Nice food, nice atmosphere

2. It's a turkey with sweet potatoes and cranberry sauce.

3. Can I try the dress in blue over there

4. The tip is usually part of the bill

STEP 4 Actual Test

Part 1

1.

M: Wow, this dress looks nice on you. Is it new?

W: _______________________________

(a) Yes. Because today I have an important interview.

(b) No. You look great today, better than yesterday.

(c) I know. It was a buy-one-get-one-free sale.

(d) OK. Do you have this in a different size?

해석_ M: 와, 이 드레스 잘 어울리는데. 새거니?

W: _______________________________

(a) 응. 오늘 중요한 면접이 있거든.

(b) 아니. 넌 어제보다 오늘 더 멋져 보여.

(c) 알아. 하나 사면 하나 덤으로 주는 세일이었어.

(d) 좋아요. 이걸로 다른 사이즈 있나요?

해설_ 새로 산 드레스인지 묻고 있으므로 이에 답하는 선택지를 고르면 된다.

어휘_ **buy-one-get-one-free sale** 하나 사면 하나 덤으로 주는 세일

정답_ (a)

2.

M: Excuse me. Could we have a table for two, please?

W: _______________________________

(a) Sure. Did you make a reservation, sir?

(b) How many do you have in your party?

(c) Yes, I can. First come, first served.

(d) I've bought a new table.

해석_ M: 실례합니다. 두 사람 앉을 테이블 있습니까?

W: _______________________________

(a) 물론이죠. 예약하셨습니까, 손님?

(b) 일행이 몇 분이세요?

(c) 예, 할 수 있습니다. 선착순이에요.

(d) 새 테이블을 샀어요.

해설_ 2인용 테이블이 있는지 묻고 있으므로 (a)가 적절하다.

어휘_ **make a reservation** 예약하다　**party** 일행　**first come, first served** 선착순

정답_ (a)

3.

W: Where did you get it?

M: _______________________________

(a) I got it for my sister's birthday present.

(b) I think you got it wrong.

(c) I will get it in the ladies section.

(d) It was a graduation gift from my parents.

해석_ W: 너 그거 어디서 났니?

M: _______________________________

(a) 여동생 생일선물로 내가 샀어.

(b) 네가 오해한 것 같아.

(c) 여성복 코너에서 살 거야.

(d) 부모님이 졸업선물로 주신 거야.

해설_ 어디서 난 건지 묻고 있으므로 (d)가 적절하다.

어휘_ **get ... wrong** ~을 오해하다

정답_ (d)

4.

M: May we have the day of brunch, please?

W: _______________________________________

(a) I am afraid time's up for brunch.

(b) I'd love to go to a buffet.

(c) All dishes look so good.

(d) Have a seat and enjoy your meal.

해석_ M: 브런치를 좀 먹을 수 있을까요?

W: _________________________________

(a) 죄송하지만, 브런치 시간은 끝났습니다.

(b) 뷔페에 가고 싶어요.

(c) 모든 요리가 아주 맛있게 보여요.

(d) 자리에 앉으셔서 맛있게 드세요.

해설_ 브런치를 주문해 먹을 수 있는지 묻고 있으므로 이에 답하는 선택지를 고르면 된다.

어휘_ **brunch** 아점(아침 겸 점심) **buffet** 뷔페

정답_ (a)

Part 2

5.

M: Do you need some help? Looking for something?

W: Oh, yes. I am looking for my glass.

M: What does it look like?

W: _______________________________________

(a) I like my glass so much.

(b) It is medium-sized and brown color.

(c) Thanks. I am just looking.

(d) It is on my own.

해석_ M: 도움이 필요하십니까? 뭐 찾으시는 거 있으세요?

W: 아, 네. 제 유리컵을 찾고 있어요.

M: 어떤 모양인데요?

W: _________________________________

(a) 전 제 유리잔을 무척 좋아해요.

(b) 중간 크기에 갈색이에요.

(c) 고맙습니다. 그냥 둘러보는 거예요.

(d) 저 혼자예요.

해설_ 찾고 있는 유리컵이 어떻게 생겼는지 묻고 있으므로 컵의 생김새를 설명하는 선택지를 고르면 된다.

어휘_ **middle-sized** 중간 크기의 **on one's own** 혼자서, 단독으로

정답_ (b)

6.

W: My sister spent a lot of money shopping yesterday.

M: Why? What did she buy?

W: I don't know. I think she has a new boyfriend now.

M: _______________________________________

(a) Really? Let's ask her about it.

(b) I have no idea.

(c) I don't think she has one.

(d) It is working out.

해석_ W: 내 여동생이 어제 쇼핑하는 데 돈을 많이 썼어.

M: 왜? 뭘 샀는데?

W: 몰라. 지금 새 남자친구가 생긴 것 같아.

M: _________________________________

(a) 정말? 걔한테 물어보자.

(b) 난 몰라.

(c) 있는 것 같지 않아.

(d) 잘돼 가고 있어.

해설_ 여동생에게 남자친구가 생긴 것 같다고 했으므로 이어지는 응답으로는 본인한테 직접 물어보자고 제안하는 (a)가 가장 적절하다.

어휘_ **work out** 잘돼 가다, 운동하다

정답_ (a)

7.

M: How may I help you?

W: Could I refund these goods? These pants are too tight for me.

M: I'm sorry. Can't refund sale items, but we'll exchange it with another item.

W: _______________________________________

(a) Do you have a bigger size than mine?
(b) I don't mind if you change your mind.
(c) At first, I could refuse his apology.
(d) Can I exchange foreign currency?

해석_ M: 어떻게 도와 드릴까요?

W: 이 상품을 환불해 주시겠어요? 이 바지가 저한테 너무 꽉 껴요.

M: 죄송합니다. 세일 품목은 환불이 안 됩니다. 하지만 다른 품목으로 교환해 드릴게요.

W: ___________________________

(a) 제 치수보다 큰 거 있나요?

(b) 생각을 바꾸셔도 상관없습니다.

(c) 우선, 그의 사과를 거절할 수 있었어요.

(d) 외화로 바꿀 수 있나요?

해설_ 환불은 불가능하고 대신 다른 것으로 바꿀 수 있다고 했으므로 구입한 바지 치수보다 더 큰 치수가 있는지 묻는 (a)가 적절하다.

어휘_ refund 환불하다   tight (몸에) 꽉 끼는   if 설사 ~일지라도   change one's mind 마음을 바꾸다   exchange 교환하다, 환전하다   foreign currency 외화

정답_ (a)

Chapter 12 의문사

STEP 1 Pattern Study

Sample

해석_ M: 서울 방문하기에 가장 좋은 시기가 언제야?

W: ___________________________

(a) 가을. 단풍에 푹 빠질 거야.

(b) 한 10분 정도 남았어.

(c) 내 다이어리에 표시해 줄래?

(d) 난 때때로 제니와 함께 방문해.

정답_ (a)

STEP 2 Clinic

Part 1

1.

해석_ W: 저것들의 용도는 뭐니?

M: ___________________________

(a) 그것들은 5개의 장비야.

(b) 그것들은 아버지가 쓰시는 도구들이야.

(c) 그들은 4년 동안 함께 있었어.

(d) 그것들은 4개의 내 가방이야.

정답_ (b)

Part 2

2.

해석_ W: 뭐 찾고 있니?

M: 아무것도 아니야. 그냥 누군가 지나가는 걸 봤어.

W: 그게 누군데?

M: ___________________________

(a) 큰 거였어.

(b) 내가 아는 사람인 것 같았어.

(c) 그냥 내 친구를 찾고 있어.

(d) 그녀가 곧 여기 올 거야.

정답_ (b)

3.

해석_ M: 그거 아직 안 읽어 보셨어요?

W: 도서관 사서가 못 빌리게 했어요.

M: 왜 못 빌려가게 했을까요?

W: _______________________________

(a) 너무 지루하다고 하더군요.

(b) 그녀는 내가 그걸 사는 것을 원치 않는 것 같아요.

(c) 그녀가 그렇게 하지 못하게 해요.

(d) 책 내용이 아주 복잡한 것 같아요.

정답_ (a)

4.

해석_ M: 샌디 씨 계십니까? 소포가 왔습니다.

W: 전데요. 배달해 주셔서 감사합니다.

M: 이 소포를 어디에 둘까요?

W: _______________________________

(a) 그냥 여기 놔 주실래요?

(b) 전 상관없어요. 당신이 원하는 것을 고르세요.

(c) 전 그게 무료로 배달되었다는 걸 알아요.

(d) 천만에요. 그게 제 일인걸요.

정답_ (a)

STEP 3 Dictation

정답_ 1. Those are some tools for my father

2. I felt as if he was my acquaintance

3. She said it was too boring

4. Would you just put it here

STEP 4 Actual Test

Part 1

1.

W: Why is she so depressed?

M: _______________________________.

(a) I think she has some problems.

(b) Yes, I like it too.

(c) I would like to have some coffee.

(d) Because I stayed up last night studying for midterms.

해석_ W: 그녀는 왜 그렇게 우울한 거야?

M: _______________________________

(a) 문제가 좀 있는 것 같아.

(b) 응, 나도 그걸 좋아해.

(c) 커피가 마시고 싶어.

(d) 내가 중간고사 공부하느라 어젯밤 늦게까지 안 잤기 때문이야.

해설_ 그녀가 우울한 이유를 묻고 있으므로 문제가 있어서 그런 것 같다는 (a)가 적절하다.

어휘_ **stay up** 자지 않고 있다

정답_ (a)

2.

W: How come you are laughing?

M: _______________________________

(a) I am studying hard for my finals.

(b) She is doing her job.

(c) I think this comic is silly but funny.

(d) It is right next to the desk.

해석_ W: 왜 웃고 있니?

M: _______________________________

(a) 기말고사를 위해 열심히 공부하고 있어.

(b) 그녀는 일을 하고 있어.

(c) 이 만화책 시시하지만 웃긴 것 같아.

(d) 그건 책상 바로 옆에 있어.

해설_ 웃고 있는 이유를 묻고 있으므로 이에 관해 언급한 선택지를 고르면 된다.

어휘_ **final** 기말고사 **silly** 바보 같은, 시시한

정답_ (c)

3.

M: Who made him see red?

W: _______________________________

(a) I think his brother did it.

(b) I will go pick up my company.

(c) Nothing can be serious.

(d) It is awful. I can't stand it.

해석_ M: 누가 그를 화나게 만들었니?

W: _______________________________

(a) 걔 동생이 그런 것 같아.

(b) 내 동료를 마중 나갈 거야.

(c) 그 어떤 것도 심각하지 않아.

(d) 지독해. 참을 수가 없어.

어휘_ **see red** 격노하다 **company** 동료 **awful** 지독한, 대
단한

정답_ (a)

4.

W: Why is the bookstore your favorite place?

M: ____

(a) I would like to read some books.

(b) They are all my favorite authors.

(c) I feel so comfortable and cozy being there.

(d) Because it was the weekend, the bookstore
was crowded with people.

해석_ W: 서점이 가장 좋아하는 장소인 이유가 뭐니?

M: ________________________________

(a) 난 책을 좀 읽고 싶어.

(b) 그들은 내가 가장 좋아하는 작가들이야.

(c) 거기 있으면 너무 편안하고 포근해.

(d) 주말이라 서점이 사람들로 붐볐기 때문이야.

해설_ 서점이 가장 좋아하는 장소인 이유를 묻고 있으므로 이에 관
한 내용이 언급된 선택지를 고르면 된다.

어휘_ **cozy** 포근한, 아늑한 **be crowded with** ~로 붐비다,
북적거리다

정답_ (c)

5.

W: How was your childhood?

M: ____

(a) I was going to say it was childish.

(b) I was too young to do it.

(c) I was a troublemaker.

(d) It was my sisterhood.

해석_ W: 어릴 때 어땠어요?

M: ________________________________

(a) 그게 유치했다고 말하려던 참이었어요.

(b) 그것을 하기에 난 너무 어렸어요.

(c) 말썽꾸러기였어요.

(d) 그건 자매의 의리였죠.

해설_ 어린 시절 어떤 아이였는지를 묻고 있으므로 (c)가 적절한 정
답이다.

어휘_ **childish** 유치한 **troublemaker** 말썽꾸러기
sisterhood 자매의 의리

정답_ (c)

Part 2

6.

W: Hi, Andrew. Where are you going now?

M: I am on the way back home.

W: Where were you coming from?

M: ____

(a) I am from Canada.

(b) I was at the doctor's office.

(c) I am fixing my car at the garage.

(d) I was doing research for that.

해석_ W: 안녕, 앤드류. 지금 어디 가?

M: 집에 돌아가는 길이야.

W: 어디 갔다 오는 건데?

M: ________________________________

(a) 난 캐나다 출신이야.

(b) 병원에 있었어.

(c) 차고에서 내 차를 고치는 중이야.

(d) 그것에 대해 연구하는 중이었어.

해설_ 어디 갔다 오는 길이었는지를 묻고 있으므로 (b)가 정답이다.
(a)는 여자의 마지막 말을 이용해 오답을 유도하려는 선택지
로, 출신지를 물을 때는 Where do you come from?으로 표
현한다.

어휘_ **doctor's office** (개인) 병원, 의원 **garage** 차고 **do
research** 연구하다

정답_ (b)

7.

M: What do you think of our suggestion?

W: There are a few points we can't accept.

M: What do you say if we meet you halfway?

W: ____

(a) I can't pinpoint it.

(b) I don't have any time to meet you.

(c) All right then. Let's compromise.

(d) They offered me a deal.

해석_ M: 우리 제안에 대해 어떻게 생각하시나요?

W: 우리가 수용할 수 없는 점이 몇 가지 있더군요.

M: 서로 조금씩 양보하는 게 어떨까요?

W: ________________________

(a) 딱 꼬집어서 말할 수는 없어요

(b) 당신을 만날 시간이 없어요.

(c) 좋아요, 그럼. 타협을 합시다.

(d) 그들이 내게 협상을 제안했어요.

해설_ 서로 조금씩 양보하자고 제안하고 있으므로 이에 응하는 (c)
가 정답이다.

어휘_ meet ... halfway ~와 타협하다, 조금씩 양보하다
pinpoint 정확하게 지적하다

정답_ (c)

Chapter 13 대화문 주제 파악하기

STEP 1 Pattern Study

Sample

해석_ M: 상점 회원카드를 만들고 싶어요.

W: 이 양식을 작성해 주세요.

M: 알겠습니다. 그리고 나서 가족 회원카드를 추가로 만들려
면 어떻게 해야 하죠?

W: 음… 가족이 몇 명이나 되시는데요?

M: 네 명이요.

W: 가족 회원카드를 원하시면 주민등록 등본 1통이 필요합니
다.

M: 음. 나중에 제출해도 되나요?

W: 상관없습니다.

Q. 대화의 주제는 무엇인가?

(a) 회원카드 만들기

(b) 상점의 새 종업원으로 함께 일하기

(c) 가족과 함께 쇼핑 가기

(d) 계약서 제출하기

정답_ (a)

STEP 2 Clinic

Part 3

1.

해석_ M: 리사! 잠자는 동안은 라디오를 끄는 게 어때? 엄마도 같은
생각이야.

W: 아빠, 난 라디오 없이 잠을 잘 수가 없어요. 그리고 헤드폰
은 귀에 좋지 않아요.

M: 하지만 잠을 제대로 잘 수가 없구나. 라디오 볼륨을 약간만
줄여 줄래?

W: 좋아요, 그럼. 오늘 밤은 그렇게 할게요.

M: 착하구나. 만약 네가 약속을 지키면 새 라디오를 사 주마.

W: 정말요? 좋아요! 고마워요, 아빠!

Q. 대화의 주요 내용은 무엇인가?

(a) 라디오가 남자가 잠자는 것을 방해한다.

(b) 남자가 헤드폰을 망가뜨렸다.

(c) 여자는 새 라디오를 사고 싶어 한다.

(d) 남자는 불면증을 앓고 있다.

2.

해석_ M: 안녕하세요.

W: 안녕하세요. 어제 3인용 테이블을 예약했는데요.

M: 알겠습니다. 성함이 어떻게 되시죠?

W: 캐시예요.

M: 죄송합니다. 성함이 명단에 있지 않네요. 잠시만요. 제가 다시 확인해 보겠습니다. 아, 예약이 내일로 잡혀 있네요.

W: 그래요? 말도 안 돼. 그럼 얼마나 오래 기다려야 하나요?

M: 음, 아마 약 20분은 기다리셔야 할 겁니다.

W: 좋아요. 대기자 명단에 제 이름을 올려 주세요.

Q. 대화의 주요 내용은 무엇인가?

(a) 여자가 예약을 잘못했다.

(b) 여자는 남자의 말을 잘못 이해했다.

(c) 남자는 20분 동안 기다릴 것이다.

(d) 남자는 여자의 테이블에 음식을 나른다.

정답_ (a)

STEP 3 Dictation

정답_ 1. Why don't you turn the radio off
How about turning down the radio a little bit
If you keep your word, I'll buy you a new radio

2. I've booked a table for three yesterday
Oh, your reservation is made tomorrow
Put me on the waiting list

STEP 4 Actual Test

Part 3

1.

M: What's the matter with you? You don't look good today.

W: I failed my economics test. I will be ashamed to take the lecture again.

M: I'm sorry to hear that.

W: I studied very hard this time. I never expected this.

M: Cheer up! You still have one more chance.

All you have to do now is concentrate on your final test.

W: Thanks. I may not be able to afford my tuition fee next year, so I have to get the scholarship.

M: That's why you are depressed. You surely can get it. I will help you with that.

Q. What is the conversation about?

(a) What the man and woman are going to do tonight

(b) What the woman is worrying about

(c) Whether the woman will be able to get a scholarship

(d) How the woman did on her test

해석_ M: 무슨 문제 있니? 오늘 안색이 안 좋아 보이네.

W: 경제학 시험에 낙제했어. 강의를 다시 들어야 해서 창피하게 됐어.

M: 그거 안됐구나.

W: 이번엔 무지 열심히 공부했는데. 이렇게 될 줄 전혀 예상 못했어.

M: 힘내! 아직 한 번 더 기회가 있잖아. 이제 기말고사에 전력을 다하기만 하면 돼.

W: 고마워. 난 내년에 등록금을 낼 수 없을지도 몰라. 그래서 장학금을 받아야만 해.

M: 그래서 우울해 있었구나. 넌 꼭 장학금을 받을 수 있을 거야. 내가 도와줄게.

Q. 무엇에 관한 대화인가?

(a) 오늘 밤 남자와 여자가 무엇을 할 건지

(b) 여자가 무엇을 걱정하고 있는지

(c) 여자가 장학금을 받을 수 있을지

(d) 여자의 시험이 어땠는지

해설_ 안색이 안 좋아 보인다며 무슨 일이 있는지 묻는 남자에게 이런저런 걱정을 늘어놓고 있으므로 정답은 (b)가 된다.

어휘_ **be ashamed to** ~을 부끄러워하다, ~하게 돼서 창피하다 **tuition** 수업료, 등록금 **depressed** 우울한 **get a scholarship** 장학금을 받다

정답_ (b)

2.

M: Hi, Sally! Long time no see!

W: Hi, Mark! How have you been? I called you up several times yesterday, but you didn't answer. You've been that busy these days?

M: No. I'm loafing around. And I didn't get any phone calls from anybody.

W: I think I know that's why. There must be a problem with your cell phone.

M: I never thought about that. I got it just a month ago. I've been wondering about why nobody called me these days. It might be broken.

W: You should go to a customer service center and get it fixed or replaced.

Q. What is the conversation about?

(a) How the man and woman have been

(b) How long the man has been using his cell phone

(c) Why the woman couldn't reach the man on the phone

(d) What the biggest problem is with the man's cell phone

해석_ M: 안녕, 샐리! 오랜만이야!

W: 안녕, 마크! 어떻게 지냈니? 어제 여러 번 전화했는데 안 받더라. 요즘 그렇게 바쁘니?

M: 아니. 빈둥거리고 있어. 그리고 아무한테도 전화 안 왔는데.

W: 그 이유를 알 것 같다. 네 휴대폰에 문제가 있는 게 틀림없어.

M: 그런 생각은 못했어. 겨우 한 달 전에 샀거든. 왜 요즘 아무한테도 전화가 안 오나 이상했었어. 고장났나 보다.

W: 고객 서비스 센터에 가서 고치든지 바꿔 달라고 해.

Q. 무엇에 관한 대화인가?

(a) 남자와 여자가 그동안 어떻게 지냈는지

(b) 남자가 휴대폰을 얼마나 오랫동안 사용해 오고 있는지

(c) 여자가 왜 남자와 통화할 수 없었는지

(d) 남자 휴대폰의 가장 큰 문제점이 무엇인지

해설_ 여자의 첫 번째 대사를 보면, 남자에게 여러 번 전화를 했는데도 전화를 받지 않았다는 내용이 나온다. 이어서 남자 역시 아무한테도 전화가 오지 않았다고 얘기하자 여자는 핸드폰이 고장 난 것 같으니 서비스 센터에 가지고 가라고 충고하고 있다. 따라서 (c)가 정답임을 알 수 있다.

어휘_ **call up** 전화를 걸다   **loaf around** 빈둥거리다   **cell phone** 휴대폰   **replace** 바꾸다, 교환하다

정답_ (c)

3.

W: I dislike this time of year. It takes us the whole month of December to make a plan for the next year.

M: What makes it require so much time? Are there too many things to consider?

W: Yes, it is more complicated than most people conceive. Last time we planned to finish it within 2 weeks but lots of mistakes were made and some parts had to be changed completely.

M: Oh, I thought it was easy.

W: So we decided it would be better to give ourselves about a month and concentrate our whole effort on it.

M: It seems like this is a pretty big deal. I can give you a hand unless you want me to carry on finishing my project immediately.

W: Thank you, but we have enough people to work on it.

Q. What is the conversation about?

(a) Why the woman doesn't like wintertime

(b) How long making year's plan will take

(c) How the woman can save time to make a plan

(d) Why the woman dislikes the last month of year

해석_ W: 난 1년 중 이때가 제일 싫어. 내년 계획 짜는 데 12월을 다 보내야 해.

M: 뭣 때문에 시간이 그렇게 많이 필요한데? 생각할 게 그렇게 많아?

W: 응, 대부분의 사람들이 생각하는 것보다 더 복잡해. 지난번엔 2주 안에 끝내려고 계획했는데, 오류가 너무 많아서 몇 군데는 완전히 바꿔야 했어.

M: 그렇군, 쉬운 일이라고 생각했는데.

W: 그래서 한 달 정도 시간을 갖고 전력을 기울이는 게 낫겠
　　다는 결정을 내렸지.

M: 꽤나 어려운 일 같아 보인다. 만약 내 프로젝트를 당장 계
　　속 진행하지 않아도 된다면 도와줄게.

W: 고마워, 하지만 지금 일하는 사람들로도 충분해.

Q. 무엇에 관한 대화인가?

(a) 여자가 왜 겨울철을 좋아하지 않는지

(b) 연간 계획을 짜는 데 얼마나 걸릴지

(c) 여자가 계획 짜는 시간을 어떻게 절약할 수 있는지

(d) 여자가 왜 한 해의 마지막 달을 싫어하는지

해설_대화 첫 부분에 핵심 내용이 나와 있다. 1년 중 12월이 가장
싫다는 얘기를 꺼내며 12월 내내 내년 계획을 짜는 데 시간을
다 보내야 한다며 불평을 늘어놓고 있으므로 (d)가 정답임을
알 수 있다.

어휘_**make a plan** 계획을 짜다　**require** 필요로 하다
conceive 생각하다, 상상하다　**give ... a hand** ~를 돕
다　**carry on** 계속 진행하다　**wintertime** 겨울(철)

정답_(d)

4.

M: Please figure out how much these are.

W: It's 87 dollars. Do you have any card for a
discount?

M: No, I didn't bring my HS card.

W: Our membership card and HS bank card
can take 10% off, too.

M: Really? How can I make the membership
card, then?

W: You can go to the Customer Service
Representatives on the 3rd floor.

M: Great. Thanks. These aren't discounted, are
these?

W: Yes. Today's products can also be
discounted.

Q. What is the conversation about?

(a) Discount of the membership card

(b) Add 10% tax

(c) Joining the HS bank card

(d) Buying the goods in the mall

해석_M: 이것들이 얼마인지 계산해 주세요.

W: 87달러입니다. 할인카드 있으세요?

M: 아니오, HS 카드를 안 가져왔어요.

W: 저희 회원카드와 HS 은행카드 역시 10% 할인됩니다.

M: 정말요?! 회원카드는 어떻게 만드나요?

W: 3층에 있는 고객 서비스 센터에 가시면 됩니다.

M: 잘됐군요. 고맙습니다. 이것들은 할인 못 받죠?

W: 아니요, 오늘 상품들도 할인받으실 수 있습니다.

Q. 무엇에 관한 대화인가?

(a) 회원카드 할인

(b) 10% 세금 추가

(c) HS 은행 카드에 가입하기

(d) 쇼핑센터에서 물건 사기

해설_상점 계산대에서 이루어지고 있는 대화다. 회원카드를 제시하
면 10% 할인이 된다는 말을 듣고 남자가 회원카드 만드는 방
법과 지금 구입한 상품들도 할인받을 수 있는지 묻고 있으므
로 (a)가 정답이다.

어휘_**figure out** 계산하다　**Customer Service
Representatives** 고객 서비스 센터　**goods** 물건, 상품

정답_(a)

5.

M: I heard you went on a business trip to
London last week.

W: Yes, I did.

M: How was the meeting with British clients? I
think they are particular about the contract.

W: You're right. I was so nervous and it was
really hard to make it, but personally they
treated me well.

M: Wow, that's great. Anything else?

W: They made me sightsee. So it was very
easy for me to travel.

Q. What is the main purpose of the conversation?

(a) Giving the woman's impressions of a
business trip

(b) Making an appointment

(c) Choosing the gift for their client

(d) Making a presentation

해석_M: 지난주에 런던으로 출장 갔다 왔다면서.

W: 응, 그랬어.

M: 영국 고객과의 미팅은 어땠어? 그들은 계약에 까다로운 것
같던데.

W: 맞아. 무척 긴장했고 계약 성사시키기 정말 힘들었어. 하
지만 개인적으로는 잘 대해 주더라.

M: 대단한데. 뭐 다른 건 없었어?

W: 관광도 시켜 줬어. 그래서 아주 편하게 여행했지.

Q. 대화의 주된 목적은 무엇인가?

(a) 여자의 출장 소감 말하기

(b) 약속 정하기

(c) 그들의 고객에게 줄 선물 고르기

(d) 발표하기

해설_ 남자는 여자가 출장 갔던 얘기를 꺼내면서 그곳에서의 일이
어땠는지 궁금해한다. 이에 출장지에서 있었던 일과 느낌에
대한 여자의 얘기가 이어지므로 (a)가 정답이다.

어휘_ particular 까다로운, 꼼꼼한 sightsee 관광하다 give
one's impressions of ~에 대한 소감[인상]을 말하다

정답_ (a)

6.

M: Oh, where are all the staplers in the office?

W: Aren't there any in the drawer?

M: I've already looked but no.

W: Ah, I think they are in the conference room.

M: Is there a meeting being held?

W: Yes, it began 30 minutes ago.

M: Oh, no. I need it now. I'll go out and come
back in a while.

W: Will you buy a stapler?

Q. What is the main topic of the conversation?

(a) The man's necessary thing right now

(b) Big meeting in the conference

(c) Going to the lost and found

(d) Waiting for the meeting

해석_ M: 아, 사무실의 호치키스가 다 어디 있지?

W: 서랍에 없어요?

M: 이미 봤는데 없어요.

W: 아, 회의실에 있는 것 같아요.

M: 회의가 열리고 있는 중인가요?

W: 네, 30분 전에 시작했어요.

M: 이런, 지금 필요한데. 나갔다 금방 올게요.

W: 호치키스 사려고요?

Q. 대화의 주제는 무엇인가?

(a) 남자가 지금 당장 필요한 것

(b) 회의실의 중요한 회의

(c) 분실물 센터 가기

(d) 회의 기다리기

해설_ 남자는 호치키스가 당장 필요한데, 그것이 회의실에 있으며
회의 중이라 들어갈 수 없다는 말을 듣자 호치키스를 사러 나
가려 한다. 따라서 정답은 (a)가 된다.

어휘_ stapler 호치키스 drawer 서랍 the lost and found
분실물 센터

정답_ (a)

STEP 1 Pattern Study

Sample

해석_ M: 안녕, 메리. 지금 어디 가는 중이니?

W: 해변가 옆 박람회에 가는 중이야. 넌 어디 가니?

M: 집에 가는 중이야.

W: 시간 있니? 나랑 같이 갈래?

M: 너랑 같이 가고 싶지만, 지금 옷을 차려 입지 않아서.

W: 상관없어. 가자! 오늘 큰 행사가 있어.

M: 정말? 거기 가야겠다.

W: 틀림없이 재미있을 거야!

Q. 남자는 왜 처음에 박람회에 가는 것을 원치 않았는가?

(a) 남자의 약속 때문에

(b) 남자의 외관 때문에

(c) 여자의 불평 때문에

(d) 여자의 재촉하는 말 때문에

정답_ (b)

STEP 2 Clinic

Part 3

1.

해석_ M: 안녕하세요. 처음 뵙겠습니다.

W: 안녕, 네가 존 친구 마이크지? 존이 네가 가장 친한 친구라
고 하더라.

M: 맞아요. 집에 들어가도 될까요?

W: 물론이지. 들어 와. 존은 지금 샤워 중이다. 콜라 마실래;
아니면 주스 마실래?

M: 고맙습니다. 주스 마실게요. 저것들이 존의 사진인가요?

W: 그래. 걘 청소년 야구 선수였어.

M: 와, 그런 얘기는 전혀 못 들었어요.

Q. 대화에 따르면 맞는 것은 어느 것인가?

(a) 남자는 그의 친구 집을 방문했다.

(b) 남자는 야구 선수가 되었다.

(c) 여자는 남자를 초대했다.

(d) 여자는 새집으로 이사를 갔다.

정답_ (a)

2.

해석_ M: 안녕. 오랜만이야, 제니.

W: 오랜만이다, 브라이언. 너 호주로 여행 갔다 왔다면서.

M: 응. 우리 할아버지가 3년째 살고 계셔. 그래서 가족들과 함
께 거기에 갔지.

W: 멋지다. 호주는 어땠어? 난 해외여행 한 번도 못해 봤어.

M: 그랬어? 아주 놀라웠지. 많은 코알라를 봤어. 아, 이건 네
선물이야.

W: 고마워! 코알라 인형이구나. 진짜 귀엽다!

M: 네가 좋아하니까 기쁘다.

Q. 대화에 따르면 맞는 것은 어느 것인가?

(a) 여자는 여행을 좋아한다.

(b) 여자는 그에게 반했다.

(c) 남자는 여행을 했다.

(d) 남자는 해외로 갈 것이다.

정답_ (c)

STEP 3 Dictation

정답_ 1. John said that you are his best friend

Would you like to drink some coke or juice

He was a junior baseball player

2. I heard you traveled in Australia

How was Australia

STEP 4 Actual Test

Part 3

1.

W: Excuse me. I live next door.

M: Hello. What may I do for you?

W: Where did you park your vehicle?

M: Oh, I forgot it. I'm sorry that I parked it in front of your house.

W: That's ok. Could you please move to another place? I should park my car now.

M: Of course. Wait a second.

Q. What does the woman want the man to do?

(a) Go to the park

(b) Wait next to door

(c) Move an automobile

(d) Set the car

해석_ W: 실례합니다. 저는 옆집에 사는데요.

M: 안녕하세요. 뭘 도와 드릴까요?

W: 차를 어디에다 주차하셨어요?

M: 앗, 깜박했어요. 당신 집 앞에 주차를 해서 죄송해요.

W: 괜찮아요. 다른 곳으로 차 좀 빼주실래요? 지금 제 차를 주차해야 해서요.

M: 물론이죠. 잠시만 기다려 주세요.

Q. 여자는 남자가 무엇을 하기를 원하는가?

(a) 공원에 가기

(b) 문 옆에서 기다리기

(c) 차 옮기기

(d) 차 가까이 대기

해설_ 여자가 집 앞에 자기 차를 주차하려는데 옆집 남자의 차가 주차돼 있는 것을 발견하고 그의 집을 찾아와 차를 빼 달라고 부탁하는 상황이므로 정답은 (c)다.

어휘_ **park** 주차하다   **vehicle** 탈것, 차   **automobile** 자동차   **set** (가까이) 갖다 대다, 접근시키다

정답_ (c)

2.

W: Honey, the night view is so wonderful, isn't it?

M: It is! Matt recommended this restaurant for our first wedding anniversary.

W: Wow, good. I'm full. All dishes were excellent.

M: We haven't had dessert yet, honey. The cheese cake we ordered will be great.

W: I suddenly have room for more.

M: Before we eat it, let's toast. To our celebration!

W: Of course!

Q. Why did they come to eat dinner at this restaurant?

(a) To congratulate their anniversary

(b) To see a great night scene

(c) To have delicious dinner

(d) To meet their friends

해석_ W: 자기야, 야경이 너무 아름답다, 그렇지 않아?

M: 그래! 매트가 우리의 결혼 1주년 기념을 위해 이 음식점을 추천해 줬어.

W: 와, 좋다. 배불러. 모든 음식이 아주 훌륭했어.

M: 우리 아직 후식 안 먹었어, 자기야. 우리가 주문한 치즈 케이크가 아주 맛있을 거야.

W: 갑자기 더 먹을 수 있을 것 같다.

M: 먹기 전에 건배하자. 우리의 결혼 기념을 위하여!

W: 물론이지!

Q. 그들은 왜 이 음식점에 저녁을 먹으러 왔는가?

(a) 기념일을 축하하기 위해

(b) 멋진 야경을 보기 위해

(c) 맛있는 저녁을 먹기 위해

(d) 친구들을 만나기 위해

해설_ 남자의 첫 번째 대사에 부부의 첫 번째 결혼 기념일을 위해 매트가 이 음식점을 추천해 주었다는 내용이 나오므로 (a)가 정답이다.

어휘_ **night view** 야경   **wedding anniversary** 결혼 기념일

정답_ (a)

3.

M: Hi, Sarah. Do you know where the nearest veterinary hospital is?

W: Is your pet sick?

M: Yes. My dog can't eat well and moans.

W: Ok. I know where it is. I think you would rather take a bus than a subway. Take the number 31 bus and get off on Washington street. Then you can see the big mall. The hospital is in that mall.

M: And how long does it take?

W: Maybe it takes around 15 minutes. I hope that your pet will get well soon.

M: I really appreciate it.

W: It's my pleasure.

Q. Why is the man going to the hospital?

(a) Because he was invited to the woman's house

(b) Because he has been sick

(c) Because his dog has died
(d) Because his pet became sick

해석_ M: 안녕, 사라. 너 여기서 가장 가까운 동물병원이 어디 있는
지 아니?

W: 애완동물이 아파?

M: 응. 우리 개가 잘 먹지도 않고 끙끙거려.

W: 알았어, 내가 위치를 알아. 지하철보다는 버스를 타는 게
나을 것 같다. 31번 버스를 타고 워싱턴 거리에서 내려. 그
러면 큰 쇼핑센터가 보일 거야. 병원은 그 쇼핑센터 안에
있어.

M: 그럼, 얼마나 걸릴까?

W: 아마 15분 정도 걸릴 거야. 네 개가 빨리 낫길 바래.

M: 정말 고마워.

W: 천만에.

Q. 남자는 왜 병원에 가려고 하는가?

(a) 여자의 집에 초대받았기 때문에

(b) 아팠기 때문에

(c) 그의 개가 죽었기 때문에

(d) 그의 애완동물이 병이 났기 때문에

해설_ 남자의 두 번째 대사를 보면 그의 개가 잘 먹지도 않고 끙끙거
린다는 내용이 나오므로 정답은 (d)다.

어휘_ **veterinary hospital** 동물병원 **moan** 신음하다, 끙끙거
리다 **get well** 병이 나아지다

정답_ (d)

4.

W: Hello, would you like something to drink,
sir?

M: Yes. What kind of beverages are there?

W: Cold drinks are coke, apple juice, beer and
hot things are green tea and coffee.

M: Oh, I'll have a cup of apple juice. Then,
when do I have the in-flight meals?

W: We are going to serve you in 20 minutes.

M: Thank you and please give me a blanket.

W: No problem.

Q. Where is the conversation likely taking
place?

(a) In an airplane

(b) At a restaurant

(c) At a grocery store

(d) At a coffee shop

해석_ W: 안녕하세요, 마실 것 좀 드릴까요?

M: 네. 어떤 종류의 음료수가 있나요?

W: 차가운 음료로는 콜라, 사과 주스, 맥주가 있고, 뜨거운 음
료로는 녹차와 커피가 있습니다.

M: 아, 저는 사과 주스 한 컵 주세요. 근데 기내식은 언제 먹나
요?

W: 20분 후에 제공해 드릴 겁니다.

M: 고마워요. 그리고 담요 한 장 주세요.

W: 알겠습니다.

Q. 대화가 어디서 이루어지고 있는 것 같은가?

(a) 기내에서

(b) 음식점에서

(c) 식료품점에서

(d) 커피숍에서

해설_ 남자의 두 번째 대사를 통해 대화가 이루어지고 있는 곳이 기
내임을 알 수 있다.

어휘_ **beverage** 음료수   **in-flight meals** 기내식   **blanket**
담요

정답_ (a)

5.

M: Excuse me. I think you sat in my seat.

W: Did I? Isn't it E45?

M: No, this is E55. I'm sorry. Your seat is in
front of here.

W: Oh, I'm really sorry. It's my mistake.

M: That's ok. Is it your handkerchief? It's nice!
Where did you get it?

W: Oh, I bought it for a reasonable price in the
duty-free shop.

M: Wow, I should go there. Thanks.

W: Enjoy your flight.

Q. Which is correct according to the conversation?

(a) The woman took her seat wrong.

(b) The woman reserved the seat.

(c) The man bought a handkerchief in the duty-
free shop.

(d) The man sells the goods.

해석_ M: 실례합니다. 당신이 제 자리에 앉으신 것 같은데요.

W: 제가요? E45번 아닌가요?

M: 아니요. 여기는 E55번입니다. 당신 자리는 여기 앞이에요.

W: 앗, 정말 미안해요. 제 실수예요.

M: 괜찮습니다. 그거 당신 손수건인가요? 멋지네요! 어디서 사셨어요?

W: 아, 면세점에서 싼 가격에 샀어요.

M: 와, 저도 거기에 가야겠군요. 고맙습니다.

W: 즐거운 여행되세요.

Q. 대화에 따르면 맞는 것은 어느 것인가?

(a) 여자는 자기 좌석이 아닌 곳에 앉았다.

(b) 여자는 좌석을 예약했다.

(c) 남자는 면세점에서 손수건을 샀다.

(d) 남자는 물건을 판다.

해설_ 대화 초반부를 통해 여자가 좌석번호를 잘못 보고 앉았음을 알 수 있다. 여자의 두 번째 대사에 자신의 실수를 깨닫고 남자에게 사과하는 내용이 나오므로 정답은 (a)다.

어휘_ handkerchief 손수건 reasonable 비싸지 않은, 합당한 duty-free shop 면세점 reserve 예약하다

정답_ (a)

6.

W: This is Karen from J&J company. How may I help you?

M: Hello. I'm your applicant. I got the mail about an interview but there is no information about the date and address.

W: Really? What is your name?

M: It's Bill.

W: Oh, we didn't give you any information. We can resend the e-mail that has all the information. Is your e-mail address bill2050@hotmail.com?

M: Yes. However, could you please send it to bill2050@yahoo.com not hotmail.com?

W: Ok. I'll send it right away.

Q. What does the man want to do?

(a) The man wants to know her e-mail address.

(b) The man wants to meet his client.

(c) The man wants to receive the e-mail included information.

(d) The man wants to apply for job openings.

해석_ W: J&J 회사의 카렌입니다. 어떻게 도와 드릴까요?

M: 안녕하세요. 귀사에 지원한 사람입니다. 인터뷰에 대한 메일을 받았는데 날짜와 주소가 없네요.

W: 정말요? 성함이 어떻게 되시죠?

M: 빌입니다.

W: 아, 저희가 아무런 정보도 드리지 않았네요. 모든 정보가 담긴 이메일을 다시 보내 드릴게요. 이메일 주소가 bill2050@hotmail.com인가요?

M: 네. 하지만 핫메일 말고 bill2050@yahoo.com으로 보내 주실래요?

W: 알겠습니다. 바로 보내 드릴게요.

Q. 남자는 무엇을 하기 원하는가?

(a) 남자는 그녀의 이메일 주소를 알기 원한다.

(b) 남자는 그의 고객을 만나기를 원한다.

(c) 남자는 정보가 포함된 이메일을 받기 원한다.

(d) 남자는 공개 채용에 지원하기를 원한다.

해설_ 남자의 첫 번째 대사를 보면 인터뷰에 대한 메일을 받았는데 날짜와 주소가 없다고 얘기하는 내용이 나온다. 따라서 (c)가 정답임을 알 수 있다.

어휘_ applicant 지원자 resend 다시 보내다 apply for ~을 지원[신청]하다 job opening 공개 채용, 일자리

정답_ (c)

Chapter 15 대화문 내용 추론하기

STEP 1 Pattern Study

Sample

해석_ W: 야, 짐! 아이스하키 시합 어땠니?

M: 근소한 차이로 졌어. 아무 말 마.

W: 앗, 정말 미안. 하지만 20분 전에는 너희 팀이 이기고 있었잖아.

M: 맞아. 하지만 우리가 자만했어. 결국 지고 말았지.

W: 너희 팀은 항상 잘하고 있잖아, 그러니까 다음번엔 이길 거야. 응원하러 갈게.

M: 정말 고마워.

Q. 대화를 통해 추론할 수 있는 것은?

(a) 여자는 하키 선수다.

(b) 오늘 오후에 다른 시합이 있다.

(c) 남자는 시합 중에 머리를 다쳤다.

(d) 여자는 다음번 시합을 보러 갈 것이다.

정답_ (d)

STEP 2 Clinic

Part 3

1.

해석_ M: 케이트! 네가 시내에 HOT 피자 가게가 있다고 했잖아. 길 좀 자세히 가르쳐 줄래?

W: 물론이지. 너 R&E 빌딩 알지?

M: 아, 중심가에 있는 거?

W: 맞아. 그 빌딩 앞에서 오른쪽으로 돈 다음, 두 블록 쭉 가면 약국 옆에 있어. 아마 많은 사람들이 줄 서 있을 거야.

M: 고마워. 피자 먹을 일이 기대된다.

W: 너도 틀림없이 나처럼 단골이 될 거야.

M: 그럴 거야. 다음번엔 나랑 같이 가.

Q. 대화를 통해 추론할 수 있는 것은?

(a) 여자는 그 피자 가게에 자주 간다.

(b) 빌딩은 피자 가게 옆에 있다.

(c) 여자는 산책을 할 것이다.

(d) 남자는 여자의 제안을 거절했다.

정답_ (a)

2.

해석_ M: 안녕하세요. 저 좀 도와주실래요?

W: 물론이죠. 무엇을 도와 드릴까요?

M: 제 이름은 제이크예요. 화이트 박사님의 조수를 구하고 있다고 들었습니다. 지원하고 싶어요.

W: 이력서 가지고 계신가요?

M: 네. 여기 있어요.

W: 좋아요. 서류전형에 통과하시면 면접 날짜를 전화로 알려 드릴게요.

M: 죄송하지만, 그가 면접 날짜를 정확히 언제로 정할지 아시나요?

W: 아마 이번주 금요일 전에 알려 드리게 될 거예요.

Q. 대화를 통해 추론할 수 있는 것은?

(a) 여자는 병원에서 일하고 있다.

(b) 여자는 남자의 불편한 점을 도왔다.

(c) 남자는 이번 금요일에 면접을 볼 것이다.

(d) 여자는 남자에게 전화할 것을 약속했다.

정답_ (a)

STEP 3 Dictation

정답_ 1. You said that there is a Hot pizza place downtown
Turn right in front of the building, then go straight two blocks and it's next to the drug store

2. I heard that your hospital is looking for Dr. White's assistant
I'm sorry, but do you know when he will decide the date exactly

STEP 4 Actual Test

Part 3

1.

M: I heard you were sick last weekend. What happened to you?

W: Right. I was attacked by influenza.

M: Are you alright now? You grew thinner than before.

W: I'm getting better. I'm going to the hospital after a while.

M: Then, you won't attend our club meeting today.

W: I'm sorry I can't. Due to the effect of medicine, I should go to bed.

M: Ok, I hope you get better soon.

W: Thank you so much.

Q. What can be inferred from the conversation?

(a) The man worried about the woman's health.

(b) The woman is probably going to the meeting.

(c) The woman couldn't have a medicine.

(d) They live in the same village.

해석_ M: 지난주 내내 아팠다면서. 무슨 일이야?

　　W: 맞아. 독감에 걸렸어.

　　M: 지금은 괜찮니? 전보다 살이 더 빠졌다.

　　W: 나아지고 있어. 좀 있다가 병원에 갈 거야.

　　M: 그럼, 오늘 우리 클럽모임에 못 오겠구나.

　　W: 유감이지만 못 가. 약효 때문에 자야 해.

　　M: 괜찮아, 곧 낫길 바랄게.

　　W: 정말 고마워.

　　Q. 대화를 통해 추론할 수 있는 것은?

　　(a) 남자는 여자의 건강을 걱정했다.

　　(b) 여자는 아마도 모임에 갈 것이다.

　　(c) 여자는 약을 먹을 수 없었다.

　　(d) 그들은 같은 마을에 산다.

해설_ 여자에게 지난주 내내 아팠다는 소식을 들었는데 무슨 일인지, 지금은 괜찮은지 묻는 것으로 보아 남자가 여자의 건강을 걱정했음을 짐작할 수 있다.

어휘_ **be attacked by** ~에 걸리다　**influenza** 독감　**grow thinner** (전보다) 여위다　**attend** 출석[참석]하다　**the effect of medicine** 약효

정답_ (a)

2.

M: Hello. I want to buy a round-trip ticket to New York.

W: This is the time table. When will you depart and arrive?

M: I'd like to leave at 4:30 pm today and come back at noon tomorrow.

W: That'll be fine. It's 25 dollars.

M: Can I pay by check?

W: I'm sorry. We can take only credit or cash.

M: It's inevitable. I'll pay with a card.

Q. What can be inferred from the conversation?

(a) They're going on a trip together.

(b) The man doesn't have enough money to buy the ticket.

(c) The man is going on a business trip.

(d) The woman is working in a booking office.

해석_ M: 안녕하세요. 뉴욕행 왕복표를 사고 싶은데요.

　　W: 이것이 시간표입니다. 언제 출발해서 언제 돌아오실 건가요?

　　M: 오늘 오후 4시 30분에 출발해서 내일 정오에 돌아오고 싶어요.

　　W: 좋습니다. 25달러예요.

　　M: 수표로 지불해도 되나요?

　　W: 죄송해요. 저희는 카드나 현금만 받습니다.

　　M: 어쩔 수 없군요. 카드로 지불할게요.

　　Q. 대화를 통해 추론할 수 있는 것은?

　　(a) 그들은 함께 여행을 갈 것이다.

　　(b) 남자는 표를 살 충분한 돈이 없다.

　　(c) 남자는 출장을 갈 것이다.

　　(d) 여자는 매표소에서 일하고 있다.

해설_ 남자의 첫 번째 대사를 통해 대화가 이루어지고 있는 장소가 공항이며, 남자가 비행기표를 사려고 하고 있음을 알 수 있다. 따라서 이 남자를 돕고 있는 여자가 매표소에서 일하는 직원임을 파악할 수 있다. 남자는 표를 살 돈이 모자란 게 아니라 단지 현금을 충분히 가지고 있지 않은 것이기 때문에 **(b)**는 틀리다.

어휘_ **time table** 시간표　**inevitable** 피할 수 없는, 부득이한　**booking office** 매표소

정답_ (d)

3.

M: Good morning. May I speak with Mr. Thompson?

W: I'm sorry but he's in a conference now. Do

you want me to take a message?

M: Actually I need to speak to him right now. I'm in a hurry.

W: I'm really sorry, sir. But Mr. Thompson told me to make sure nobody interrupts the conference.

M: Then when would I be able to reach him?

W: The conference should be over in 10 minutes.

M: Well, that's not a long time. Thank you very much.

Q. What can be inferred from the conversation?

(a) The man will visit Mr. Thompson's office.

(b) The man will call back once the conference is over.

(c) The woman will call the man back when the conference is over.

(d) The conference will be put off until this afternoon.

해석_ M: 안녕하세요. 톰슨 씨와 통화할 수 있을까요?

W: 죄송하지만, 그는 지금 회의 중이에요. 메시지 남겨 드릴까요?

M: 실은 지금 바로 그와 통화해야 하는데요. 제가 좀 급해서요.

W: 정말 죄송합니다, 선생님. 하지만 톰슨 씨가 아무도 회의를 방해하지 않도록 하라고 하셨어요.

M: 그럼 언제 그와 연락할 수 있을까요?

W: 회의는 10분 후에 끝날 겁니다.

M: 음, 그렇게 긴 시간은 아니네요. 정말 고마워요.

Q. 대화를 통해 추론할 수 있는 것은?

(a) 남자는 톰슨 씨의 사무실을 방문할 것이다.

(b) 남자는 회의가 끝나자마자 다시 전화할 것이다.

(c) 여자는 회의가 끝날 때 남자에게 다시 전화할 것이다.

(d) 회의는 오늘 오후까지 연기될 것이다.

해설_ 남자의 두 번째 대사를 보면, 그는 톰슨 씨와 바로 통화하길 원하고 있다. 하지만 여자로부터 지금은 회의 중이라 통화가 불가능하고 10분 후에 회의가 끝날 거라는 얘기를 들었으므로 그가 10분 후에 바로 다시 전화할 것임을 짐작할 수 있다.

어휘_ **be in a hurry** 급하다 **interrupt** 방해하다 **put off** 미

루다, 연기하다

정답_ (b)

4.

M: I've made a decision to quit my job.

W: For real? I think you're the only person who is suitable for this job. And you loved your job here. What made you do that?

M: Yeah, I know. But I'm fed up with doing the same stuff everyday.

W: Well, I feel that way sometimes. But at least they give us good things to compensate for that. Good salary, working circumstances, people.

M: I used to think like you, but not any more. I've felt like I was losing my own life. I want to do what I really want to.

W: So, what do you really want to do?

M: Well, I want more active and lively jobs like in a sales department or a public relations department.

W: Are you planning anything now?

M: After quitting my job, I'll travel around Asia for a month. And then I'll go to business school.

Q. What can be inferred from the conversation?

(a) The man wants to be a CEO.

(b) The man is going to study for his new job.

(c) The woman will quit her job after the man does.

(d) The man works in a sales department.

해석_ M: 나 일 그만두기로 결심했어.

W: 정말로? 네가 이 일에 적합한 유일한 사람이라고 생각하는데. 그리고 여기 일을 무척 좋아했잖아. 뭣 땜에 그래?

M: 그래, 나도 알아. 하지만 매일 같은 일을 하는 데 질렸어.

W: 음, 나도 가끔씩 그렇게 느껴. 하지만 최소한 그것에 대한 보상으로 좋은 것들을 제공해 주잖아. 높은 봉급, 좋은 근무 환경, 좋은 사람들.

M: 나도 너처럼 생각했었지만 더 이상은 아니야. 내 자신의 삶을 잃어버리고 있는 것처럼 느꼈어. 내가 정말로 원하는 걸

하고 싶어.

W: 그래서 넌 정말로 뭘 하기를 원하는데?

M: 음, 판매부나 홍보부처럼 좀 더 활동적이고 활기찬 일을 하고 싶어.

W: 지금 뭐 계획하고 있는 거라도 있어?

M: 일을 그만둔 후에 한 달 동안 아시아를 여행할 거야. 그리고 나서 경영대학원에 갈 거야.

Q. 대화를 통해 추론할 수 있는 것은?

(a) 남자는 최고 경영자가 되기를 원한다.

(b) 남자는 그의 새 직업을 위해 공부할 것이다.

(c) 여자는 남자가 그만둔 뒤 그녀의 일을 그만둘 것이다.

(d) 남자는 판매부에서 일한다.

해설_ 남자의 마지막 대사를 보면, 일을 그만둔 뒤 여행을 다녀와서 경영대학원에 갈 거라는 내용이 나온다. 따라서 그가 새로운 직업을 위해 공부할 것임을 짐작할 수 있다.

어휘_ **be suitable for** ~에 적합하다 **be fed up with** ~에 싫증이 나다, 넌더리나다 **compensate** 보상하다 **active** 활동적인 **lively** 활기에 넘친 **public relations department** 홍보부 **business school** 경영대학원 **CEO(= chief executive officer)** 최고 경영자

정답_ (b)

5.

W: May I help you?

M: Yes, I'm taking professor Jeffery's English literature class, but I don't know what the textbook is.

W: Which class are you taking, medieval or contemporary?

M: Oh, my class is about medieval.

W: Then this is the main textbook.

M: How much is it?

W: It's $20. Don't you need an auxiliary textbook?

M: Sure. Is there any price cutting if I buy both of them?

W: Yes, we discount the price 5%. So it'll be $25.

Q. What can be inferred from the conversation?

(a) The man is selling used books.

(b) Professor Jeffery has three English literature lectures.

(c) The man can get a 10% discount if he buys three books.

(d) The original price of the main textbook and the auxiliary book is not $25.

해석_ W: 무엇을 도와 드릴까요?

M: 예, 제프리 교수님의 영문학 강좌를 수강할 건데요. 교재가 어떤 건지 잘 몰라서요.

W: 어떤 강좌를 들으시는 건가요? 중세문학인가요, 아님 현대문학인가요?

M: 아, 중세문학이에요.

W: 그럼 이게 주교재예요.

M: 얼마예요?

W: 20달러입니다. 다른 부교재는 안 필요하세요?

M: 네. 둘 다 사면 할인 혜택이 있나요?

W: 네, 5% 할인해 드려요. 그럼 25달러가 되겠네요.

Q. 대화를 통해 추론할 수 있는 것은?

(a) 남자는 중고책을 팔고 있다.

(b) 제프리 교수는 세 개의 문학 강좌를 맡고 있다.

(c) 남자는 책 세 권을 사면 10% 할인받을 수 있다.

(d) 주교재와 부교재의 원가는 25달러가 아니다.

해설_ 주교재와 부교재를 모두 살 경우 할인 혜택이 있냐는 남자의 질문에 5% 할인해서 25달러라고 했으므로 (d)가 정답임을 알 수 있다.

어휘_ **medieval** 중세의 **contemporary** 현대의 **auxiliary** 보조의, 부수적인 **price cutting** 할인, 가격 인하 **used book** 중고책 **original price** 원가

정답_ (d)

Chapter 16 담화문 요지 파악하기

STEP 1 Pattern Study

Sample

해석_ 폭풍으로부터 추가적으로 보호받을 수 있는 방법이 있나요? 우리의 토지 위에 공습대피소 같은 건물을 짓는 것이 실용적인가요? 날씨가 잠잠하면 이런 식으로 생각하는 것이 어리석게 보입니다. 그러나 바람이 거세게 불고 있었을 때 토네이도가 우리의 집을 휩쓴다면 세상의 모든 돈으로도 우리를 구해 줄 수 없다고 생각할 수밖에 없었죠. 특히 지금처럼 날씨 유형이 더욱 맹렬한 바람을 동반할 것 같을 때 더더욱 그렇습니다.

Q. 담화의 요지는 무엇인가?

(a) 폭풍으로부터 보호하는 방법

(b) 재난으로부터 돈을 지키는 방법

(c) 폭풍이 지난 후 길을 보수하는 방법

(d) 폭풍을 예측하는 방법

정답_ (a)

STEP 2 Clinic

Part 4

1.

해석_ 우리는 이런 나라에 삽니다. 동네에는 가스 공급이 되지 않아 집 안의 모든 것을 전기로 가동시키죠. 관리비는 당연히 너무도 비쌉니다! 7월에는 312달러, 8월에는 283달러였죠. 우리는 에어컨조차 없어요. 우리는 땅을 파서 설치한 수영장, 냉동고, 전기 온수기가 있으며, 지하실에는 제습기를 가동해야 합니다. 그러나 그것 말고는, 우리는 낮에 집에 있지 않으며 밤에 방을 나갈 때면 늘 불을 끕니다. 그렇다면 전력은 모두 어디로 가고 있는 거죠?

Q. 담화의 요지는 무엇인가?

(a) 화자는 전기세가 지나치게 비싼 이유를 모른다.

(b) 화자는 에어컨 때문에 전기세를 많이 내야 한다.

(c) 화자는 전기를 아끼기 위해 노력하고 있다.

(d) 정부는 전기 요금을 인상할 것이다.

정답_ (a)

2.

해석_ 당신의 피부를 보호하는 가장 중요한 방법은 태양으로부터 보호하는 것이다. 자외선, 즉 눈에 보이진 않지만 태양으로부터의 강렬한 빛은 깊은 주름, 건조하고 거친 피부, 기미, 그리고 양성 및 악성 피부 종양과 같은 보다 심각한 병을 유발하면서 피부를 손상시킨다. 사실 노화 피부에서 보여지는 대부분의 변화는 태양에 노출된 수명에 의해 야기된다.

Q. 담화의 요지는 무엇인가?

(a) 햇빛은 건강에 해롭다.

(b) 햇빛을 쬐는 것이 피부를 보호하는 가장 좋은 방법이다.

(c) 누구나 늙지 않기를 원하는 것은 사실이다.

(d) 피부 노화의 진행은 햇빛에 의해 야기된다.

정답_ (d)

STEP 3 Dictation

정답_ 1. There is no gas service on our street
turn off lights whenever we leave rooms at night
So where is all the electricity going
2. The most important way to take care of your skin
most of the changes seen in aging skin are actually caused by a lifetime of sun exposure

STEP 4 Actual Test

Part 4

1.

When the weather's cold, chilies can warm you from the inside while a crackling fire warms you from the outside. Heat, however, can be too much of a good thing sometimes. But don't let one painful experience sour you on chilies — they will grow on you over time. I once thought that jalapeno peppers were hot. I now consider them only zesty and quite delicious.

Q. Which of the following best summarizes the talk?

(a) A pungent food can be palatable.

(b) People who have a weak stomach had better avoid spicy foods.

(c) You may have a stomachache if you have too much spicy food.

(d) Recently many people enjoy having spicy foods.

해석_ 날씨가 추울 때 우지직우지직 소리 내며 타오르는 불이 외부로부터 당신을 따뜻하게 해주는 반면, 칠리는 당신의 내부를 따뜻하게 해줍니다. 그렇지만 열은 이따금씩 지나치게 좋아 오히려 해가 될 수 있죠. 하지만 고통스런 경험 때문에 칠리를 싫어하는 일이 생기지 않도록 하세요. 시간이 지날수록 점점 좋아하게 될 것입니다. 전 한때 할라피뇨 칠리가 맵다고 생각한 적이 있었습니다. 지금은 단지 맛이 강할 뿐 아주 맛있다고 생각합니다.

Q. 담화를 가장 잘 요약한 것은 어느 것인가?

(a) 매운 음식이라도 즐거울 수 있다.

(b) 위가 약한 사람은 매운 음식을 피하는 것이 낫다.

(c) 매운 음식을 너무 많이 먹으면 위가 아플 수도 있다.

(d) 최근 들어 많은 사람들이 매운 음식을 즐긴다.

해설_ 너무 매워 고통스러운 경험을 겪기도 하지만, 시간이 지날수록 좋아하게 될 거라는 내용이므로 (a)가 가장 적절하다.

어휘_ **chili** 칠리 고추, 그것으로 만든 향신료 **crackling** 우지직우지직 소리 내는 **sour on** ~을 싫어하다 **grow on** (~의 마음에) 점점 들게 되다 **zesty** 강한 맛이 나는, 자극적인 **pungent** 매운, 자극성의 **palatable** 비위에 맞는, 즐거운 **avoid** 피하다 **spicy** 매운

정답_ (a)

2.

How did you learn to ride your bike? Someone probably gave you a few lessons and then you practiced a lot. You can learn how to study in much the same way. No one is born knowing how to study. You need to learn a few study skills and then practice them when preparing for a test or even doing your homework. If you get study skills, you can study well.

Q. What is the main point the speaker is trying to make?

(a) Before you start something, you should do it step by step.

(b) You might prepare perfectly to make a presentation.

(c) Learning study skills is better than studying without reserve.

(d) Anyone who studies hard gets a good grade in an exam.

해석_ 자전거 타는 방법을 어떻게 배웠습니까? 누군가 가르쳐 줬을 테고, 그 후 연습을 많이 했을 것입니다. 공부하는 방법 역시 아주 똑같은 방식으로 배울 수 있습니다. 누구도 공부하는 방법을 알고 태어나는 사람은 없습니다. 몇 가지 공부 방법을 배운 다음, 시험을 준비하거나 심지어 숙제를 할 때도 연습해야 합니다. 공부 방법을 터득한다면 공부를 잘할 수 있습니다.

Q. 화자가 말하고자 하는 요점은 무엇인가?

(a) 무언가를 시작하기 전에 단계적으로 해야 한다.

(b) 발표를 하기 위해 완벽히 준비할 수 있다.

(c) 무조건 공부하는 것보다 공부 방법을 익히는 것이 더 낫다.

(d) 열심히 공부하는 사람만이 시험에서 좋은 성적을 거둔다.

해설_ 자전거 타는 방법을 터득한 방식대로 공부 방법을 터득하면 공부를 잘할 수 있다는 내용이므로 (c)가 정답이다.

어휘_ **give lessons** 가르치다 **practice** 연습하다 **in much the same way** 매우 동일한 방법으로 **skill** 기술 **step by step** 단계적으로 **make a presentation** 발표하다 **without reserve** 무조건, 거리낌 없이

정답_ (c)

3.

Now on its 15th Year, Cinema One Originals 2009 Film Festival will provide directors, writers and film enthusiasts an opportunity for expressing their original stories. A 1,000,000 pound grant will be awarded to each of the chosen five finalists to produce their movie. The festival and awards will be in November.

Q. What is the main purpose of this announcement?

(a) To notify various Movie Festivals in many country

(b) To notify people of the film event

(c) To inform you that a job fair will be closed in November

(d) To inform you how to join the Film Festival

Q. 이 광고의 주된 목적은 무엇인가?

(a) 많은 국가에서 열리는 다양한 영화 축제를 알리기 위해

(b) 사람들에게 영화 행사를 알리기 위해

(c) 취업 설명회가 11월에 끝난다는 것을 알리기 위해

(d) 영화 축제에 참가하는 방법을 알리기 위해

해설_ 15주년 영화 축제가 11월에 열릴 예정이라고 했으므로 (b)가
정답이다.

어휘_ **director** 감독 **enthusiast** 열성적인 사람, ~팬(fan)
grant 상금 **finalist** 결승 진출자 **notify** 통지하다, 공고
하다 **job fair** 취업 설명회

정답_ (b)

4.

Just as higher gas prices have changed driving habits, rising food prices are shifting grocery shopping patterns. Consumers are buying less and sticking to the staples, observes one grocer on the front lines. "People are just buying what they need," said Sindy Moore, customer service manager with Matt's Grocery, a family-owned grocery chain with five stores around the state. But there are signs that food prices won't follow the dramatic drop of gasoline.

Q. Which of the following best summarizes the talk?

(a) A scholar anticipated that gas prices will increase dramatically.

(b) The market is now on sale in the mall.

(c) A consumer market is decreasing because of soaring food prices.

(d) Consumer habits are changed by comfortable living.

Q. 담화를 가장 잘 요약한 것은 어느 것인가?

(a) 한 학자는 기름 값이 급격히 오를 것이라고 예상했다.

(b) 식료품점은 쇼핑몰에서 현재 세일 중이다.

(c) 치솟는 음식 값 때문에 소비자 시장이 감소하고 있다.

(d) 소비 습관은 편리한 생활에 의해 바뀐다.

해설_ 음식 값이 오르자 소비자들의 소비가 줄었다는 내용이므로
(c)가 정답이다.

어휘_ **shift** 바뀌다, 위치가 변경되다 **stick to** ~에 집착하다[달
라붙다] **staple** 기본 식료품 **observe** ~이라고 말하다
grocer 식료 잡화상 **on the front lines** 최전선에서, 현
장에서 **dramatic** 극적인 **drop** 하락 **scholar** 학자
decrease 감소하다 **ballooning oil prices** 급등하는
유가

정답_ (c)

5.

In Houston and Harris County, over 85,000 dogs and cats must be euthanized every year because they are unwanted. You can be a responsible pet owner by spaying or neutering your pet to help reduce this number. Spaying/neutering is good for your pet. It reduces the chances of reproductive cancer; prevents females from having heat cycles; reduces chances males will spray to mark their territory and reduces the pet overpopulation problem.

Q. What is the main idea of the talk?

(a) People who keep animals need to have responsibilities.

(b) People never euthanize their pet.

(c) You ought to go to the veterinary hospital immediately if your pet is sick.

(d) The pets which have cancer has recently increased.

해석_ 휴스턴과 해리스 지역에서는 매년 8만 5천 마리가 넘는 강아지와 고양이가 쓸모없다는 이유로 안락사됩니다. 당신은 이 같은 숫자를 줄이도록 당신의 애완동물의 난소를 제거하거나 거세를 시킴으로써 책임감 있는 애완동물 주인이 될 수 있습니다. 난소를 제거하거나 거세를 시키는 것은 당신의 애완동물에게 좋습니다. 번식하는 암의 가능성을 줄이며, 열 순환을 막음으로써 암컷 애완동물을 보호하고, 수컷 애완동물의 번식 기회를 줄일 수 있으며, 애완동물 과잉 문제를 줄일 수 있습니다.

Q. 담화의 요지는 무엇인가?

(a) 동물을 기르는 사람은 책임감을 가져야 한다.

(b) 사람들은 자신의 애완동물을 절대 안락사시키지 않는다.

(c) 애완동물이 아프면 즉시 동물병원으로 가야 한다.

(d) 암에 걸린 애완동물이 최근 증가했다.

해설_ 매년 8만 5천 마리의 개와 고양이들이 안락사된다는 사실을 언급하면서, 이렇게 안락사되는 숫자를 줄이기 위해 애완동물의 난소를 제거하거나 거세를 시킴으로써 책임감 있는 애완동물 주인이 될 수 있다고 말했으므로 (a)가 정답이다.

어휘_ **euthanize** 안락사시키다 **unwanted** 불필요한, 쓸모없는 **spay** 난소를 제거하다 **neuter** 거세하다 **reproductive** 번식하는 **territory** 영역 **overpopulation** 인구 과잉

정답_ (a)

6.

Bike-friendly cities in Europe have retimed traffic lights in bike corridors to correlate with man powered speeds instead of automobile speed limits. The practice is called "green wave." San Francisco is preparing it. A preliminary study conducted on San Francisco's Valencia Street suggests that retiming lights for vehicles moving 12 mph would make the road safer for everyone by reducing the number of bikers running red lights and reducing the likelihood of bike/car collisions.

Q. What is the main point the speaker is trying to make?

(a) Bikes and automobiles should keep a stop line.

(b) All countries should practice "green wave."

(c) Bicyclists in Europe have increased steadily.

(d) Traffic lights in bike corridors can prevent an accident.

해석_ 유럽에서 자전거가 익숙한 도시들은 자동차 제한 속도 대신에 사람의 힘의 속도와 관련시키기 위해 자전거 전용도로의 신호등 시간을 재조정했다. 이러한 실행은 "녹색 움직임"이라고 불린다. 샌프란시스코는 이를 준비 중에 있다. 샌프란시스코의 발렌시아 거리에서 실시된 사전준비 연구는 시속 12마일로 움직이는 차들에 대해서 신호를 조정하는 것이 적신호를 무시하고 달리는 자전거 수를 줄이고, 자전거나 자동차 충돌의 가능성을 줄임으로써 모두에게 더 안전한 길을 만들어 줄 것이라고 제안한다.

Q. 화자가 말하고자 하는 요점은 무엇인가?

(a) 자전거와 오토바이는 정지선을 지켜야 한다.

(b) 모든 나라가 "녹색 움직임"을 실행해야 한다.

(c) 유럽에서 자전거 타는 사람이 꾸준히 늘었다.

(d) 자전거 전용도로의 신호등은 사고를 줄일 수 있다.

해설_ 자전거 전용도로의 신호등 시간을 재조정함으로써 모두에게 안전한 길을 만들어 주고 교통 혼잡과 위험을 줄이자는 내용이므로 (d)가 적절한 정답이다.

어휘_ **retime traffic lights** 교통 신호등 시간을 재조정하다 **bike corridor** 자전거 전용도로 **correlate** ~와 관련시키다 **speed limit** 제한 속도 **preliminary** 예비적인 **conduct** 수행[실행]하다 **mph(= miles per hour)** 시속 **likelihood** 가능성 **collision** 충돌 **bicyclist** 자전거 타는 사람 **steadily** 꾸준히, 착실하게

정답_ (d)

Chapter 17 담화문 내용 파악하기

STEP 1 Pattern Study

Sample

해석_ 오늘 한 밴쿠버 소년이 정지 신호를 무시하고 자신의 자전거를 타고 가다가 트랜 버스와 충돌하여 부상당했다고 경찰이 말했습니다. 밴쿠버 Arts and Academics 학교에 다니는 7학년생 매튜는 아침 9시 24분 충돌 후 레가시 엠마누엘 아동 병원에서 중태에 빠졌습니다.

Q. 보도에 따르면 사실인 것은 어느 것인가?

(a) 소년은 병원으로 후송되었다.
(b) 경찰이 맨 먼저 사고를 발견했다.
(c) 버스는 빨간 신호등을 무시하고 운전했다.
(d) 거리에는 두 명의 목격자가 있었다.

정답_ (a)

STEP 2 Clinic

Part 4

1.

해석_ 활력이 넘치고 성장하는 수입업체에서 저희 팀에 합류할 활동적인 회계 보조를 찾고 있습니다. 지원자들은 지급 계정과 수취 계정 분야에서 최소 3년의 경험이 있어야 합니다. 지원자들은 긍정적인 태도와 다중 업무 처리 능력을 지향하고 위기의식을 지니고 있어야 합니다. denny@brain.com으로 희망 연봉과 함께 이력서를 제출해 주세요.

Q. 담화에 따르면 사실이 아닌 것은 어느 것인가?

(a) 이 회사는 컴퓨터에 능한 직원을 원한다.
(b) 지원자는 동종 업계에서의 경험을 가지고 있어야 한다.
(c) 이 광고에 관심 있는 지원자는 이메일로 이력서를 보낼 수 있다.
(d) 이 회사는 회계 보조를 구하고 있다.

정답_ (a)

2.

해석_ 지금 outdoors link를 클릭하시면 누구든지 Michigan.org 사이트의 골프 페이지에서 골프 시작 시간 예약과 원하시면 숙박 예약도 하실 수 있습니다. 저희는 최근 사이트를 개선하였습니다. 일단 사이트에 들어가시면 지역별, 코스별 또는 날짜별로 검색하실 수 있습니다. 갑자기 금요일 아침에 시간이 비어 북쪽으로 드라이브하고 싶은 생각이 간절하시다면, 이 사이트가 골프 경기가 가능한 곳을 알려주고 그곳을 예약할 수 있게 해줄 것입니다. 놀랍게도 그 (북쪽 지역의) 주에는 선택 가능한 골프 코스가 850군데나 있습니다.

Q. 광고에 따르면 맞는 것은 어느 것인가?

(a) 이 회사는 여행 관련 사업을 한다.
(b) 고객은 인터넷 웹사이트에서 예약할 수 있다.
(c) 웹사이트는 한 달 후에 개선될 것이다.
(d) 금요일 코스를 원한다면 가능한 빨리 예약해야 한다.

정답_ (b)

STEP 3 Dictation

정답_ 1. Candidates should have at least 3 years of experience in
Please submit resume with salary requirements

2. We improved our site recently. Once there, you can search by region, course or date
The site will tell you what tee times are open and where

STEP 4 Actual Test

Part 4

1.

As the prices of everyday household expenses like gas and groceries continue to climb, many families are cutting back on eating out. However, if you'd still like to enjoy an occasional meal out with your family or spouse, try cutting out coupons before you cut out the fun of dining out. It isn't hard to find good coupons for restaurants you like if you know where to look. You can find discounted prices for these books at www.coupon.com in the Restaurant Coupon section.

Q. What is being advertised?

(a) Web site
(b) New grocery store
(c) Restaurants in your town
(d) Famous souvenir in their town

해석_가스, 식료품 같은 생활비가 계속 오르면서 많은 가정들이 외식을 줄이고 있습니다다. 그러나 만일 여전히 가족들이나 배우자와 특별한 외식을 즐기고 싶다면 밖에서 식사하는 즐거움을 없애기 전에 쿠폰을 잘라 보세요. 만일 어딜 찾아봐야 하는지 안다면 좋아하는 레스토랑의 괜찮은 쿠폰을 찾는 것은 어렵지 않습니다. www.coupon.com의 레스토랑 쿠폰 분류에서 할인된 가격의 이러한 책들을 찾으실 수 있습니다.

Q. 무엇을 광고하고 있는가?

(a) 웹사이트

(b) 새로운 식료품점

(c) 동네 레스토랑들

(d) 그들 지역의 유명한 기념품

해설_늘어나는 생활비 때문에 외식을 줄이고 있지만, 할인 쿠폰을 활용해 외식을 즐길 수 있으며, 그러한 쿠폰 책자들을 자기네 웹사이트에서 찾을 수 있다고 했으므로 (a)가 정답임을 알 수 있다.

어휘_**household expenses** 가사 비용 **cut back** (수량, 크기를) 줄이다, (비용을) 삭감하다 **eat[dine] out** 외식하다 **occasional** 이따금씩의, 특별한 경우를 위한 **spouse** 배우자 **cut out** 잘라내다, 제거하다 **souvenir** 기념품

정답_(a)

2.

Immigrant families from Africa, Asia and Latin America have changed metro Atlanta. Latinos make up key work forces in the construction, landscaping, hospitality, poultry and agricultural industries, and a growing number of Latinos are moving into the middle class. In all, one in 10 people in metro Atlanta was born outside the United States.

Q. What happened in Atlanta?

(a) The government will change an immigration law.
(b) The racial discrimination sometimes occurs.
(c) The various human races are being mixed more and more.
(d) Students don't study Latin anymore.

해석_아프리카, 아시아, 그리고 라틴 아메리카에서 온 이민 가정들이 메트로 애틀랜타를 바꿔 놓았다. 라틴 아메리카인들은 건설업, 조경업, 호텔·요식업, 양계업과 농업에서 중요한 노동력을 구성한다. 그리고 증가하는 라틴 아메리카인들의 숫자는 중산층으로 이동하고 있다. 모두 합치면, 메트로 애틀랜타의 10명 중 1명은 미국 밖에서 태어났다.

Q. 애틀랜타에서 무슨 일이 일어났는가?

(a) 정부는 이민법을 바꿀 것이다.

(b) 인종 차별이 가끔씩 발생한다.

(c) 다양한 인종이 점점 더 혼합되고 있다.

(d) 학생들은 더 이상 라틴어를 공부하지 않는다.

해설_애틀랜타의 라틴 아메리카인들이 여러 분야에서 노동력을 제공하고 있으며, 애틀랜타 인구에서 10명 중 1명은 다른 나라에서 태어난 사람들이라고 말했으므로, 다양한 인종이 점점 더 혼합되고 있다는 (c)가 정답이다.

어휘_**immigrant** 이민, 이주자 **metro Atlanta** 메트로 애틀랜타 (애틀랜타를 중심으로 그 주위를 둘러싸고 있는 거주 생활권) **Latino** 라틴 아메리카 사람 **make up** 구성하다 **key** 기본적인, 중요한 **work force** 노동력 **construction** 건설업 **landscaping** 조경업 **hospitality** 호텔·요식업 **poultry** 양계업 **agricultural industry** 농업 **racial discrimination** 인종 차별 **occur** 일어나다, 발생하다 **human race** 인종

정답_(c)

3.

A 3-year-old girl injured in the crash of a small plane in southeast Alaska that killed four members of an Oregon family remained in critical condition Saturday morning in Seattle's Harborview Medical Center. Her grandmother, Mindy Mayer, 60, of Oregon City, was in serious condition, a hospital spokeswoman said. Mayer and her granddaughter were flown to the hospital after the sightseeing plane they were flying in crashed near Ketchikan.

Q. Which of the following is true according to the report?

(a) Four passengers were killed by a plane accident.
(b) The girl is the only survivor.
(c) The criminal was arrested by her grand-mother.
(d) The accident was caused by bad weather conditions.

해석_ 오리건 주에 사는 한 가족 중 4명의 목숨을 앗아간, 알래스카 동남부에서 발생한 소형 비행기 충돌 사고로 부상당한 3살짜리 소녀가 시애틀의 하버뷰 의학 센터에서 토요일 아침 중태에 빠졌습니다. 그녀의 할머니인 60세 민디 메이어 씨도 상태가 심각하다고 병원 대변인은 전했습니다. 메이어와 그녀의 손녀는 그들이 타고 있던 관광 비행기가 케치칸 근처에서 충돌한 후 병원으로 후송되었습니다.

Q. 기사에 따르면 맞는 것은 어느 것인가?

(a) 비행기 사고로 4명의 승객이 목숨을 잃었다.

(b) 그 소녀가 유일한 생존자이다.

(c) 범인은 그녀의 할머니에 의해서 체포됐다.

(d) 그 사고는 나쁜 날씨 조건 때문에 일어났다.

해설_ 한 가족 중 4명이 사망했다는 내용이 나오므로 정답은 (a)다.

어휘_ **in the crash of** ~의 충돌로 **in critical[serious] condition** 중태의 **spokeswoman** (여성) 대변인 **fly** 비행기로 나르다[태워 가다] **sightseeing plane** 관광 비행기 **survivor** 생존자 **criminal** 범인 **arrest** 체포하다

정답_ (a)

4.

The University of Portland is steering hundreds of freshmen to off-campus apartments next fall because its dorms lack sufficient room to handle an unexpected surge in enrollment. The university expects 3,800 freshmen next fall, a 400-student increase, which will exceed dorm space and force it to provide more classes and services.

Q. How many were students in this semester approximately?

(a) 3,400 students
(b) 3,800 students
(c) 4,000 students
(d) 4,800 students

해석_ 포틀랜드 대학교는 수백 명의 신입생들이 다음 가을 학기에는 캠퍼스 밖의 아파트에서 거주하도록 권고하고 있습니다. 왜냐하면 학교 기숙사에는 예상치 못하게 늘어난 등록 수를 처리하기에 충분한 방이 없기 때문입니다. 그 대학교는 다음 가을 학기에 기숙사 공간을 초과하고 더 많은 수업과 편의 제공을 요하게 될, 400명이 더 늘어난 3,800명의 신입생을 예상하고 있습니다.

Q. 이번 학기에는 학생들이 대략 몇 명이었는가?

(a) 3,400명

(b) 3,800명

(c) 4,000명

(d) 4,800명

해설_ 다음 가을 학기에는 400명이 더 늘어나 3,800명이 될 것으로 예상했으므로 이번 학기엔 3,400명임을 알 수 있다.

어휘_ **steer** 나아가게 하다, 이끌다 **off-campus** 캠퍼스 밖의 **dorm** 기숙사 **sufficient** 충분한 **handle** 다루다, 처리하다 **unexpected** 예기치 않은 **surge** 급상승 **enrollment** 등록 **exceed** 초과하다

정답_ (a)

5.

The second day of 2009 has been unusually warm. Our low this morning of 64° is what the normal high should be. Warm, moist air continues to flow into Southeast Texas. Meanwhile, to our west, a developing upper-level storm system is poised to plow into that warm air and touch off showers and thunderstorms while you sleep tonight into Saturday morning.

Q. Which is correct according to the weather forecast?

(a) The temperature tomorrow morning will be in the 64s.
(b) The typhoon is approaching Southeast Texas.
(c) The warm temperature will continue until Saturday morning.

(d) The storm's center is now located in the Pacific Ocean.

해석_ 2009년의 두 번째 날은 평소와 달리 따뜻했습니다. 오늘 아침의 낮은 64도는 보통의 높은 기온이어야 하는 것입니다. 따뜻하고 습한 공기는 텍사스 남동부 쪽으로 계속 흘러들 것입니다. 그사이 서쪽으로는 상위권에서 발달하고 있는 태풍이 따뜻한 공기와 충돌해 오늘 밤부터 토요일 아침까지 소나기가 내리고 천둥번개가 칠 것으로 예상됩니다.

Q. 기상예보에 따르면 맞는 것은 어느 것인가?

(a) 내일 아침 기온은 64도일 것이다.
(b) 태풍이 텍사스 남동부에 접근하고 있다.
(c) 따뜻한 기온이 토요일 아침까지 이어질 것이다.
(d) 폭풍의 중심은 현재 태평양 연안에 있다.

해설_ 텍사스 남동부 쪽으로는 따뜻하고 습한 공기가 흘러들 것이라고 했으므로 (b)는 내용에 어긋난다. 또 오늘 아침 온도가 64도라고 했으므로 (a) 역시 틀리며, (d)는 언급된 바 없다. 따라서 정답은 (c)가 된다.

어휘_ **unusually** 평소와 달리, 이상하게 **moist** 축축한, 습한 **flow into** ~로 흘러들다 **be poised to** ~할 준비가 돼 있다, ~할 태세를 갖추다 **plow into** 충돌하다, 들이받다 **touch off** 유발하다 **shower** 소나기 **thunderstorm** 천둥번개 **approach** 접근하다

정답_ (c)

6.

Marcus's store three-day sale kick-off begins Friday (Nov 21) and includes women's designer and couture clothing, handbags and shoes and men's clothing and shoes. Save as much as 40 percent off big-name designer duds. Store's card users save an additional 15 percent. This is at the La Cantera store on La Cantera Parkway at Loop 1604.

Q. According to the talk, how can you save much money?

(a) You can save money if you have membership card.
(b) You should go to the store because it is having a big sale.
(c) You will buy clothes for 100 dollars in the store.

(d) If you make a membership card, you'll be provided with 40% off.

해석_ 마커스 상점의 3일간 할인 행사 개시가 금요일(11월 21일)에 시작되며, 디자이너 여성복과 기성복, 핸드백과 신발, 남성 의류와 신발을 포함합니다. 유명 디자이너의 의상을 무려 40%까지 할인받으세요. 상점 카드 사용자는 15% 추가 할인을 받습니다. 이 행사는 룹 1604의 라 칸테라 파크웨이에 있는 라 칸테라 상점에서 열립니다.

Q. 이야기에 따르면, 어떻게 많은 돈을 절약할 수 있는가?

(a) 회원카드를 가지고 있다면 돈을 절약할 수 있다.
(b) 대규모 세일을 하고 있으므로 그 상점에 가야 한다.
(c) 그 상점에서 100달러어치의 옷을 살 것이다.
(d) 회원카드를 만들면 40% 할인을 제공받을 것이다.

해설_ 상점에서 할인 행사를 하는데 40%까지 할인해 주며, 카드 사용자에게는 15% 추가 할인해 준다고 했으므로 정답은 (a)다.

어휘_ **kick-off** 시작, 개시 **couture** (고급 여성복 디자이너가 만든) 여성복 **big-name** 유명한 **duds** (한 벌의) 옷

정답_ (a)

7.

We live on a lake and the water level is high. The house is 13 years old and has a six feet high basement. The basement has some water spots on the walls and in two corners. It seems that the spots started where the floor and the walls meet. I would like to paint the walls with waterproof paint.

Q. What is the main problem with the house?

(a) The wall in the house is wet due to environmental causes.
(b) There is no way to buy waterproof paint.
(c) This area had a flood repeatedly.
(d) A writer couldn't wait for the painter because of another appointment.

해석_ 우리는 호수 위에 살고 있으며, 그 호수의 수위는 높다. 집은 13년이 되었고 6피트 높이의 지하실이 있다. 그 지하실에는 벽과 두 개의 모퉁이에 물이 있었던 흔적이 있다. 그 흔적은 바닥과 벽이 만난 지점에서 시작한 듯이 보인다. 나는 방수 페인트로 그 벽을 칠하고 싶다.

Q. 이 집의 주된 문제점은 무엇인가?

(a) 집 안의 벽이 환경적 원인 때문에 축축하다.

(b) 방수 페인트를 살 방법이 없다.

(c) 이 지역은 홍수가 잦았다.

(d) 글쓴이는 다른 약속 때문에 페인트공을 기다릴 수 없었다.

해설 호수 위에 살고 있는데 지하실의 벽에 물이 있었던 흔적이 보여 방수가 되는 페인트로 벽을 칠하고 싶다고 했으므로 (a)가 정답이다.

어휘 **water level** 수위 **spot** 반점, 얼룩 **floor** 바닥 **waterproof** 방수의 **environmental cause** 환경적 원인 **repeatedly** 되풀이하여, 거듭 **painter** 페인트공

정답 (a)

Chapter 18 담화문 추론하기

STEP 1 Pattern Study

Sample

해석 케냐의 우디 카렐은 목요일 밤 100미터 경기에서 승리하며 세계 기록을 수립했으며, 수월하게 하는 바람에 결승점에 골인하기 전에 카메라를 향해 포즈를 취했습니다. 카렐은 결승점까지 20여 미터를 앞두고 양손을 떨어뜨리고 컨디션을 잃었음에도 불구하고 10.9초를 기록했습니다. 그녀는 머리 위의 비디오 화면을 힐끗 보며 왼쪽으로 가는 듯이 보였다가, 양손을 낮추고 결승점에 가까워지면서 속도를 늦췄습니다. 그러나 그녀는 오늘 아침 400미터 경기에서는 지고 말았습니다.

Q. 이 기사로부터 언급될 수 있는 것은?

(a) 그녀는 케냐에서 금메달을 딴 유일한 사람이다.

(b) 아무도 그녀가 그 경기에 이길 것이라고 예상치 못했다.

(c) 그녀는 다음날 아침 400미터 경기에 이길 것이다.

(d) 그녀는 금메달을 받았다.

정답 (d)

STEP 2 Clinic

Part 4

1.

해석 토끼가 내쫓긴 지하실로 내려갔을 때, 우리는 우리의 부드러운 털을 가진 친구의 흔적을 찾아볼 수 없었다. 엄마는 자신이 잘못해서 문을 열어 놓고 나갔을 때 뛰쳐나간 것이 틀림없다고 말했다. 하지만 엄마를 너무 몰아붙이면 안 된다. 엄마는 토끼를 지지하는 사람들의 모임인 '어떻게 토끼를 돌보는가'와 '애완동물로서 토끼를 기르는 것은 어떠한가'에 관한 발표회에 참석할 기회가 단 한 번도 없었다. 그래서 우리는 동물에 관한 책을 사고 토끼를 기르기로 결정했다.

Q. 담화를 통해 추론할 수 있는 것은?

(a) 가족은 토끼를 집에서 발견했다.

(b) 어머니는 다양한 동물 지식을 가지고 있다.

(c) 토끼는 차 사고로 아팠다.

(d) 가족은 어떠한 동물도 키우고 싶어 하지 않는다.

정답 (a)

2.

Q. 담화를 통해 추론할 수 있는 것은?

(a) 카페인은 인간의 건강에 가장 위험한 물질 중 하나다.

(b) 카페인은 해롭지 않다.

(c) 2~3컵의 커피에 들어 있는 카페인 양은 당뇨병 환자에게 도움이 된다.

(d) 아데노신 효과는 혈관이 넓어지는 것을 돕는다.

정답_ (d)

STEP 3 Dictation

정답_ 1. When we went down to the basement, where the rabbit had been banished Mom said that it must have hopped out when she accidentally left the door open

2. two cups of coffee a day is not harmful in people without high blood pressure a hormone that helps keep them widened

STEP 4 Actual Test

Part 4

1.

Two UC Irvine students who proposed construction of the "Ultra Capacitor" were declared the winners Thursday of the $25,000 "Crazy Green Idea" contest sponsored by the Prize Foundation. Kyle Good and Bryan Le, both 19 and both second-year students at UC Irvine, submitted one of the 133 Youtube videos explaining an idea, and learned last week that their concept was one of three finalists.

Q. What can be inferred from the report?

(a) Two students won the competition.

(b) Two students invented a new video game.

(c) Two students donated $25,000 to charity.

(d) The Prize Foundation held the contest.

Q. 기사를 통해 추론할 수 있는 것은?

(a) 두 학생은 대회에서 우승했다.

(b) 두 학생은 새로운 비디오 게임을 발명했다.

(c) 두 학생은 자선 단체에 2만 5천 달러를 기부했다.

(d) 프라이즈 재단이 콘테스트를 개최했다.

정답_ (a)

2.

Ray Gomez is a quiet man, nothing flashy. Gomez is 79 years old, with a head of white hair, neatly styled and he is a famous hairdresser. People came to him not just for a $17 haircut, but for a few moments of peace in a busy world. All customers are satisfied with his haircut. However, he is retiring Dec. 31 after 58 years of cutting hair.

Q. What can be inferred from the talk?

(a) Gomez will cut his last hair at the end of the month.

(b) He has been working his job for over 70 years.

(c) People want to know his cutting skill.

(d) He was a famous designer's assistant.

해석_ 레이 고메즈는 조용하고 조금도 화려하지 않은 사람입니다. 머리가 하얗고 깔끔한 스타일을 한 79세의 고메즈는 유명한 미용사죠. 사람들은 단지 17달러짜리 컷을 위해서가 아니라 바쁜 세상 속에서 잠깐의 평화를 얻고자 그에게 왔습니다. 모든 손님들은 그의 머리 자르는 솜씨에 만족합니다. 하지만 그는 12월 31일, 머리를 잘랐던 58년의 세월로부터 퇴직할 것입니다.

Q. 담화를 통해 추론할 수 있는 것은?

(a) 고메즈는 월말에 마지막으로 머리를 자를 것이다.

(b) 그는 70년 넘게 그의 일을 해왔다.

(c) 사람들은 그의 컷 기술을 알고 싶어 한다.

(d) 그는 유명한 디자이너 보조였다.

해설_ 12월 31일에 미용사를 그만둘 것이라고 했으므로 (a)가 정답임을 알 수 있다. (b)는 맨 마지막 문장에 58년 동안 머리를 잘랐다는 내용이 나오므로 틀리다.

어휘_ **flashy** 화려한 **neatly** 깔끔하게 **retire** 퇴직하다

정답_ (a)

3.

Chocolate isn't just a taste sensation, it's an experience that enlivens all the senses. Consider touch: How quickly does the chocolate melt in your hand or mouth? The quicker the better, as this indicates a greater amount of cocoa butter. Sound also enters the equation. The crystalline structure of cocoa butter gives the excellent chocolate a "snap" when broken.

Q. What can be known through the talk?

(a) A factor destroying the texture of chocolate

(b) A chocolate depository

(c) A chocolate melting time in your hand or mouth

(d) How to select good chocolate

해석_ 초콜릿은 단지 맛의 감각이 아닙니다. 모든 감각에 생기를 주는 경험이죠. 촉감에 대해 생각해 보십시오. 얼마나 빨리 초콜릿이 여러분의 손과 입에서 녹습니까? 빠를수록 더 좋습니다. 이것은 더 많은 양의 코코아버터가 들었다는 것을 암시하기 때문입니다. 소리도 마찬가지죠. 코코아버터의 수정 같은 구조는 아주 질 좋은 초콜릿이 깨질 때 '뚝' 소리를 내게 해 줍니다.

Q. 담화를 통해 무엇을 알 수 있는가?

(a) 초콜릿 감촉을 파괴하는 요소

(b) 초콜릿 보관 장소

(c) 초콜릿이 손이나 입에서 녹는 시간

(d) 좋은 초콜릿을 고르는 방법

해설_ 빨리 녹을수록 더 많은 양의 코코아버터가 들은 것이고, 깨질 때 '뚝' 소리 나는 것이 좋은 초콜릿이라는 얘기를 하고 있으므로 (d)가 정답임을 알 수 있다.

어휘_ **sensation** 감각 **enliven** 활기 있게 만들다 **touch** 촉감 **melt** 녹다 **indicate** 나타내다, 암시하다 **enter the equation** 마찬가지이다 **crystalline** 수정 같은 **snap** 뚝 소리 냄, 툭 끊어짐 **factor** 요소 **texture** 감촉, 결 **depository** 보관소

정답_ (d)

4.

In a charity race Saturday, more than 5,000 runners ran two miles to a downtown Raleigh doughnut shop, ate a dozen glazed doughnuts each and returned to North Carolina State University in less than an hour. That's 2,400 calories and 144 grams of fat consumed while burning about 400 calories during the run. The student-run doughnut Challenge raised about $35,000 for the North Carolina Children's Hospital.

Q. What can be inferred from the report?

(a) People collected contributions for children.

(b) People are trying to lose their weight.

(c) Doughnuts are the worst food in North Carolina.

(d) People who ran consist of former racers.

해석_ 토요일 자선 경주에서 5천 명이 넘는 경주자들이 중심가의 롤리 도넛 가게까지 2마일을 달렸습니다. 각자 12개의 글레이즈드 도넛을 먹고 한 시간이 채 되기도 전에 노스캐롤라이나 주립대학으로 돌아왔습니다. 2,400칼로리와 144그램의 지방을 섭취했는데 달리는 동안 400칼로리가 태워졌습니다. 학생이 운영하는 도넛 먹기 대회에서는 노스캐롤라이나 아동 병원을 위해 약 3만 5천 달러를 모았습니다.

Q. 기사를 통해 추론할 수 있는 것은?

(a) 사람들은 아이들을 위한 기부금을 모았다.

(b) 사람들은 자신의 몸무게를 줄이려고 노력하고 있다.

(c) 도넛은 노스캐롤라이나에서 가장 나쁜 음식이다.

(d) 달리기 했던 사람들은 이전의 달리기 선수들로 구성되어 있다.

해설_ 글 마지막 부분의 아동 병원을 위해 돈을 모았다는 내용을 통해 (a)가 정답임을 알 수 있다.

어휘_ charity 자선 glazed doughnut 글레이즈드 도넛(설탕 시럽, 젤라틴 등을 입힌 도넛) consume 소비하다 burn 태우다 raise (돈을) 모으다 contribution 기부금 lose one's weight 체중을 줄이다 consist of ~으로 구성되다 former 이전의

정답_ (a)

Final Test 1

Part 1

1.

W: How is your mother's condition?

M: ___________________________________

(a) She has taken a turn for the worse since last weekend.
(b) It's my mother who wears red shirts.
(c) Great. I'm improving on my coryza.
(d) Nothing special except that it was too big.

해석_ W: 당신 어머니 상태는 어떠세요?

　　 M: ___________________________________

　　 (a) 지난주부터 더 나빠지셨어요.
　　 (b) 빨간 셔츠를 입고 계신 분이 제 어머니세요.
　　 (c) 좋아요. 코감기가 나아지고 있어요.
　　 (d) 너무 컸던 거 빼곤 특별한 게 없어요.

해설_ 어머니의 몸 상태가 어떤지 묻고 있으므로 상태가 더 악화됐다고 언급한 (a)가 정답이다.

어휘_ **take a turn for the worse** 병세가 악화되다　**coryza** 코감기

정답_ (a)

2.

M: Could you please pick a blue one on top of the shelf?

W: ___________________________________

(a) Wait a minute. I'll bring something.
(b) Please put it on another shelf.
(c) No thanks. I can carry it by myself.
(d) Do you know where the blue one is?

해석_ M: 선반 꼭대기에 있는 파란 것 좀 집어 주실래요?

　　 W: ___________________________________

　　 (a) 잠깐 기다려요. 뭐 좀 가져올게요.
　　 (b) 다른 선반 위에 좀 놓아 주세요.
　　 (c) 아니, 괜찮아요. 저 혼자 옮길 수 있어요.
　　 (d) 파란 거 어디 있는지 알아요?

해설_ 선반 위에 있는 걸 집어 달라고 부탁하고 있으므로 이에 응하는 (a)가 정답이다.

어휘_ **on top of** ~의 위에

정답_ (a)

3.

M: Congratulations! You're nominated to the top five of the scholarship student list.

W: ___________________________________

(a) Don't mention it. I just gave it to you without meaning.
(b) I think he is incompetent to decide it.
(c) Thank you for selecting me.
(d) Are you sure? Where did you get it?

해석_ M: 축하해! 네가 장학생 명단 5명에 지명됐어.

　　 W: ___________________________________

　　 (a) 천만에. 별 뜻 없이 준 거야.
　　 (b) 난 그가 그것을 결정할 능력이 없다고 생각해.
　　 (c) 날 뽑아 줘서 고마워.
　　 (d) 확실하니? 어디서 입수한 거야?

해설_ 자신이 장학생 명단에 들었다는 말을 듣고 남자에게 확실한지 되묻는 (d)가 정답이다.

어휘_ **nominate** 지명하다　**incompetent** 무능한　**select** 고르다, 뽑다

정답_ (d)

4.

W: What are you going to do this Sunday?

M: ___________________________________

(a) I think I will be in New York City with my parents.
(b) I don't think I can finish this until Sunday.
(c) They are leaving for Las vegas on that day.
(d) I think it was great and fabulous.

해석_ W: 이번 일요일에 뭐 할 거야?

　　 M: ___________________________________

　　 (a) 부모님과 함께 뉴욕에 있을 것 같아.
　　 (b) 일요일까지 이거 못 끝낼 것 같아.
　　 (c) 그들을 그날 라스베이거스로 떠날 거야.

(d) 그거 진짜 대단하고 멋졌던 것 같아.

해설_ 일요일에 무슨 계획이 있는지 묻고 있으므로 (a)가 정답이다.
참고로, will과 be going to는 둘 다 미래에 할 일을 나타내지
만, will은 계획되지 않은 일에 대해, be going to는 계획된 일
에 대해 말할 때 사용한다.

어휘_ **leave for** ~로 떠나다 **fabulous** 멋진, 굉장한

정답_ (a)

5.

M: How did you get to the hotel?
W: ________________________________

(a) It was on the right side.
(b) It was pretty comfortable and cozy.
(c) I took a shuttle bus to the airport.
(d) You should look around the city.

해석_ M: 호텔에 어떻게 갔어요?
W: ____________________________

(a) 오른편에 있었어요.
(b) 꽤 아늑하고 편했어요.
(c) 공항에서 셔틀버스를 탔어요.
(d) 당신은 그 도시를 둘러보는 게 좋겠어요.

해설_ 호텔까지 어떻게 갔는지 묻고 있으므로 교통수단이 언급된 선
택지를 고르면 된다.

어휘_ **cozy** 아늑한, 편안한 **look around** 둘러보다

정답_ (c)

6.

W: What is your new year's resolution?
M: ________________________________

(a) I didn't find a solution yet.
(b) I hope you have a great year, too.
(c) I am thinking of studying Spanish more
    diligently this year.
(d) She is doing well.

해석_ W: 새해 결심이 뭐야?
M: ____________________________

(a) 아직 해결책을 못 찾았어.
(b) 너도 좋은 한 해를 보내길 바래.
(c) 올해는 스페인어 공부를 좀 더 열심히 할 생각이야.
(d) 그녀는 잘하고 있어.

해설_ 새해 결심을 묻고 있으므로 이에 관한 내용이 담긴 (c)가 정답
이다.

어휘_ **resolution** 결심 **diligently** 열심히, 부지런히

정답_ (c)

7.

M: Good morning. I'd like to speak with Dr.
   Katherine.
W: ________________________________

(a) It's me speaking.
(b) I'd like to speak with Kate, too.
(c) You should wait for the reservation.
(d) She always speaks to people loudly.

해석_ M: 안녕하세요. 캐서린 선생님과 통화하고 싶은데요.
W: ____________________________

(a) 저예요.
(b) 저도 케이트와 통화하고 싶어요.
(c) 예약을 기다리셔야 합니다.
(d) 그녀는 항상 사람들과 큰 소리로 얘기해요.

해설_ 캐서린 선생님과 통화하고 싶다고 했으므로 바로 본인이라고
말한 (a)가 정답이다. (c)는 진료 예약 시 나옴직한 응답.

어휘_ **loudly** 큰 소리로

정답_ (a)

8.

W: How far is the central city?
M: ________________________________

(a) It is only for 5 people.
(b) We are almost there.
(c) She is on her way to the city.
(d) You should take it.

해석_ W: 센트럴 시티 멀었어?
M: ____________________________

(a) 딱 5인용이야.
(b) 거의 다 왔어.
(c) 그녀는 그 도시에 가는 중이야.
(d) 넌 그걸 받아들여야 해.

해설_ 센트럴 시티까지 아직 멀었는지 묻고 있으므로 거의 다 왔다
고 응답한 (b)가 정답이다.

어휘_ **be on one's way to** ~에 가는 길이다

정답_ (b)

9.

W: Do you know why the number 51 bus was delayed this morning?

M: _______________________________________

(a) It is reported that the bus collided with a motorcycle.
(b) Well. Let me ask a bus driver.
(c) The bus comes every 10 minutes.
(d) If you were in the bus, you would be surprised.

해석_ W: 51번 버스가 오늘 아침 왜 연착됐는지 아니?

    M: _______________________________________

    (a) 버스가 오토바이와 충돌했다고 보도됐어.

    (b) 글쎄. 버스 운전사에게 물어볼게.

    (c) 버스는 10분마다 와.

    (d) 네가 버스에 타고 있었다면 놀랐을 거야.

해설_ 버스가 연착된 이유를 묻고 있으므로 이에 관해 언급한 (a)가 정답이다.

어휘_ **delay** 지연하다, 미루다   **collide with** ~와 충돌하다   **motorcycle** 오토바이

정답_ (a)

10.

M: How did you get to the stadium?

W: _______________________________________

(a) I am at the stadium with my brother.
(b) It was a great game.
(c) It was so crowded.
(d) I used a bicycle.

해석_ M: 경기장에 어떻게 갔어?

    W: _______________________________________

    (a) 남동생이랑 경기장에 있어.

    (b) 정말 멋진 경기였어.

    (c) 너무 혼잡했어.

    (d) 자전거 탔어.

해설_ 경기장까지 뭘 타고 갔는지 교통수단을 묻고 있으므로 (d)가 정답이다.

어휘_ **stadium** 경기장   **be crowded** 붐비다

정답_ (d)

11.

W: Do you agree that the renovation on the 1st floor is a good idea?

M: _______________________________________

(a) I am against this opinion. It won't be efficient.
(b) I am sure that the building is not under construction yet.
(c) If you want to make a presentation, I can't dissuade you from making it.
(d) You do? I don't think it will be repaired.

해석_ W: 당신은 1층을 개조하는 것이 좋은 생각이라는 데 동의하십니까?

    M: _______________________________________

    (a) 저는 이 의견에 반대합니다. 그건 능률적이지 않을 겁니다.

    (b) 그 건물이 아직 공사 중은 아니라고 확신합니다.

    (c) 발표하기를 원하시면 막을 수 없죠.

    (d) 당신은 그래요? 제 생각엔 그게 수리될 것 같지 않아요.

해설_ 동의하는지 여부를 묻고 있으므로 (a)가 정답이다.

어휘_ **renovation** 개조   **efficient** 능률적인   **under construction** 공사 중인   **dissuade from** ~을 단념하게 하다

정답_ (a)

12.

M: How long does it take from here to the nearest bus terminal?

W: _______________________________________

(a) Maybe it takes fifteen minutes approximately.
(b) It's around 2 kilometers from here.
(c) It takes an hour from here to Texas by airplane.
(d) I told you before. I ought to drive my son to the school.

해석_ M: 여기서 가장 가까운 버스 터미널까지 얼마나 걸리나요?

    W: _______________________________________

    (a) 아마 대략 15분쯤 걸릴 겁니다.

    (b) 그건 여기서 약 2km 떨어져 있어요.

(c) 여기서 텍사스까지 비행기로 한 시간 걸려요.

(d) 전에 말했잖아요. 저는 아들을 학교까지 태워다 줘야 해요.

해설_ 버스 터미널까지 가는 데 걸리는 시간을 묻고 있으므로 (a)가
정답이다. (b)는 얼마나 먼지 거리를 물었을 때 가능한 응답.

어휘_ approximately 대략

정답_ (a)

13.

W: Wow, this movie is what I want to see. You have all kinds of DVDs.

M: _______________________________

(a) My brother is shooting a film now.

(b) This movie ticket is already sold out.

(c) Do you get it now? I'm a collector of these.

(d) I'm listening to the OST of that movie.

해석_ W: 와, 이 영화 내가 보고 싶은 건데. 넌 모든 종류의 DVD를
가지고 있구나.

M: _______________________________

(a) 우리 형은 지금 영화 촬영 중이야.

(b) 이 영화표는 이미 매진됐어.

(c) 지금 알았어? 나 이들 수집가야.

(d) 그 영화의 OST를 듣고 있어.

해설_ 모든 종류의 DVD를 다 가지고 있는 걸 보고 놀라워하는 여자
에게 DVD 수집가라고 얘기해 주는 (c)가 적절한 응답이다.

어휘_ shoot a film 영화를 찍다   sell out 상품이 매진되다
collector 수집가

정답_ (c)

14.

W: Do you have non-smoking seats available?
M: _______________________________

(a) I'm sorry, it's full, but smoking seats are possible.

(b) No. That's enough.

(c) Could you please smoke out of the restaurant?

(d) I can reserve the affordable seat.

해석_ W: 비흡연석 있나요?

M: _______________________________

(a) 죄송해요. 다 찼어요. 하지만 흡연석은 가능합니다.

(b) 아니요. 그걸로 충분해요.

(c) 식당 밖에서 담배 피워 주실래요?

(d) 저는 적당한 가격의 자리를 예약할 수 있어요.

해설_ 비흡연석이 있는지 묻고 있으므로 이에 답하는 선택지를 고르
면 된다.

어휘_ reserve 예약하다   affordable (가격이) 알맞은

정답_ (a)

15.

M: Who recommended you for a promotion?
W: _______________________________

(a) Do you happen to know? I can't imagine who did.

(b) Yes. He recommended me to the job.

(c) I think the CEO will be selected by the ex-CEO.

(d) Mr. Kim is also difficult to manage.

해석_ M: 누가 당신을 승진하도록 추천했죠?

W: _______________________________

(a) 당신은 혹시 알아요? 전 누가 그랬는지 전혀 안 떠올라요.

(b) 네. 그가 그 일자리에 절 추천해 줬어요.

(c) 제 생각엔 전 최고 경영자가 최고 경영자를 뽑을 것 같아
요.

(d) 김 씨 또한 다루기 힘든 사람이에요.

해설_ 승진을 추천한 사람이 누군지 묻고 있으므로 이에 어울리는
응답은 (a). Do you happen to ...?는 확신이 없는 사실에 대
해 '혹시 ~하나요?'라고 물을 때 쓸 수 있는 표현이다.

어휘_ promotion 승진   ex- 전(前)의   manage 다루다, 취급
하다

정답_ (a)

Part 2

16.

M: Did you watch the movie last night?

W: I couldn't because I had to finish my assignment.

M: What kind of assignment was that?

W: _______________________________

(a) I was scared after watching it.

(b) It is related to the movie.

(c) The movie was made in 1995.

(d) It is sort of statistics.

해석_ M: 지난밤에 영화 봤니?

W: 숙제 끝내야 해서 못 봤어.

M: 어떤 숙제였는데?

W: ________________________

(a) 그거 보고 나서 무서웠어.

(b) 그 영화와 관련된 거야.

(c) 그 영화는 1995년에 만들어졌어.

(d) 통계학 같은 거야.

해설_ 숙제의 종류를 묻고 있으므로 이를 언급한 (d)가 정답이다.

어휘_ **assignment** 숙제 **scared** 겁에 질린 **be related to** ~와 관계가 있다 **sort of** 말하자면 **statistics** 통계학

정답_ (d)

17.

M: Did you hear the news? Jack emigrated with his family to Canada last week.

W: What? Why did they decide to leave suddenly?

M: His father was transferred to the Canada branch.

W: ________________________

(a) Oh, dear. I didn't say good-bye.

(b) Cool. When does he come back?

(c) Is it true? I was born in Canada.

(d) It's sad. I am left to myself.

해석_ M: 너 소식 들었니? 잭이 지난주에 가족과 함께 캐나다로 이민 갔대.

W: 뭐라구? 왜 갑자기 떠날 결심을 했지?

M: 아버지가 캐나다 지사로 발령 받으셨어.

W: ________________________

(a) 이런. 작별 인사도 못했네.

(b) 멋진데. 그는 언제 돌아와?

(c) 정말이야? 나 캐나다에서 태어났어.

(d) 슬프다. 나 혼자 남겨졌어.

해설_ 잭이 갑자기 이민 갔다는 말에 인사도 못했다며 안타까워하는 (a)가 가장 자연스럽다.

어휘_ **be transferred to** 발령받다 **branch** 지점, 지사 **be left to oneself** 혼자 남겨지다

정답_ (a)

18.

W: What is the best landmark in your country?

M: It must be the Statue of liberty when all is said and done.

W: I want to go sightseeing in New York. It is called Big apple!

M: ________________________

(a) Come and see me. I'll be your guide.

(b) I don't think it is big enough to look around the city for a week.

(c) Let me see. It doesn't matter.

(d) If you want to see it, you should take a ship.

해석_ W: 너희 나라에서 최고의 건축물이 뭐야?

M: 모든 걸 따져봤을 때, 자유의 여신상이 틀림없어.

W: 뉴욕으로 관광 여행 가고 싶다. 빅 애플이라고 불리잖아!

M: ________________________

(a) 나 보러 와. 내가 안내해 줄게.

(b) 일주일 동안 그 도시를 둘러볼 만큼 크지는 않은 것 같아.

(c) 어디 보자. 별거 아냐.

(d) 그걸 보고 싶으면 배를 타야 해.

해설_ 남자가 살고 있는 뉴욕으로 여행 가고 싶다고 했으므로, 이어질 응답으로는 (a)가 가장 자연스럽다.

어휘_ **landmark** 역사적 건조물 **when all is said and done** 최종적으로, 뭐니 뭐니 해도 **go sightseeing** 관광 여행 가다 **Big apple** 뉴욕을 가리키는 애칭 **take a ship** 배를 타다

정답_ (a)

19.

W: How was the party the other night?

M: It was so funny. Why weren't you there?

W: I was out of town.

M: ________________________

(a) How come?

(b) When are you coming back?

(c) I was in the city, too.

(d) I went to town as well.

해석_ W: 요전날 밤 파티 어땠어?

M: 아주 재밌었어. 왜 안 왔니?

W: 다른 데 갔었어.

M: ___________________________

(a) 왜?

(b) 언제 돌아올 거야?

(c) 나도 그 도시에 있었어.

(d) 나도 시내에 갔었어.

해설_ 파티에 오지 않은 이유를 묻는 질문에 다른 데 갔었다고 말했으므로, 이어질 내용으로는 그 이유를 묻는 (a)가 자연스럽다. How come?은 Why?와 같은 의미로 회화체에서 흔히 쓰이는 표현이다.

어휘_ **be out of town** 다른 곳에 가다, 출장 나가다

정답_ (a)

20.

M: Welcome to my home! Was it easy to find my house?

W: Yes, but I wandered about in the cross street.

M: Right. The buildings all look the same.

W: ___________________________

(a) How about do you change a spot?

(b) I thought you should open instead of me.

(c) If there was a sign, it could be found easily.

(d) The villa won't be built until next month.

해석_ M: 저희 집에 오신 것을 환영해요! 집 찾기 쉬우셨나요?

W: 네, 하지만 교차로에서 헤맸어요.

M: 맞아요. 건물들이 다 똑같죠.

W: ___________________________

(a) 성격을 고치는 게 어때요?

(b) 저는 당신이 제 대신 문을 열어야 한다고 생각했어요.

(c) 표지판이 있었다면 쉽게 찾을 수 있었을 거예요.

(d) 그 빌라는 다음 달까지 지어지지 않을 거예요.

해설_ 교차로에서 헤맸다는 여자의 말에 건물들이 모두 똑같이 생겨서 그렇다고 했으므로 표지판이 있었으면 쉽게 찾았을 거라는 (c)가 적절한 응답이다.

어휘_ **wander about** 헤매다　**cross street** 교차로, 골목길　**change a spot** 성격을 고치다

정답_ (c)

21.

W: Mike, what about this white laptop computer? It's simple and neat.

M: Well. It can be easy to become dirty.

W: You really pick and choose.

M: ___________________________

(a) I'd like to use it as long as possible.

(b) Don't worry about the money. I'll treat you.

(c) I didn't know that I said that to you.

(d) Of course I can buy on the internet.

해석_ W: 마이크, 이 하얀 노트북 어때? 심플하고 깔끔한데.

M: 글쎄. 그건 더러워지기 쉬울 수 있어.

W: 넌 정말 신중히 골라.

M: ___________________________

(a) 난 가능한 한 오래 사용하고 싶어.

(b) 돈 걱정은 하지 마. 내가 낼게.

(c) 내가 너한테 그렇게 말했는지 몰랐어.

(d) 물론 인터넷으로 살 수 있지.

해설_ 신중하게 고른다는 말에 그 이유를 언급한 (a)가 적절한 응답이다.

어휘_ **neat** 깔끔한　**pick and choose** 신중히 고르다

정답_ (a)

22.

M: Mom. Guess what?

W: Let me see. I think you must have good news.

M: How did you know? I got a new job.

W: ___________________________

(a) I've already known about the article.

(b) Oh, it's unbelievable!

(c) Are you making a compliment to me?

(d) You will begin the work on Tuesday.

해석_ M: 엄마. 맞춰 보세요.

W: 어디 보자. 좋은 소식이 틀림없는 것 같은데.

M: 어떻게 아셨어요? 저 새 직장 얻었어요.

W: ___________________________

(a) 난 이미 그 기사에 대해 알았어.

(b) 오, 믿을 수가 없구나!

(c) 나 칭찬하는 거니?

(d) 넌 화요일에 일을 시작할 거야.

해설_ 아들이 새 직장을 얻었다는 말에 놀라워하는 (b)가 정답이다.

어휘_ **make a compliment to** ~를 칭찬하다

정답_ (b)

23.

M: Oh my god! What a pretty baby! She is your daughter.

W: Thank you.

M: Your baby has the same eyes as you.

W: ______________________________________

(a) Whenever I met people, they said like that.

(b) My daughter prefers a cell phone to a doll.

(c) I am having a baby in August.

(d) You're right. She has a killing smile like her dad.

해석_ M: 세상에! 아기가 정말 예뻐요! 당신 딸이군요.

　　 W: 고맙습니다.

　　 M: 아기가 당신 눈을 쏙 빼닮았어요.

　　 W: ______________________________

　　 (a) 만나는 사람마다 그렇게 얘기했어요.

　　 (b) 우리 딸은 인형보다 휴대폰을 더 좋아해요.

　　 (c) 저는 8월에 아기를 낳을 거예요.

　　 (d) 맞아요. 그녀는 아빠처럼 아주 멋진 미소를 지녔어요.

해설_ 아기가 엄마 눈을 닮았다는 칭찬에 이어지는 응답으로 (a)가 자연스럽다.

어휘_ **prefer ... to** ~보다 …을 더 좋아하다　**have a baby** 아기를 낳다[가지다]

정답_ (a)

24.

M: Hello. This is WD corporation. I'd like to check your order.

W: Ok. Who is a responsible person?

M: Mr. Nick Johnson.

W: ______________________________________

(a) Just a minute. I'll put Mr. Johnson on the phone.

(b) He hasn't ordered the products yet.

(c) Could you leave a message for him?

(d) I'm sorry but there is no seat available.

해석_ M: 안녕하세요. WD 주식회사입니다. 주문을 확인하고 싶은데요.

　　 W: 알겠습니다. 누가 책임자죠?

　　 M: 닉 존슨 씨입니다.

　　 W: ______________________________

　　 (a) 잠깐만요. 존슨 씨 바꿔 드릴게요.

　　 (b) 그가 아직 제품들을 주문하지 않았어요.

　　 (c) 그에게 메시지 좀 전해 주시겠어요?

　　 (d) 죄송하지만, 자리가 없습니다.

해설_ 책임자가 닉 존슨이라고 했으므로 그 사람을 바꿔 주겠다는 (a)가 이어지는 것이 자연스럽다.

어휘_ **a responsible person** 책임자

정답_ (a)

25.

M: Mom. I'd like to travel in Thailand alone.

W: Alone? I can't accept your decision. It's too dangerous to go alone.

M: Please. I'll be an adult next month.

W: ______________________________________

(a) You should go on your own way.

(b) Without permission, you can't enter here.

(c) You'd better go travel alone.

(d) Should father approve it, I would consent.

해석_ M: 엄마. 혼자 태국으로 여행 가고 싶어요.

　　 W: 혼자? 네 결정을 받아들일 수 없구나. 혼자 가는 건 너무 위험해.

　　 M: 제발요. 다음 달이면 저도 성인이라구요.

　　 W: ______________________________

　　 (a) 넌 네 방식대로 가야 해.

　　 (b) 허락 없이 여기 못 들어와.

　　 (c) 넌 혼자 여행 가는 게 좋겠다.

　　 (d) 아빠가 승낙하면 나도 승낙할게.

해설_ 아들이 엄마에게 혼자 여행 가는 걸 허락해 달라고 졸라대는 상황으로, 대화의 흐름상 자연스러운 응답은 (d)다.

어휘_ **permission** 허가, 허락　**consent** 승낙하다, 찬성하다

정답_ (d)

26.

W: Jack, it's snowing now. You should change tires.

M: Oh. It's a nuisance.

W: But you have to do it. Safety is first.

M: __________________________________

(a) I'm sorry but it wasn't your business.
(b) Right. Then could you help me?
(c) I will finish it much faster.
(d) I couldn't move a step because of heavy snow.

해석_ W: 잭, 지금 눈이 내리고 있어. 타이어를 바꾸는 게 좋겠다.
　　 M: 아. 성가시네.
　　 W: 하지만 해야 돼. 안전이 우선이야.
　　 M: ___________________________
　　 (a) 미안하지만, 네가 상관할 바가 아니었잖아.
　　 (b) 맞아. 그럼 나 좀 도와줄래?
　　 (c) 훨씬 빨리 끝낼 거야.
　　 (d) 눈이 많이 와서 한 발짝도 움직일 수 없었어.
해설_ 안전이 우선이라는 여자의 말에 공감하며 도와 달라고 부탁하는 (b)가 자연스러운 응답이다.
어휘_ a nuisance 성가신[귀찮은] 것 safety 안전
정답_ (b)

27.

M: Hi, Michelle. How was the trip to Germany?
W: It was great.
M: Good. I heard Germans are cold, aren't they?
W: __________________________________

(a) It's true but not for everyone.
(b) The weather is always sunny and warm.
(c) Most of German people love to drink draft beer.
(d) They applauded as soon as the performance finished.

해석_ M: 안녕, 미쉘. 독일 여행은 어땠니?
　　 W: 아주 좋았어.
　　 M: 잘됐구나. 독일 사람들은 차갑다던데, 그렇지 않니?
　　 W: ___________________________
　　 (a) 사실이지만 모두 그런 건 아니야.
　　 (b) 날씨가 항상 맑고 따뜻해.
　　 (c) 독일 사람들은 대부분 생맥주를 즐겨 마셔.
　　 (d) 그들은 공연이 끝나자마자 박수를 쳤어.
해설_ 독일 사람들의 성격이 차갑지 않냐고 묻고 있으므로 이에 관

해 언급한 (a)가 정답이다.
어휘_ draft beer 생맥주 applaud 박수 치다
정답_ (a)

28.

M: Oh, no! I had a big mistake.
W: What's up?
M: The teacher has become aware of my homework which copied Jake's.
W: __________________________________

(a) I'm concerned about your thinking.
(b) No. She won't know how to use it.
(c) Tell her the truth frankly before she says it.
(d) She didn't notice that you left the class.

해석_ M: 이런! 큰 실수를 했다.
　　 W: 무슨 일이야?
　　 M: 선생님이 제이크 거 베낀 숙제를 알게 되셨어.
　　 W: ___________________________
　　 (a) 난 네 생각에 관심이 있어.
　　 (b) 안 돼. 그녀는 사용법을 모를 거야.
　　 (c) 그녀가 말하기 전에 솔직히 사실을 얘기해.
　　 (d) 그녀는 네가 수업을 빠져나간 것을 눈치 못 챘어.
해설_ 선생님이 숙제 베낀 사실을 알고 있다고 걱정하는 남자에게 그녀가 먼저 말하기 전에 솔직히 털어놓으라고 조언해 주는 (c)가 적절하다.
어휘_ become aware of ~을 알게 되다 frankly 솔직하게
정답_ (c)

29.

W: You can choose one side dish.
M: Could you tell me what kind of things you have?
W: Sure. Sweet potato, potato, corn and bread.
M: __________________________________

(a) Then, are they all baked?
(b) After we have supper, you will wash the dishes.
(c) How about french fries?
(d) Could I make a decision tomorrow morning?

해석_W: 사이드 메뉴 한 가지를 고르실 수 있습니다.

M: 어떤 종류가 있는지 말씀해 주시겠어요?

W: 네. 고구마, 감자, 옥수수 빵이 있습니다.

M: ________________________________

(a) 그럼, 그것들은 모두 구워진 건가요?

(b) 우리가 저녁 먹고 나면 당신이 설거지를 할 거예요.

(c) 감자튀김 어때요?

(d) 내일 아침에 결정할 수 있을까요?

해설_ 음식점에서 종업원이 주문을 받으면서 이루어지는 대화 내용
이다. 종업원이 사이드 메뉴의 종류를 말해 주었으므로 이에
대해 언급한 (a)가 자연스럽다.

어휘_ **side dish** 곁들이는 요리 **have supper** 저녁 식사를 하
다 **wash the dishes** 설거지하다

정답_ (a)

30.

M: This is South Inn. May I help you?

W: Hello. I'd like to stay in your Inn on January 3rd.

M: Ok. Which room is better, visible outside or not?

W: ________________________________

(a) Is it possible to use the swimming pool?

(b) Both are good for you.

(c) Great. And I want to stay in the double room.

(d) I don't mind. What is room's price difference?

해석_ M: 사우스 여관입니다. 무엇을 도와 드릴까요?

W: 안녕하세요. 1월 3일에 당신네 여관에 묵고 싶은데요.

M: 알겠습니다. 어느 방이 나으세요, 밖이 보이는 곳이요, 아
니면 안 보이는 곳이요?

W: ________________________________

(a) 수영장을 사용하는 게 가능한가요?

(b) 둘 다 당신을 위한 거예요.

(c) 좋군요. 그리고 2인용 방에 묵고 싶어요.

(d) 상관없어요. 방값 차이는 어떻게 되나요?

해설_ 밖이 보이는 방을 원하는지 여부를 묻고 있으므로 이에 답하
는 선택지를 고르면 된다.

어휘_ **double room** 2인용 방

정답_ (d)

Part 3

31.

M: What is this? Looks so yummy.

W: It's something with the cheese and the olive oil. Watch out, you will stick yourself.

M: Can I have some more dressing here?

W: How about this one? I have tried in ten different ways and I think this is the best one.

M: Is that edible with the salad? I had no idea about that.

W: Why not? It's well matched with vegetable.

M: Let me try this.

Q. What are the speakers doing?

(a) They are arguing about the meal.

(b) They are looking for something delicious.

(c) They are making dinner together.

(d) They are having a meal.

해석_ M: 이게 뭐지? 너무 맛있어 보인다.

W: 치즈하고 올리브 오일이 곁들여진 거야. 조심해, 달라붙겠
다.

M: 드레싱을 좀 더 뿌릴까?

W: 이건 어때? 10가지 방법으로 먹어 봤는데 이게 제일 나은
것 같아.

M: 샐러드랑 같이 먹을 수 있어? 그거에 대해선 잘 몰라.

W: 그럼. 야채랑 잘 어울려.

M: 내가 먹어볼게.

Q. 화자들은 무엇을 하고 있는가?

(a) 식사에 대해 언쟁을 벌이고 있다.

(b) 맛있는 것을 찾고 있다.

(c) 함께 저녁 식사를 준비하고 있다.

(d) 식사를 하고 있는 중이다.

해설_ 어떤 요리를 앞에 두고 먹는 방법에 대해 얘기를 주고받는 것
으로 보아 그들이 식사 중에 나누는 대화 내용임을 알 수 있다.

어휘_ **yummy** 맛있는 **stick** 달라붙다 **edible** 먹을 수 있는,
식용에 맞는 **matched** 어울리는, 조화된

정답_ (d)

32.

M: I am so nervous. I think I messed up and

my parents will scold me as they see the room.

W: Why? What's wrong with that?

M: I tried to tidy out my room before my parents arrived from their trip to Malibu. But it is still remaining untidy. I don't know how to start up again.

W: Did you make your bed in the morning?

M: Oh, gosh, I didn't. I am really bad at making the bed.

W: Here you go. Go clean your room again. Don't forget to make your bed first.

M: Thanks, I will. Thanks again!

Q. What is the main idea of the conversation?

(a) He is trying to make furniture before his parents come back.

(b) He likes to be tidy and neat all the time.

(c) Their parents will punish him about a messy room.

(d) He will clean his room again by making the bed.

해석_ M: 불안해 죽겠어. 방을 너저분하게 늘어놔서 부모님이 보면 혼내실 거야.

W: 왜? 뭐가 문제야?

M: 부모님이 말리부 여행에서 돌아오시기 전에 정리하려고 했어. 그런데 여전히 지저분하다. 어떻게 다시 시작해야 할지 모르겠어.

W: 아침에 침대 정리했어?

M: 맙소사, 안했어. 난 침대 정리를 너무 못한다니까.

W: 자, 시작하자. 가서 방을 다시 청소해. 먼저 침대 정리하는 거 잊지 말고.

M: 고마워, 그럴게. 다시 한 번 고마워!

Q. 대화의 주제는 무엇인가?

(a) 그는 부모님이 돌아오시기 전에 가구를 만들려고 노력하고 있다.

(b) 그는 항상 깨끗하고 깔끔한 것을 좋아한다.

(c) 그들의 부모님이 지저분한 방 때문에 그를 혼낼 것이다.

(d) 그는 침대 정리를 하면서 방 청소를 다시 할 것이다.

해설_ (c)를 정답으로 착각할 수 있으나 두 사람이 남매지간은 아니므로 their parents라고 말한 게 틀리다. 따라서 정답은 (d).

어휘_ **mess up** 어질러 놓다, 지저분하게 만들다 **scold** 꾸짖다 **tidy out** 깨끗하게 하다, 정리하다 **Malibu** 말리부(미국 로스앤젤레스 서쪽의 해양 휴양지) **start up** 일을 시작하다 **make the bed** 침대 정리를 하다 **here you go** 시작하다, 출발하다 **punish** 벌하다

정답_ (d)

33.

W: Hey, John. Where were you at the moment? Did you get my message?

M: Sorry. I was in the car on the way to the meeting and couldn't use my cell phone at the moment.

W: Then, you should've texted me when you arrived. I was waiting for your response.

M: I am sorry I forgot it. I was in a real hurry though.

W: So, did you make it to the meeting well?

M: Yes, it was great joining the meeting on time.

W: Okay. Don't forget to text me when you have time.

Q. Which is correct according to the conversation?

(a) The man went to the meeting with the woman.

(b) The woman was waiting for the man to go to the meeting.

(c) The woman was already in the meeting waiting for the man.

(d) The woman didn't get the man's message.

해석_ W: 야, 존. 그때 어디 있었어? 내 메시지 받았어?

M: 미안. 회의 가는 차 안이어서 휴대폰을 쓸 수가 없었어.

W: 그럼 도착했을 때 문자 메시지라도 보냈어야지. 답변 기다렸잖아.

M: 깜박해서 미안. 근데 내가 정말 급했거든.

W: 그래서, 회의 시간에 잘 맞춰 갔어?

M: 응, 정시에 회의에 참석해서 정말 좋았어.

W: 좋아. 시간 있을 때 메시지 보내는 거 잊지 마.

Q. 대화에 따르면 맞는 것은 어느 것인가?

(a) 남자는 여자와 함께 회의에 갔다.

(b) 여자는 회의에 가기 위해 남자를 기다리고 있었다.

(c) 여자는 남자를 기다리며 이미 회의 중이었다.

(d) 여자는 남자의 메시지를 받지 않았다.

해설_ 남자가 메시지를 보내지 않은 것에 대해 불평을 했으므로 (d)
가 정답이다.

어휘_ **text** 문자 메시지를 보내다   **response** 응답

정답_ (d)

34.

M: How was Disney World in Florida?

W: I felt like a little kid all over again and the weather was fabulous except for one day it rained.

M: What was the best ride?

W: It is called "The Tower of Terror." I was able to go on it a lot because there weren't long lines.

M: I am so jealous of you. That is why your voice is so hurt?

W: Yes, I screamed so much for the first time that my voice hurt.

Q. Which is correct according to the conversation?

(a) The woman injured her neck by the ride called "The Tower of Terror."

(b) The woman enjoyed a lot at Disney World and the weather was perfect.

(c) The woman had such a fun time at Disney World.

(d) The woman was waiting in a long line.

해석_ M: 플로리다 디즈니 월드 어땠어?

W: 다시 어린 아이가 된 기분이었어. 날씨도 비가 온 하루만
빼고는 끝내주게 좋았어.

M: 뭐 타는 게 제일 재밌었어?

W: "공포의 탑" 이라고 불리는 거. 줄 서 있는 사람이 많지 않
아서 많이 탈 수 있었어.

M: 너무 부럽다. 그래서 목소리가 그렇게 쉬었구나?

W: 응, 처음으로 내 목소리가 쉴 만큼 소리를 많이 질렀어.

Q. 대화에 따르면 맞는 것은 어느 것인가?

(a) 여자는 "공포의 탑" 이라고 불리는 것을 타다가 목을 다쳤
다.

(b) 여자는 디즈니 월드에서 아주 즐거운 시간을 보냈고 날씨
도 완벽했다.

(c) 여자는 디즈니 월드에서 매우 재미있는 시간을 보냈다.

(d) 여자는 긴 줄에서 기다리고 있었다.

해설_ 그녀가 디즈니 월드에서 즐거운 시간을 보낸 것은 맞지만, 하
루는 비가 왔으므로 날씨가 완벽한 것은 아니었다. 따라서 정
답은 (c).

어휘_ **all over again** 반복하여, 또 한번   **be jealous of** ~가
부럽다   **scream** 소리 지르다

정답_ (c)

35.

M: Hey, Jennie! Where are you headed for?

W: I am on the way to grab something. I was in the library all day to finish the homework.

M: You going to Kelly diner?

W: Yeah, I need some coffee and bagels to refresh my mind. It took me so long to get done with that assignment. I need a break for coffee.

M: What's the class? Is it a Bio 310 and professor John Devor from France?

W: Yes, he can barely speak English and speaks too fast. That is why it is hard to keep up with the class.

M: I heard his class forces you to learn for yourself and do an independent assignment to keep up.

Q. Which is correct according to the conversation?

(a) The woman is taking an English class and will have a presentation tomorrow.

(b) The class is demanding.

(c) The woman didn't finish her assignment at the moment.

(d) The woman is doing a team project in the class.

해석_ M: 야, 제니! 너 어디 가?

W: 뭐 좀 사 먹으려고 가는 중이야. 하루 종일 숙제 끝내려고

도서관에 있었어.

M: 켈리 식당에 가는 길이야?

W: 응, 머리를 식히기 위해 커피와 베이글이 필요해. 그 숙제 끝내는 데 무지 오래 걸렸어. 커피 마시면서 쉬어야겠어.

M: 그 수업이 뭐야? 생물 310, 프랑스에서 오신 존 데버 교수님 거야?

W: 응, 그는 영어를 거의 못하고 말이 너무 빨라. 그래서 수업 따라잡기가 힘들어.

M: 그 교수님 수업은 네 스스로 공부하고 개별적인 숙제를 해서 따라잡도록 한다고 들었어.

Q. 대화에 따르면 맞는 것은 어느 것인가?

(a) 여자는 영어 수업을 받고 있고 내일 발표를 할 것이다.

(b) 수업은 큰 노력을 요한다.

(c) 여자는 현재 숙제를 끝마치지 않았다.

(d) 여자는 그 수업의 팀 프로젝트를 하고 있다.

_ 숙제를 하는 데 시간도 많이 걸리고 수업을 따라잡기 힘들다고 했으므로 (b)가 정답이다.

_ **head for** ~로 향하다 **grab something** 간단히 먹다 **bagel** 베이글(도넛 모양의 딱딱한 빵의 일종) **refresh one's mind** 기분을 상쾌하게 하다 **get done with** ~을 마치다, 끝내다 **barely** 거의 ~ 않다 **keep up with** ~에 뒤지지 않다 **independent** 독립된, 독자적인 **keep up** 뒤지지 않고 따라가다 **demanding** 큰 노력을 요하는

_ (b)

36.

W: Do you know who just got promoted recently?

M: You mean Rudy Melanie in the Sales division?

W: Yes, I heard he is not only very nice but also very cooperative.

M: I think he was in a marketing part in second floor before he joined the sales team.

W: That is why he had a grasp on the subject at hand. He seems so enthusiastic about a new project.

M: He seems to be putting a lot of effort into it. I will look into that project seriously.

Q. What is the main idea of the conversation?

(a) They have a totally new employee in the company.

(b) Rudy is quite laid back in his position.

(c) Rudy wants to go back to the marketing division.

(d) Rudy looks so passionate about working in the sales division.

_ W: 최근에 승진한 사람 알아?

M: 판매 부서에 있는 루디 멜라니 말이지?

W: 응, 그 사람 착할 뿐만 아니라 아주 협조적이래.

M: 판매팀에 합류하기 전에 2층 마케팅 부서에 있었던 것 같아.

W: 그래서 그 사람이 그 과제를 금방 파악했구나. 새로운 프로젝트에 무척 열정적인 것 같더라.

M: 그는 거기에 많은 노력을 쏟고 있는 것 같아. 나도 그 프로젝트를 진지하게 연구해 봐야겠다.

Q. 대화의 주제는 무엇인가?

(a) 그들의 회사에 완전 신참 직원이 있다.

(b) 루디는 그의 직무에 매우 태만하다.

(c) 루디는 마케팅 부서로 돌아가길 원한다.

(d) 루디는 판매 부서에서 일하는 것에 매우 열정적으로 보인다.

_ 루디가 신입사원은 아니므로 (a)는 틀리다. 또 그가 판매부에서 태만했는지 알 수 없다. 판매부의 프로젝트에 매우 열정적이라는 내용이 나오므로 (d)가 정답이다.

_ **cooperative** 협조적인 **have a grasp** 이해하다, 파악하다 **at hand** 금방, 가까이 **enthusiastic** 열정적인 **put into** (시간, 노력을) 들이다 **be laid back** 마음을 놓다, 안심하다

_ (d)

37.

M: Hey! Jane. Are you looking forword to the weekend?

W: Why? Because of the blind date on Saturday?

M: I am sure you are. Do you have any idea who is going to come?

W: My friend told me he is his old friend from high school and he is working at a consulting firm. That is the only thing I know so far.

M: Where are you going on that day? Going to

the movies?

W: I think it would be better not to go to the movies.

M: Of course. You should have more time to chat to know him.

Q. Which is correct according to the conversation?

(a) The woman is planning to go to the movies with the man.

(b) The woman knows the man very well because they went to the same high school.

(c) The woman would not watch a movie on the first date.

(d) The woman wants to go out with the man.

해석_ M: 안녕! 제인. 너 주말을 기대하고 있니?

W: 왜? 토요일 소개팅 때문에?

M: 그럴 거라고 확신해. 누가 나올지 아니?

W: 친구가 그러는데 자기 고등학교 친구이고 컨설턴트 회사에 다닌대. 지금까지 아는 건 그게 다야.

M: 그날 어디 갈 거야? 영화 보러 갈 거야?

W: 영화 보러 안 가는 게 나을 것 같아.

M: 물론이지. 그를 알기 위해 얘기 나누는 시간을 좀 더 갖는 게 좋아.

Q. 대화에 따르면 맞는 것은 어느 것인가?

(a) 여자는 남자와 영화 보러 가는 것을 계획하고 있다.

(b) 여자는 같은 고등학교에 다녔기 때문에 남자를 매우 잘 안다.

(c) 여자는 첫 데이트 때 영화를 보지 않을 것이다.

(d) 여자는 남자와 데이트하기를 원한다.

해설_ 여자의 마지막 대사에서, 영화는 안 보는 게 나을 것 같다고 얘기했으므로 (c)가 정답이다.

어휘_ **blind date** 소개팅 **consulting firm** 컨설턴트 회사 **chat** 수다떨다, 담소를 나누다 **go out with** ~와 데이트하다

정답_ (c)

38.

M: Honey. What will you cook for dinner? I'd like to eat a hamburger.

W: Never! I told you that you shouldn't have junk food anymore.

M: I know, but I really want to eat.

W: The doctor said that you can't have fat because you are overweight. I'm preparing a green salad for dinner.

M: You're right. I'm sorry. I will listen to your advice from now on.

W: You can say that again!

Q. What is the main topic of the conversation?

(a) The man's health care

(b) The woman's preparation of dinner

(c) The woman's worry about her weight

(d) The man's big mistake

해석_ M: 자기. 저녁에 무슨 요리 할 거야? 나 햄버거 먹고 싶은데.

W: 안 돼요! 더 이상 패스트푸드를 먹어서는 안 된다고 했잖아요.

M: 나도 알아, 하지만 정말 먹고 싶어.

W: 의사가 당신은 과체중이라 지방을 먹지 말라고 했어요. 저녁으로 그린 샐러드를 준비하는 중이에요.

M: 당신 말이 맞아. 미안해. 이제부터 당신 조언을 잘 따를게.

W: 내 말이 그 말이에요!

Q. 대화의 주제는 무엇인가?

(a) 남자의 건강 관리

(b) 여자의 저녁 식사 준비

(c) 여자의 체중에 대한 걱정

(d) 남자의 큰 실수

해설_ 햄버거가 먹고 싶다는 남편에게 과체중 때문에 먹어선 안 되며, 저녁으로 그린 샐러드를 준비하고 있다고 했으므로 (a)가 정답이다.

어휘_ **junk food** 영양가 없는 음식, 인스턴트 식품 **fat** 지방 **overweight** 과체중의 **green salad** 그린 샐러드(주로 양상추와 청색 야채 샐러드)

정답_ (a)

39.

M: This music is cool, isn't it? What's the name of the song?

W: Yes. It is *I stay in love* by Mariah Carey. What kind of music do you like recently?

M: I like all kinds of pop music. What about

you?
W: I'm crazy about jazz and my hobby is listening to music.
M: Jazz? Wow, it sounds great. I've never heard jazz before.
W: No way! I will send you a jazz file by e-mail. What is your e-mail address?
M: Oh, thanks. My address is jack22@hotmail.com.
W: Check your e-mail tonight.

Q. What is the main topic of the conversation?

(a) Preference for music
(b) Playing a musical instrument
(c) How to send e-mail
(d) How to listen to music through the internet

해석_ M: 이 음악 멋지다, 그렇지 않니? 노래 제목이 뭐야?

W: 응. 머라이어 캐리의 '나는 여전히 사랑하고 있어요'. 넌 요즘 어떤 음악이 좋아?

M: 대중음악은 다 좋아해. 넌 어때?

W: 난 재즈를 너무 좋아하고, 취미가 음악 듣는 거야.

M: 재즈? 와, 멋진데. 난 재즈 들어 본 적이 없는데.

W: 말도 안 돼! 내가 이메일로 재즈 파일을 보내 줄게. 이메일 주소가 뭐니?

M: 아, 고마워. 이메일 주소는 jack22@hotmail.com이야.

W: 오늘 밤에 이메일 확인해 봐.

Q. 대화의 주제는 무엇인가?

(a) 음악 선호도
(b) 악기를 연주하는 것
(c) 이메일 보내는 방법
(d) 인터넷에서 음악 듣는 방법

해설_ 서로 좋아하는 음악 장르에 대한 얘기를 나누고 있으므로 (a) 가 정답이다.

어휘_ **cool** 멋진, 근사한   **be crazy about** ~에 푹 빠져 있다   **musical instrument** 악기

정답_ (a)

40.

M: Hello. This is Mark.
W: Hello. This is from Jessica Mum corporation. Did you apply for the intern?

M: Yes, I did.
W: Congratulations. You passed the documentation.
M: Oh, my god! Thanks.
W: You have an interview this Thursday morning at 10 o'clock. Don't be late.
M: Sure! Oh, I have a question. How many candidates are picked for the interview?
W: There are approximately 25 people.

Q. What is the main topic of the conversation?

(a) Informing the man of interview date
(b) Direction of the working place
(c) Warning not to be late
(d) Preparing the interview

해석_ M: 안녕하세요. 마크입니다.

W: 안녕하세요. 멈 주식회사의 제시카입니다. 인턴에 지원하셨나요?

M: 네, 지원했어요.

W: 축하드립니다. 서류 전형에 합격하셨습니다.

M: 세상에! 감사합니다.

W: 이번 목요일 아침 10시에 면접이 있습니다. 늦지 마세요.

M: 물론이죠! 아, 질문이 하나 있습니다. 면접에 몇 명의 지원자가 뽑혔나요?

W: 대략 25명 정도요.

Q. 대화의 주제는 무엇인가?

(a) 남자에게 면접 날짜 알려주기
(b) 근무처의 위치
(c) 늦지 말라는 경고
(d) 면접 준비

해설_ 서류 심사에 통과한 사실과 함께 면접 날짜를 알려주고 있으므로 정답은 (a)다. 늦지 말라는 얘기도 있었지만 여자가 전화를 건 주요 용건은 면접 날짜를 알려주기 위한 것이므로 (c)는 정답이 될 수 없다.

어휘_ **corporation** 주식회사   **intern** 수습사원   **pass the documentation** 서류 전형에 합격하다

정답_ (a)

41.

M: Mom, I think I should go to see a doctor.
W: What's wrong with you?

M: Look at these. I got nettle rash on my arms.

W: Oh my god! What is it? What did you eat yesterday?

M: I don't know why. I had same meal as usual.

W: Anyway let's go to see a doctor.

M: First, I have to inform my class teacher.

W: Sure, I'll call now.

Q. Which is correct according to the conversation?

(a) The man has urticaria.

(b) The woman will drive to her son's school.

(c) The man didn't have anything yesterday.

(d) The woman reported her son's illness.

해석_ M: 엄마, 병원에 가 봐야 할 것 같아요.

W: 어디 안 좋은 데 있니?

M: 이것들 좀 보세요. 팔에 두드러기가 났어요.

W: 맙소사! 그게 뭐니? 너 어제 뭐 먹었어?

M: 저도 이유를 모르겠어요. 늘 먹던 대로 먹었어요.

W: 어쨌든 병원에 가자.

M: 먼저, 담임 선생님한테 알려야 해요.

W: 그래, 지금 전화할 거야.

Q. 대화에 따르면 맞는 것은 어느 것인가?

(a) 남자는 두드러기가 났다.

(b) 여자는 그의 아들의 학교로 운전하고 갈 것이다.

(c) 남자는 어제 어떤 것도 먹지 않았다.

(d) 여자는 그의 아들의 병을 알렸다.

해설_ 팔에 두드러기가 나 병원에 가 봐야겠다고 했으므로 (a)가 정답이다.

어휘_ nettle rash = urticaria 두드러기 as usual 평소와 같이

정답_ (a)

42.

M: Ashely! Come here, hurry up!

W: Bob, why are you in a hurry?

M: Look at that! It's a beautiful rainbow, isn't it?

W: Wow, it's amazing! I have seen the rainbow for the first time in my life. How beautiful the rainbow is!

M: I'll take a picture of you with the rainbow. Take your pose. Cheese!

W: Thank you. I will take a picture of you, too.

M: Thanks. Great.

W: I think everything will be fine because of the rainbow.

Q. Why is the woman surprised?

(a) Because the woman saw a rainbow for the first time

(b) Because the rainbow was wonderful

(c) Because it started raining suddenly

(d) Because the man took her picture without saying

해석_ M: 애슐리! 이리 와봐, 서둘러!

W: 밥, 왜 그렇게 급해?

M: 저것 좀 봐! 아름다운 무지개야, 그렇지 않니?

W: 와, 놀랍다! 무지개는 난생 처음 봐. 정말 아름다운 무지개다!

M: 무지개를 배경으로 네 사진을 찍어 줄게. 포즈를 취해 봐. 치즈!

W: 고마워. 나도 네 사진을 찍어 줄게.

M: 고마워. 정말 좋구나.

W: 무지개 때문에 모든 일이 잘될 거라는 생각이 들어.

Q. 여자는 왜 놀랐나?

(a) 처음으로 무지개를 보았기 때문에

(b) 무지개가 굉장히 멋있었기 때문에

(c) 갑자기 비가 오기 시작했기 때문에

(d) 남자가 말도 없이 그녀의 사진을 찍었기 때문에

해설_ 여자의 두 번째 대사에 무지개를 난생 처음 봤다는 얘기가 나오므로 정답은 (a)가 된다.

어휘_ amazing 놀랄 만한, 굉장한 take one's pose 포즈를 취하다

정답_ (a)

43.

W: I heard you were going to quit your job in five days. Is that true?

M: Yes, it is. Who told you that?

W: Some guys in a lounge were talking about

it, so I heard unintentionally. Anyway, what are you going to do after then?

M: I'm going to travel all around the world. I've been looking forward to this for 5 years. I've worked here to save money for my trip.

W: Wow! That's a kind of exciting life. I wish I could do that some day.

M: Yes, you can. You are still young and don't need to take your life too seriously.

Q. What can be inferred from the conversation?

(a) The woman is going to quit her job and travel the world.

(b) The man will not be working anytime soon.

(c) The woman will save her money for her trip.

(d) The man will be on a trip for 5 years.

해석_ W: 5일 후에 직장 그만둔다면서. 진짜야?

M: 그래, 맞아. 누구한테 들었어?

W: 휴게실에서 몇몇 사람들이 그 얘기를 하고 있어서 우연히 들었지. 그건 그렇고, 그만두고 나서 뭐할 거야?

M: 세계여행 갈 거야. 5년 동안 기다려왔어. 여기서 일한 것도 여행비를 모으기 위한 거였어.

W: 와! 흥미로운 삶인데. 언젠가 나도 그랬으면 좋겠다.

M: 그래, 넌 할 수 있어. 넌 아직 젊고, 삶을 너무 심각하게 받아들일 필요 없어.

Q. 대화를 통해 추론할 수 있는 것은?

(a) 여자는 직장을 그만두고 세계여행을 할 것이다.

(b) 남자는 빠른 시일 내에 일을 하지는 않을 것이다.

(c) 여자는 여행을 위해 돈을 모을 것이다.

(d) 남자는 5년 동안 여행할 것이다.

해설_ 5일 후 직장을 그만두고 세계여행을 갈 거라고 했으므로 금방 다른 일을 하지 않을 것임을 알 수 있다. 따라서 정답은 (b).

어휘_ **lounge** (호텔 등의) 로비, 휴게실 **unintentionally** 무심코, 우연히 **anytime soon** 조만간

정답_ (b)

44.

M: What's going on, Kelly?

W: Hi, John! I have good news. You might know that. It's about Jeniffer.

M: A good news about Jeniffer? I have no idea. It's been ages since I saw her.

W: She will get married in a month.

M: Really? To whom? Joshua? When I last saw her, she was with Joshua.

W: No. They were broken up about one and a half years ago. She will marry a singer. And his name is Jake Thompson.

M: I think I heard of that name before.

W: You might have. He is famous for his songs these days.

M: Wow! She got lucky.

Q. What can be inferred from the conversation?

(a) Thompson is one of the most popular singers.

(b) It's been more than about 18 months since the man last saw Jeniffer.

(c) The woman will marry with Joshua in a month.

(d) The man will go to Kelly's wedding.

해석_ M: 무슨 일이니, 켈리?

W: 안녕, 존! 좋은 소식이 있어. 네가 알지도 모르겠다. 제니퍼에 대한 거야.

M: 제니퍼에 대한 좋은 소식? 모르겠는데. 걔 본 지 오래됐어.

W: 한 달 후에 결혼할 거야.

M: 정말? 누구랑? 조슈아? 걔 마지막으로 봤을 때 조슈아랑 같이 있었는데.

W: 아니. 걔네들은 한 1년 반쯤 전에 헤어졌어. 제니퍼는 가수와 결혼할 거야. 그 사람 이름은 제이크 톰슨이고.

M: 전에 그 이름 들어 본 것 같은데.

W: 아마 그랬을 거야. 요즘 그의 노래로 유명하거든.

M: 와! 걘 운이 좋구나.

Q. 대화를 통해 추론할 수 있는 것은?

(a) 톰슨은 가장 인기 있는 가수 중 한 명이다.

(b) 남자가 제니퍼를 마지막으로 본 지가 약 18개월이 넘었다.

(c) 여자는 한 달 후에 조슈아와 결혼할 것이다.

(d) 남자는 켈리의 결혼식에 갈 것이다.

해설_ 제니퍼를 마지막으로 봤을 때 그녀가 조슈아랑 같이 있었다는 남자의 말에 여자가 그들은 1년 반쯤 전에 헤어졌다고 말했으므로 (b)가 정답임을 알 수 있다.

정답_ (b)

45.

M: Hello. What has brought you here today?

W: Good morning. My left ankle has a sprain.

M: Oh, it swelled up badly. When did you hurt it?

W: Yesterday. When I cleaned the window, I fell off the chair.

M: First, you should have an X-ray. Please go to the department of radiology and come back here again.

W: Where is it?

M: It's on the 2nd floor.

Q. What can be inferred from the conversation?

(a) The woman is going to go to the 2nd floor.

(b) The man got hurt in his foot.

(c) The woman has been waiting for a X-ray.

(d) The man is majoring in radiology.

해석_ M: 안녕하세요. 오늘 여기 무슨 일로 오셨나요?

W: 안녕하세요. 왼쪽 발목을 삐었어요.

M: 아, 심하게 부었군요. 언제 다치셨나요?

W: 어제요. 창문을 닦을 때 의자에서 떨어졌어요.

M: 우선 엑스레이를 찍어 봐야 합니다. 방사선과에 갔다가 다시 이리로 오세요.

W: 어디에 있죠?

M: 2층에 있습니다.

Q. 대화를 통해 추론할 수 있는 것은?

(a) 여자는 2층에 갈 것이다.

(b) 남자는 발을 다쳤다.

(c) 여자는 엑스레이를 기다리고 있다.

(d) 남자는 방사선학을 전공하고 있다.

해설_ 남자가 엑스레이를 찍어야 한다고 했으므로 여자는 2층 방사선과로 갈 것이다. 따라서 정답은 (a).

어휘_ **ankle** 발목 **sprain** (손목, 발목 등을) 삐다 **swell up** (손, 발 등이) 부어오르다 **fall off** ~에서 떨어지다 **radiology** 방사선학 **major** 전공하다

정답_ (a)

Part 4

46.

Investigators have linked icy conditions on a freeway bridge north of San Antonio to a fatal accident Wednesday morning near the Bexar County and Comal County line. Keith Edward Olsen was southbound on U.S. 281 in a Ford pickup near Cibolo Creek about 7 a.m. when a large utility truck in the northbound lanes lost control and collided with Olsen's truck, according to the Texas Department of Public Safety.

Q. What is the report about?

(a) Traffic accident

(b) Traffic regulations on the freeway

(c) Highway's safety supervision

(d) Traffic condition

해석_ 수사관들은 벡사와 코말 지역 경계 근처에서 수요일 아침 발생한 치명적인 사건을 꽁꽁 얼어붙은 북쪽 샌안토니오 고속도로 다리와 연관지었습니다. 텍사스 공공 안전팀에 의하면, 케이스 에드워드 올젠 씨는 북쪽 차선의 대형 다용도 트럭이 통제력을 잃고 자신의 트럭과 충돌한 시각인 7시경, 시볼로 호수 근처에서 포드 차량을 타고 U.S. 281번 지방도로의 남쪽 차선을 달리고 있었다고 합니다.

Q. 무엇에 관한 보도인가?

(a) 교통사고

(b) 고속도로에서의 교통 규칙

(c) 고속도로의 안전 관리

(d) 교통 상황

해설_ 트럭끼리 충돌했다는 사고 소식을 전하고 있으므로 (a)가 정답이다.

어휘_ **investigator** 수사관 **link** 관련짓다 **freeway** 고속도로 **fatal** 치명적인 **southbound** 남행의 **pickup** 소형 트럭 **creek** (바다, 강, 호수의) 작은 만 **utility truck** 다용도 소형 트럭 **lose control** 통제력을 잃다 **regulation** 규정 **supervision** 감독

정답_ (a)

47.

Long-term global warming is prompting North

American birds to winter farther north — a trend more noticeable in Alaska than anywhere else in the nation, according to a new study by the National Audubon Society. Climate-induced changes in vegetation are also altering the summer habitat of Alaska birds, and while some species may thrive amid the change, others won't, reported Matt Kirchhoff, director of bird conservation at Audubon Alaska.

Q. What is the main focus of the news?

(a) Global warming causes the surface of the ocean to rise.
(b) Global warming brings more feathered friends north in winter.
(c) Global warming helps all Alaska birds to winter.
(d) Global warming is attacking the Earth.

해석_ 장기적인 지구 온난화가 북미 철새들이 보다 먼 북쪽에서 겨울을 나도록 촉구하고 있습니다. 국립 오듀본 협회의 새로운 연구에 따르면, 이러한 추세는 다른 어느 지역에서보다도 알래스카에서 더욱 두드러진다고 합니다. 또한 기후가 초래한 식물의 변화들은 알래스카 새들의 여름 서식지에도 변화를 준다고 합니다. 그리고 몇몇 종들은 그러한 변화 속에서 잘 자랄 수 있는 반면, 다른 종들은 그러지 못할 것이라고 오듀본 알래스카의 새 보호지역 감독, 매트 키르히호프가 전했습니다.

Q. 뉴스의 주제는 무엇인가?

(a) 지구 온난화는 해수면 상승을 일으킨다.
(b) 지구 온난화는 겨울에 더 많은 깃털 달린 친구들을 북쪽으로 데려간다.
(c) 지구 온난화는 모든 알래스카 새들이 겨울을 나는 데 도움이 된다.
(d) 지구 온난화가 지구를 공격하고 있다.

해설_ 장기적인 지구 온난화가 철새들을 보다 먼 북쪽으로 가게 하고 있으며, 이러한 추세가 알래스카에서 더욱 두드러진다는 내용이 이어지므로 정답은 (b)가 된다.

어휘_ **noticeable** 현저한, 두드러진 **climate-induced** 기후가 초래한 **vegetation** 한 지방의 식물 **alter** 변경하다, 바꾸다 **habitat** 서식지 **species** 종 **thrive** 번성하다, 잘 자라다 **amid** ~의 한복판에 **conservation** (자연 환경의) 보호, 자연보호 지역 **feathered** 깃털이 난

48.

The nice folks at Verizon Wireless recently loaned me an LG Dare, a new touch screen phone exclusive to Verizon. The Dare is Verizon's best touch screen yet, despite a few shortcomings. Like all touch-screen phones, the Dare is dominated by a large display covering almost the entire front surface. It has a motion sensor inside that tells whether you're holding it horizontally or vertically.

Q. What is the main function in this product?

(a) You can contact the display of the device with a finger.
(b) You can use a videophone anytime.
(c) You can touch the screen with only touch pen.
(d) It has the smallest antenna in the world.

해석_ 버라이즌 와이어리스 사의 좋은 사람들이 최근 내게 버라이즌 독점의 새 터치스크린폰 LG Dare를 빌려 주었다. Dare는 몇 가지 결점에도 불구하고 지금까지 나온 버라이즌 최고의 터치스크린이다. 모든 터치스크린 방식의 휴대폰들처럼 Dare는 거의 전면을 커버하는 대형 화면에 의해 조절된다. Dare에는 휴대폰을 수평으로 들고 있는지, 또는 수직으로 들고 있는지를 식별하는 모션 센서가 내장돼 있다.

Q. 이 제품의 주요 기능은 무엇인가?

(a) 손가락 하나로 휴대폰 화면에 접촉할 수 있다.
(b) 언제든지 화상 전화를 사용할 수 있다.
(c) 오직 터치펜으로만 스크린을 만질 수 있다.
(d) 세상에서 가장 작은 안테나를 가지고 있다.

해설_ touch screen phone이라고 했으므로 정답은 (a)가 된다.

어휘_ **loan** 빌려 주다 **exclusive** 한정된, 독점적인 **shortcoming** 결점, 단점 **dominate** 지배하다 **motion** 동작, 움직임 **sensor** 감지기 **horizontally** 수평적으로 **vertically** 수직적으로

49.

Registration is open until Friday for a three-day

workshop with Santa Fe artist Gasali Adeyemo, who will share resist and dyeing techniques of his native Nigerian Yoruba culture. Participants will leave with fabric they've dyed using three techniques. The workshop is 10 a.m.~4 p.m. Feb. 20~22. Cost is $240 for the three days. Space is limited. Call Southwest School of Art & Craft at (210) 224-1848 or e-mail trodriguez@swschool.org for more details or to register.

Q. Which of the following is correct according to the advertisement?

(a) You can learn about dyeing art with an artist.
(b) Gasali Adeyemo is well known in Nigeria.
(c) The workshop fee is included with a free lunch.
(d) The workshop invites participants only by e-mail.

해석_ 산타페의 예술가 가살리 아데예모와 함께하는 3일간의 워크숍을 위한 등록은 금요일까지 할 수 있습니다. 가살리 아데예모는 그의 출생지인 나이지리아 요르바 문화의 방염 및 염색 기법을 알려줄 것입니다. 참가자들은 세 가지 기법을 사용하여 자신들이 염색한 천을 가지고 그곳을 떠날 것입니다. 워크숍은 2월 20일부터 22일까지 오전 10시에서 오후 4시까지 열리며 3일간의 비용은 240달러입니다. 공간은 제한되어 있습니다. 더 자세한 정보나 등록을 위해서는 Southwest School of Art & Craft (210) 224-1848로 연락 하 거 나 trodriguez@swschool.org로 이메일을 보내 주세요.

Q. 광고에 따르면 맞는 것은 어느 것인가?

(a) 예술가과 함께 염색 예술에 대해 배울 수 있다.
(b) 가살리 아데예모는 나이지리아에서 유명하다.
(c) 워크숍 비용에 무료 점심이 포함돼 있다.
(d) 워크숍은 오직 이메일로 참가자들을 초대한다.

해설_ 산타페의 예술가와 함께 하는 워크숍이라고 했고, 그 예술가가 나이지리아 요르바 문화의 염색 기법을 알려줄 것이라고 했으므로 (a)가 정답이다.

어휘_ **registration** 등록 **resist** 방염 **dyeing** 염색 **participant** 참가자 **fabric** 직물, 천 **limited** 제한된, 한정된 **register** 등록하다

정답_ (a)

50.

The annual San Antonio Stock Show & Rodeo gets going again this week with events and concerts kicking off Thursday on the grounds of the AT Center. And, as usual, there are lots of kid-friendly attractions to be found, including the Buddy's Kid's Corral, pony rides, carnival and more. For more information, go to www.rodeo.com.

Q. Which is correct according to the report?

(a) You can go to the web site, if you want to know more.
(b) There will be many famous singers.
(c) You should make a reservation if you want to join this event.
(d) This event will be held for the first time in the city.

해석_ 해마다 열리는 샌 안토니오 가축 품평회 및 로데오 대회가 AT 센터 경기장에서 목요일 시작하는 각종 행사 및 콘서트와 함께 이번주 다시 시작합니다. 그리고 늘 그렇듯이 Buddy's Kid's Corral, 조랑말 타기, 카니발 등을 포함하여 아이들을 위한 행사들이 많이 있습니다. 더 많은 정보를 얻으시려면 www.rodeo.com을 방문하세요.

Q. 기사에 따르면 맞는 것은 어느 것인가?

(a) 더 많이 알고 싶으면 웹사이트로 가면 된다.
(b) 유명한 가수들이 많이 있을 것이다.
(c) 이 행사에 참가하고 싶으면 예약을 해야 한다.
(d) 이 행사는 그 도시에서 처음으로 열릴 예정이다.

해설_ 글 마지막 부분에 더 많은 정보를 얻으려면 웹사이트를 방문하라는 얘기가 나오므로 (a)가 정답이다.

어휘_ **annual** 해마다 **kick off** 시작하다 **kid-friendly** 아이들에게 맞는, 아이들을 위한 **attraction** 사람의 마음을 끄는 것, 인기거리

정답_ (a)

51.

The second heavy snowfall to hit Britain this week caused major travel delays on Thursday, and roads and airports in neighboring Ireland also suffered snow-related shutdowns. The city was still recovering from its heaviest snowfall in almost 20 years on Monday, when schools were closed, public transport all but collapsed and millions of workers stayed home.

Q. Which is the correct according to the weather forecast?

(a) A storm of snow blanketed the city during this week.
(b) It has been snowing in Britain from Monday to tonight.
(c) The school event last weekend was snowed off.
(d) It is reported that this snowfall has never happened before.

해석_ 이번주 영국에 두 번째 폭설이 내려 목요일에는 주요 교통이 지연되었고, 이웃하는 아일랜드의 도로와 공항들도 눈으로 인해 폐쇄되었습니다. 학교도 문을 닫고 대중교통 시설도 거의 무너져 내려 수백만 명의 근로자들이 쉬어야 했던 월요일, 거의 20년 만에 가장 심했던 폭설로부터 도시는 아직 회복 중에 있었습니다.

Q. 기상 예보에 따르면 맞는 것은 어느 것인가?

(a) 폭설이 이번주 동안 도시를 온통 뒤덮었다.
(b) 월요일부터 오늘 밤까지 영국엔 눈이 내리고 있다.
(c) 지난주 학교 이벤트는 폭설 때문에 취소되었다.
(d) 보도에 따르면 이런 강설은 이전에 발생한 적이 없다고 한다.

해설_ 월요일에 아주 심한 폭설이 내린 데 이어 목요일에도 폭설이 내렸다고 했으므로 (a)가 정답이다.

어휘_ **snowfall** 강설 **neighboring** 이웃의 **shutdown** 일시 휴업, 휴점 **recover** 회복하다 **all but** 거의 **collapse** 무너지다 **a storm of snow** 폭설 **blanket** 온통 뒤덮다 **be snowed off** 폭설 때문에 최소되다

정답_ (a)

52.

The Lee County Sheriff's Office is investigating the death of a person found in a car parked at the Albertson's Store in Estero. Around 5 p.m. deputies received a call about a vehicle that had been parked in the store's lot for several days. The caller said it appeared that a person was in the vehicle. Responding deputies found that the vehicle matched the description of a vehicle belonging to a woman, who had been reported missing by her family earlier this week.

Q. What is the main topic of the report?

(a) A car which was driven by the girl
(b) Deputies who received a call about a broken vehicle
(c) The Sheriff's Office which is waiting for the outcome of the autopsy
(d) The death of a woman who was found in a car

해석_ 리 카운티 보안관실은 에스테로에 있는 엘버슨 가게에 주차된 차 안에서 발견된 사람의 죽음에 대해 조사 중에 있습니다. 오후 5시경, 경찰관들은 며칠 동안 가게 주차장에 주차돼 있던 차량에 대해 한 통의 전화를 받았는데요. 전화를 건 사람은 그 차량 안에 사람이 있는 것처럼 보였다고 말했습니다. 신고를 받고 출동한 경찰관들은 그 차량이 이번주 초 가족들에 의해 실종 신고됐던 여자의 차량과 일치함을 발견했습니다.

Q. 기사의 주제는 무엇인가?

(a) 소녀가 운전한 차
(b) 고장 난 차량에 대해 전화를 받은 경찰관들
(c) 부검 결과를 기다리고 있는 보안관 사무실
(d) 차 안에서 발견된 한 여자의 죽음

해설_ 차 안에서 발견된 사람의 죽음에 대해 조사 중이며, 그 차량이 실종 신고됐던 여자의 차량과 일치했다는 내용에 대한 기사이므로 정답은 (d)가 된다.

어휘_ **county** 군 **sheriff** 보안관(미국의 지역 경찰은 City Police와 County Sheriff의 두 종류로 나눠진다. City Police는 시 경계 내의 치안을 전담하고, County Sheriff는 군의 시에서 제외되는 부분을 전담한다. 그리고 County Sheriff에서 일하는 경찰관들은 Sheriff's Deputies라고 부른다.) **lot** 주차장 **description** 묘사 **outcome** 결과 **autopsy** 부검

정답_ (d)

53.

An association of all six Vineyard finance committees this week called for every Island public employee to forego an annual cost of living increase amid the growing national economic crisis. The association put out a statement on Monday asking employees to band together to help avoid layoffs in the coming year. The group has even asked employees covered by unions to effectively refuse any cost of living increase they are offered as a part of a standing union contract.

Q. Which is the most appropriate title for this report?

(a) Finance Leaders Call on Town Workers to Give Up Pay Raises
(b) Effective Productivity of Employees Covered by Unions
(c) Furious Employees to Band Together to Help Avoid Layoffs in the Coming Year
(d) The Demonstration of the Local Fired Workers

해석_ 모두 6명의 포도밭 재정 위원회 협회는 이번주 모든 아일랜드 공공 근로자들에게 국가 경제 위기가 고조되는 가운데 연 생활비 인상을 포기할 것을 요청했습니다. 월요일에 협회는 근로자들에게 내년에 해고를 피하도록 단결할 것을 요청하는 성명을 발표했습니다. 협회는 심지어 조합에 의해 보호받는 근로자들에게도 영구적인 조합 계약의 일부로서 그들에게 제공되는 생활비 인상을 효과적으로 거부할 것을 요청했습니다.

Q. 이 기사에 가장 적절한 제목은 어느 것인가?

(a) 재정 대표들이 마을 근로자들에게 봉급 인상 포기 요구
(b) 조합에 의해 보호받는 직원의 효과적인 생산성
(c) 내년 해고를 피하기 위해 단결한 성난 직원들
(d) 지역 해고 근로자들의 시위

해설_ 재정 위원회 협회에서 모든 근로자들에게 생활비 인상을 포기할 것을 요청한 사실에 대한 내용을 담고 있으므로 (a)가 가장 적절하다.

어휘_ association 협회 vineyard 포도밭 forego ~ 없이 지내다, 보류하다, 버리다 cost of living 생활비, 생계비 put out 발표하다 band together 단결하다 layoff 해고 union 조합 standing 영구적인, (규칙 등이) 계속 효력을 갖는 call on 요구하다 productivity 생산성 furious 격노한 demonstration 시위, 데모

정답_ (a)

54.

With the fragile ceasefire still in force, The Art Newspaper has learned that Gaza's only museum has been damaged and other heritage sites and buildings may also be at risk. The Antiquities Museum of Gaza, privately founded and run by Gazan contractor and collector Jawdat Khoudary, was badly damaged during Israel's 22 days of air and land strikes.

Q. What is the main idea of the report?

(a) The Art Newspaper learned Gaza's other heritage sites.
(b) Between Israel and Gaza, a bridge is being built now.
(c) Gaza has many heritage sites and buildings.
(d) The museum in Gaza was badly damaged by Israel's strikes.

해석_ 여전히 유효한, 깨지기 쉬운 휴전 속에서, The Art Newspaper(영국 미술 신문)는 가자의 유일한 박물관이 손상되었고, 다른 유적지와 건물들 또한 위험에 처해 있을 수 있다는 것을 알았습니다. 가자인 토건업자와 수집가 조댓 쿠데리에 의해 사설로 설립되어 운영된 가자의 고대 박물관이 이스라엘의 22일간의 공수 공격 동안 심하게 손상되었습니다.

Q. 기사의 주제는 무엇인가?

(a) The Art Newspaper는 가자의 다른 유적지를 알았다.
(b) 이스라엘과 가자 사이에 다리를 현재 건설 중에 있다.
(c) 가자에는 많은 유적지와 건물들이 있다.
(d) 가자의 박물관이 이스라엘의 공격으로 심하게 파손되었다.

해설_ 이스라엘이 공격하는 동안 박물관이 몹시 손상되었다는 내용을 담고 있으므로 정답은 (d)다.

어휘_ fragile 깨지기 쉬운, 허약한 ceasefire 휴전, 정전 in force 유효한 damage 손상을 입히다 heritage site 유적지 antiquities 옛 기물[미술품], (고대의) 유물

privately 개인으로서 **found** 설립하다 **contractor** 토
건업자

정답_ (d)

55.

Congratulations go to Oak Harbor High School senior Jennifer Jansen on being named the Wendy's High School Heisman winner. For the past 14 years, Wendy's Restaurants have teamed up with the Heisman Memorial Trophy Committee to create this award. The award honors high school students who excel in academics, athletics and student leadership.

Q. What is the main topic of the announcement?

(a) Jansen wins Wendy's Heisman award.
(b) Jansen will continue her athletic career at Northwestern College.
(c) Wendy's restaurants have joined a union.
(d) The award honors high school students who excel in academics, athletics and student leadership.

해석_ 웬디즈 고등학교 하이즈만 수상자로 지명된 오크 하버 고등학교 상급생 제니퍼 얀센에게 축하를 드립니다. 지난 14년 동안 웬디즈 레스토랑은 하이즈만 기념 트로피 위원회와 함께 이 상을 주기 위해 협력해 왔습니다. 이 상의 영예는 학업, 운동, 학생 리더십에 뛰어난 고등학생들에게 돌아갑니다.

Q. 발표의 주제는 무엇인가?

(a) 얀센이 웬디즈 하이즈만 상을 탄다.
(b) 얀센은 노스웨스턴 대학에서 운동 경력을 계속 쌓을 것이다.
(c) 웬디즈 레스토랑은 조합에 가입할 것이다.
(d) 이 상의 영예는 학업, 운동, 학생 리더십에 뛰어난 고등학생들에게 돌아간다.

해설_ 웬디즈 하이즈만 수상자로 얀센이 지명됐다는 소식을 알리는 내용이므로 (a)가 정답이다.

어휘_ **team up with** 협력하다 **create** 주다 **excel** 뛰어나다
athletics (각종) 운동 경기, 스포츠

정답_ (a)

56.

The Lodi City Council is paying $1.2 million to an environmental pollution lawyer it had fired and then sued for fraud and negligence. Attorney Michael C. Donovan had already received roughly $14 million for his work over a number of years. The Wednesday night settlement came six weeks before the city was set to go to trial against Donovan.

Q. Which is correct according to the report?

(a) Fired Lawyer gets $1.2 million.
(b) The Lodi City Council is paying $14 million.
(c) The City will go to trial against Donovan.
(d) Donovan was fired and then sued for fraud and negligence.

해석_ 로디 시의회는, 해고시킨 후 사기와 태만으로 고소했던 환경 오염 전문 변호사에게 120만 달러를 지불할 것입니다. 마이클 C. 도노반 변호사는 이미 몇 년 동안 일한 대가로 대략 1,400만 달러를 받았습니다. 수요일 밤 합의는 시가 도노반을 상대로 재판을 받을 예정이었던 6주 전에 이루어진 것이었습니다.

Q. 기사에 따르면 맞는 것은 어느 것인가?

(a) 해고된 변호사는 120만 달러를 받는다.
(b) 로디 시의회는 1,400만 달러를 지불할 것이다.
(c) 시는 도노반을 상대로 재판을 받을 것이다.
(d) 도노반은 해고되고 나서 사기와 태만으로 고소당했다.

해설_ 기사 첫 부분에 도노반을 해고시킨 후 사기와 태만으로 고소했다는 내용이 나오므로 (d)가 정답이다.

어휘_ **environmental pollution** 환경 오염 **sue for** ~에 대해 소송을 걸다 **fraud** 사기 **negligence** 태만 **attorney** 변호사(= lawyer) **roughly** 대충, 대략 **settlement** (사건 등의) 해결, 합의 **go to trial** 재판에 회부되다, 재판을 받다

정답_ (d)

57.

A Lodi father pleaded not guilty Tuesday to charges that he used a clothes iron to burn his 6-year-old daughter, as well as beating her with a stick. The burns were severe enough that the girl will have scars for life, Detective

Steve Maynard said. He had not released details, but a prosecutor said in court Tuesday that the weapon used was an iron.

Q. What is the report about?

(a) The father who was arrested last Friday
(b) The police who are on suspicion of torture
(c) The case of a father abusing child
(d) A prosecutor's statement about this case

해석_ 로디의 아버지는 그의 6살 난 딸을 다리미를 사용해 화상을 입히고 막대기로 때린 혐의에 대해 화요일 무죄를 주장했습니다. 화상은 소녀가 평생 흉터를 가질 정도로 심각하다고 스티브 메이너드 형사는 말했습니다. 그는 자세한 내용을 공개하지 않았지만, 검사는 흉기로 사용된 것이 다리미였다고 화요일 법정에서 말했습니다.

   Q. 무엇에 대한 기사인가?

   (a) 지난 금요일 체포된 아버지
   (b) 고문 혐의를 받고 있는 경찰
   (c) 아버지가 아이를 학대한 사건
   (d) 이 사건에 대한 검사의 진술

해설_ 아버지가 어린 딸을 때리고 다리미로 화상을 입힌 사건을 중점적으로 다루고 있으므로 정답은 (c)다.

어휘_ plead not guilty 무죄를 주장하다 **charge** 혐의 **iron** 다리미 **beat** 때리다 **severe** 심한 **scar** 흉터, 상처 **detective** 형사 **release** 공개하다, 발표하다 **prosecutor** 검사 **court** 법정 **suspicion** 혐의, 의심 **case** 사건, 사례 **abuse** 학대하다 **statement** 진술

정답_ (c)

58.

"No." That is a mother's usual response to a request from a child for permission to get a tattoo. "Not till you move out," is dad's usual answer. The excuse that "everyone has them" leads to the question: "Would you jump off a bridge if everyone else did?" Obviously not, but getting a tattoo is certainly not as drastic as jumping off a bridge. Saying that everyone has a tattoo is an exaggeration, but tattoos are becoming increasingly popular on Tokay High School campus.

Q. What is the main idea of the talk?

(a) You can jump off a bridge if everyone else did.
(b) The school graduated its senior class on June 12.
(c) Saying that everyone has a tattoo is an exaggeration.
(d) Tattoos are becoming increasingly popular in Tokay High School campus.

해석_ "안 돼." 엄마들은 보통 아이가 문신을 하겠다고 허락을 받으려 할 때 이렇게 반응한다. 아빠들은 보통 "다 크기 전까지는 안 돼."라고 대답한다. '모든 사람이 문신을 가지고 있다' 는 이유를 대면 "모든 사람이 그러면 너도 다리에서 뛰어내릴래?"라는 질문이 날아온다. 명백하게 아니다. 하지만 문신을 하는 것이 다리에서 뛰어내리는 것만큼 그렇게 극적인 것은 아니다. 모든 사람이 문신을 가지고 있다고 말하는 것은 과장이라고 할 수 있지만, 토케이 고등학교 캠퍼스에서는 문신의 인기가 점점 높아지고 있다.

   Q. 담화의 주제는 무엇인가?

   (a) 모든 사람이 그러면 당신도 다리에서 뛰어내릴 수 있다.
   (b) 학교는 6월 12일 상급생들을 졸업시켰다.
   (c) 모든 사람이 문신을 가지고 있다고 말하는 것은 과장이다.
   (d) 토케이 고등학교 캠퍼스에서 문신의 인기가 점점 높아지고 있다.

해설_ 부모들은 문신을 하는 것에 대해 부정적인 반응을 보이고, 문신을 하는 것이 그렇게 극적인 것도 아니지만, 그럼에도 토케이 고교생들 사이에서는 문신의 인기가 점점 높아지고 있다는 것이 중심 내용이므로 정답은 (d)가 된다.

어휘_ get a tatto 문신을 하다 **move out** 이사 가다 **jump off** ~에서 뛰어내리다 **exaggeration** 과장

정답_ (d)

59.

ZOObilee 2009 is scheduled for Feb. 20 at the Naples Zoo. Presented by Fifth Third Bank, the event will celebrate the zoo's 40th anniversary. It includes food, drinks, live entertainment, dancing, a live auction conducted by Naples Mayor Bill Barnett, and wildlife experiences.

Q. What is mostly referred in the announcement?

(a) Zoobilee 2009
(b) Naples Mayor
(c) Distinguished Conservation Award
(d) The entertainment company

해석_ 2009 쥬빌리가 나폴리 동물원에서 2월 20일로 예정돼 있습니다. Fifth Third 은행에 의해 제공되는 그 행사는 동물원 40주년을 축하할 것입니다. 음식, 음료수, 라이브 쇼, 춤, 나폴리 시장 빌 바넷에 의해 행해지는 공개 경매, 그리고 야생 생물 체험이 포함돼 있습니다.

Q. 안내 방송에 대부분 언급되어진 것은?

(a) 2009 쥬빌리
(b) 나폴리 시장
(c) 저명한 자연보호 상
(d) 연예회사

해설_ 2월 20일에 열릴 예정인 쥬빌리 행사에 대한 안내 방송이므로 정답은 (a)다.

어휘_ **be scheduled for** ~로 예정되어 있다 **live entertainment** 라이브 쇼 **live auction** 공개 경매 **wildlife** 야생 생물의 **distinguished** 저명한, 뛰어난 **entertainment company** 연예회사

정답_ (a)

60.

Godfrey Seward's 7-year-old heart stopped Jan. 25 for no apparent reason. His death pushed his unemployed, single mother into near despair when she found out she could not afford to bury him. Through a series of coincidences, different parts of the Lee County community rallied to raise money for a funeral. Plans call for Godfrey to be buried after 11 a.m. services at Mt. Sinai Baptist Church on Saturday.

Q. Which is correct according to the report?

(a) A Woman died for no apparent reason.
(b) A Woman could not afford to raise her son.
(c) Different parts of the community rallied to raise money for a funeral.
(d) A 7-year-old boy hurt because of stopping running.

해석_ 7살 된 고드프리 슈어드의 심장이 명백한 이유 없이 1월 25일 멈췄습니다. 그의 죽음은 아이를 묻을 돈이 없다는 것을 알았을 때 무직의 편모인 아이의 어머니를 절망으로 밀어 넣었습니다. 동시에 발생한 일련의 사건들로 인해 리 카운티 공동체 일부는 장례식을 위한 기금을 모으기 위해 다시 모였습니다. 고드프리는 토요일 시내산 침례교회에서 11시 예배가 끝난 후 매장될 계획입니다.

Q. 기사에 따르면 맞는 것은 어느 것인가?

(a) 여자가 명백한 이유 없이 죽었다.
(b) 여자는 그녀의 아들을 양육할 형편이 못 됐다.
(c) 공동체 일부가 장례식 기금 마련을 위해 모였다.
(d) 7살 된 소년이 달리다 멈춰서 다쳤다.

해설_ 명백한 이유 없이 죽은 7살 된 소년의 어머니가 그의 장례식비를 치를 형편이 안 되자 기금 마련을 위해 공동체 일부가 다시 모였다는 내용이므로 (c)가 정답이다.

어휘_ **push into** ~로 밀어 넣다 **unemployed** 실직한, 무직의 **despair** 절망 **bury** 묻다, 매장하다 **coincidence** 동시에[우연히 같이] 일어난 사건 **rally** 다시 모이다 **funeral** 장례식 **Mt. Sinai** 시내산(모세가 신에게서 십계명을 받은 곳) **Baptist church** 침례교회

정답_ (c)

Final Test 2

Part 1

1.

M: Would you like to drink one more beer?

W: ______________________________

(a) Sorry, I can't take it anymore.

(b) No, thanks. I am a casual drinker.

(c) Why not? You may be under the weather.

(d) You should have stopped drinking liquor.

해석_ M: 맥주 한 병 더 드릴까요?

W: ______________________________

(a) 미안해요, 더 이상 못 참겠어요.

(b) 아니, 괜찮아요. 잘 못 마시거든요.

(c) 그럼요. 당신 몸이 편치 않은 것 같군요.

(d) 당신은 술을 그만 마셨어야 했어요.

해설_ 맥주를 한 병 더 마시겠냐는 권유에 사양하는 (b)가 정답이다.

어휘_ **casual drinker** 가끔씩 술 마시는 사람, 술 못 마시는 사람 *cf.* heavy drinker 술 많이 마시는 사람 **be under the weather** 몸이 불편하다, 기분이 안 좋다

정답_ (b)

2.

W: Could you please check if this is available now?

M: ______________________________

(a) I am sure it is in stock.

(b) I don't like investing money on it.

(c) She has already done.

(d) I really appreciate it.

해석_ W: 이거 지금 구입 가능한지 확인 좀 해주실래요?

M: ______________________________

(a) 재고가 확실히 있습니다.

(b) 그것에 돈을 투자하고 싶지 않아요.

(c) 그녀가 이미 끝냈어요.

(d) 정말 감사합니다.

해설_ 물건을 지금 구입할 수 있는지 여부를 묻고 있으므로 (a)가 정답이다.

어휘_ **in stock** 재고가 있는(↔ out of stock 품절된) **invest** 투

자하다

정답_ (a)

3.

M: This blue dress looks good on you.

W: ______________________________

(a) Thanks. I bought this for Prom.

(b) Yes, I am looking for some blue dress.

(c) Well, I don't know what to do.

(d) So do you. You look so good today.

해석_ M: 이 파란색 드레스 너한테 잘 어울린다.

W: ______________________________

(a) 고마워. 졸업파티 때 입으려고 샀어.

(b) 네, 파란색 드레스를 찾는데요.

(c) 글쎄, 뭘 해야 할지 모르겠어.

(d) 너도 그래. 오늘 아주 근사해 보인다.

해설_ 드레스가 잘 어울린다고 칭찬하고 있으므로 고마움을 표하는 (a)가 자연스럽다.

어휘_ **look good on** ~에게 잘 어울리다 **Prom** (고교 · 대학 등에서 학년말이나 졸업 때 여는) 무도회, 댄스 파티

정답_ (a)

4.

M: I am so worried that she could misunderstand me.

W: ______________________________

(a) I want to give her a big hug.

(b) I will never see her again.

(c) I am sure she doesn't think of you like that.

(d) She did it on purpose.

해석_ M: 그녀가 날 오해했을까 봐 무지 걱정돼.

W: ______________________________

(a) 그녀를 안아 주고 싶어.

(b) 다신 그녀를 안 볼 거야.

(c) 그녀는 분명 널 그렇게 생각하지 않을 거야.

(d) 그녀가 일부러 그랬어.

해설_ 남자가 걱정을 하고 있으므로 이에 대한 위로나 조언이 담긴

선택지를 고르면 된다.

어휘_ misunderstand 오해하다(= get ... wrong) **give ... a hug** ~를 안아 주다 **on purpose** 고의로, 일부러

정답_ (c)

5.

W: I am sorry I couldn't send you a fax this afternoon.

M: _______________________________

(a) I don't think it was easy.
(b) Good luck on your finals.
(c) Never mind. I still have enough time.
(d) I have never thought about it.

해석_ W: 오늘 오후에 팩스를 보내 드리지 못해서 죄송해요.

M: _______________________________

(a) 전 그게 쉬운 일이었다고 생각지 않아요.
(b) 기말시험 잘 봐.
(c) 걱정 마세요. 아직 시간 충분히 있어요.
(d) 그 점에 대해서 한 번도 생각해 본 적이 없어요.

해석_ 팩스를 보내지 못한 것에 대해 사과하고 있으므로 이를 받아들이는 응답 표현이 적절하다. Never mind.는 상대방의 사과에 대해 '걱정하지 마라', '괜찮다'고 말할 때 쓸 수 있는 표현으로, That's all right.이나 That's ok.와 마찬가지다.

어휘_ finals 기말고사

정답_ (c)

6.

M: It was great seeing you New Years Eve!
W: _______________________________

(a) Me too. It was good to see you that night.
(b) It is right down the street from my house.
(c) I don't have a New Year's resolution yet.
(d) I am so happy to know you.

해석_ M: 한 해의 마지막 날 널 만나서 정말 기뻤어!

W: _______________________________

(a) 나도. 그날 밤 널 만나서 좋았어.
(b) 우리 집 바로 앞길이야.
(c) 난 아직 새해 결심을 세우지 않았어.
(d) 널 알게 돼서 너무 기쁘다.

해석_ 남자가 한 해의 마지막 날 만나서 기뻤다고 말하고 있으므로

여자도 즐거웠다고 말하는 (a)가 자연스럽다.

어휘_ down the street 길 아래로 **resolution** 결심, 결단

정답_ (a)

7.

W: She is on the line. Would you like to hold?

M: _______________________________

(a) That's alright. I'll fax it to her.
(b) She'll hold a big concert next month.
(c) I've just left an urgent message.
(d) No, my wife must lie in a hammock.

해석_ W: 그녀는 통화 중입니다. 잠시 기다려 주시겠습니까?

M: _______________________________

(a) 괜찮아요. 그녀에게 팩스로 보낼게요.
(b) 그녀는 다음 달에 대규모 콘서트를 열 거예요.
(c) 지금 막 긴급 메시지를 보냈어요.
(d) 아뇨, 집사람은 그물 침대에 누워 있어야 해요.

해석_ 통화 중이니 잠시 기다려 달라는 말에 그냥 팩스로 보내겠다는 (a)가 적절한 응답이다.

어휘_ on the line 통화 중인 **hammock** 그물 침대

정답_ (a)

8.

M: The flight 205 has been delayed an hour. Thank you for your patience.

W: _______________________________

(a) You're welcome. I think it was an unavoidable delay.
(b) It happened because of the heavy rainstorm.
(c) Could you tell me where your destination is?
(d) You're welcome. It's my duty.

해석_ M: 205 항공편이 1시간 지연됐습니다. 참고 기다려 주셔서 감사합니다.

W: _______________________________

(a) 천만에요. 어쩔 수 없는 지연이었다고 생각해요.
(b) 강한 폭풍우 때문에 발생했습니다.
(c) 당신의 목적지가 어딘지 말씀해 주시겠습니까?
(d) 천만에요. 제가 해야 할 일인걸요.

해석_ 지연된 비행기를 참고 기다려 준 데 대해 감사의 뜻을 전하고 있으므로 (a)가 이어져야 적절하다.

9.

W: Could you get in touch with him as soon as possible?
M: _______________________________________

(a) I am waiting for him as well.
(b) I will do it right away.
(c) I think it has 252 pages.
(d) He is on the right way.

해석_ W: 가능한 한 빨리 그에게 연락할 수 있나요?
   M: _______________________________________

   (a) 저도 그를 기다리는 중이에요.
   (b) 당장 그렇게 하겠습니다.
   (c) 그건 252페이지로 돼 있는 것 같아요.
   (d) 그는 오른쪽에 있어요.
해설_ 남자에게 빨리 연락을 취해 달라고 부탁하고 있다. 따라서 바로 연락하겠다고 응답한 (b)가 정답이다.
어휘_ **get in touch with** ~와 연락하다
정답_ (b)

10.

M: You can't buy the ticket, because your passport already expired.
W: _______________________________________

(a) So, should I renew my passport?
(b) Why not? I purchased it last week.
(c) I guess the contract will have expired next year.
(d) Could I check your license?

해석_ M: 여권이 이미 만료되어 표를 구매하실 수 없습니다.
   W: _______________________________________

   (a) 그럼 여권을 갱신해야 하나요?
   (b) 그럼요, 지난주에 구매했어요.
   (c) 그 계약은 내년에 만기될 것으로 생각합니다.
   (d) 면허증을 확인할 수 있을까요?
해설_ 여권 기한이 만료되어 표를 살 수 없다고 했으므로 갱신해야 하는지 묻는 (a)가 적절하다.

11.

W: How was the trip to Melbourne?
M: _______________________________________

(a) Good. I think it will be a great opportunity.
(b) I was young and stupid.
(c) I am sorry to hear that.
(d) Great. You should go see how peaceful it is.

해석_ W: 멜버른 여행 어땠어?
   M: _______________________________________

   (a) 좋아. 좋은 기회가 될 것 같아.
   (b) 난 어렸고 어리석었어.
   (c) 그 소식을 듣게 돼서 유감이다.
   (d) 좋았어. 그곳이 얼마나 평화로운지 가서 봐야 해.
해설_ 여행이 어땠는지 묻고 있으므로 이에 관해 언급한 선택지를 고르면 된다.
어휘_ **stupid** 어리석은 **peaceful** 평화로운
정답_ (d)

12.

W: Who is in charge of this position?
M: _______________________________________

(a) It is free of charge.
(b) I think John is handling that.
(c) She is in the meeting now.
(d) I don't think it is free.

해석_ W: 누가 이 일을 맡고 있나요?
   M: _______________________________________

   (a) 무료입니다.
   (b) 존이 그 일을 다루고 있는 것 같아요.
   (c) 그녀는 지금 회의 중입니다.
   (d) 무료가 아닌 것 같은데요.
해설_ in charge of는 '~을 맡고 있는'의 뜻으로, 담당자가 누군지 묻고 있다. 따라서 그 사람을 언급한 (b)가 정답이다. (a)와 (d)는 charge의 의미를 이용한 함정.
어휘_ **in charge of** ~을 맡고 있는 **free of charge** 무료로 **handle** 다루다, 처리하다

정답_(b)

13.

W: I heard you got a new position.

M: ___________________________________

(a) Wow, congratulations!
(b) I've just heard about the news.
(c) Right. I was promoted a few days ago.
(d) What kind of job do you want?

해석_W: 새 직책을 얻었다면서요.

M: ___________________________________

(a) 와, 축하해요!
(b) 방금 그 소식을 들었어요.
(c) 맞아요. 며칠 전에 승진했어요.
(d) 어떤 종류의 직업을 원하세요?

해설_ 새 직책을 얻었다는 소식을 들었다는 여자의 말에 며칠 전에
승진했다고 응답하는 (c)가 적절하다.

어휘_ promote 승진시키다

정답_ (c)

14.

W: How often do you go to the shopping mall?

M: ___________________________________

(a) It is second floor on the right.
(b) I should have a savings account.
(c) Yes, I have a 30% discount card.
(d) Not much. I guess once a month.

해석_W: 쇼핑센터에 얼마나 자주 가세요?

M: ___________________________________

(a) 오른쪽 2층에 있어요.
(b) 저는 보통예금 계좌가 있어야 해요.
(c) 네, 30% 할인카드를 가지고 있어요.
(d) 그리 자주 가진 않아요. 한 달에 한 번 정도인 것 같아요.

해설_ 쇼핑센터에 얼마나 자주 가는지를 묻고 있으므로 빈도수가 언
급된 선택지를 고르면 된다.

어휘_ saving account 보통예금 계좌

정답_ (d)

15.

M: What do you want to grab for lunch?

W: ___________________________________

(a) I think I will have some chicken.
(b) I will have my lunch in the cafeteria.
(c) That is already over and you should change
the menu.
(d) You can get whatever you want.

해석_M: 점심으로 뭘 먹고 싶니?

W: ___________________________________

(a) 난 치킨을 좀 먹을까 하는데.
(b) 난 구내 식당에서 점심을 먹을 거야.
(c) 그건 이미 끝나서 메뉴를 바꾸셔야 합니다.
(d) 네가 원하는 건 뭐든 얻을 수 있어.

해설_ 점심으로 뭘 먹고 싶은지 묻고 있으므로 음식 종류가 언급된
선택지를 고르면 된다.

어휘_ cafeteria 구내 식당

정답_ (a)

Part 2

16.

M: Anything wrong with you?
W: Nothing wrong.
M: Then why do you look so down?

W: ___________________________________

(a) I have a headache.
(b) I am not feeling down.
(c) It is up to you.
(d) You are my angel.

해석_M: 무슨 문제 있니?

W: 아무 문제 없어.

M: 그럼 왜 그렇게 우울해 보이니?

W: ___________________________________

(a) 머리가 아파.
(b) 우울하지 않아.
(c) 그건 너한테 달렸어.
(d) 넌 나의 천사야.

해설_ 왜 우울해 보이는지 묻고 있으므로 그 이유가 될 만한 선택지
를 고르면 된다.

어휘_ down 의기소침한, 음울한   headache 두통   feel
down 기분이 가라앉다, 우울하다

정답_ (a)

17.

W: Have you ever read the article in the magazine?

M: No, I haven't had time to do it.

W: You should read that as soon as possible.

M: ___________________________________

(a) I am sure I will.

(b) Let me do this.

(c) I will take it.

(d) That is too bad.

해석_ W: 잡지에서 그 기사 읽어 본 적 있어?

　　　M: 아니, 그럴 시간이 없었어.

　　　W: 가능한 한 빨리 읽어 봐.

　　　M: ___________________________

　　　　(a) 꼭 그렇게.

　　　　(b) 내가 이거 할게.

　　　　(c) 내가 가져갈게.

　　　　(d) 너무 안됐다.

해설_ 가능하면 빨리 그 기사를 읽어 보라고 권유하고 있으므로 이에 응하는 (a)가 적절하다.

어휘_ **magazine** 잡지

정답_ (a)

18.

M : My grandfather passed away yesterday.

W : Oh my god! He loved you very much.

M : I know. I'm heartsick over the death.

W : ___________________________________

(a) I express my condolences.

(b) He tried to keep the faith.

(c) Thank you for the advice.

(d) It wasn't expected.

해석_ M: 우리 할아버지가 어제 돌아가셨어.

　　　W: 세상에! 널 무척 사랑하셨는데.

　　　M: 나도 알아. 마음이 많이 아프다.

　　　W: ___________________________

　　　　(a) 삼가 조의를 표한다.

　　　　(b) 그는 신의를 지키려 노력했어.

　　　　(c) 충고 고마워.

　　　　(d) 그건 예상 못했어.

해설_ 할아버지를 잃고 마음 아파하는 남자에게 애도의 뜻을 전하는

(a)가 자연스럽다. '조의를 표하다', '애도의 뜻을 표하다'라고 할 때 express one's condolence를 사용해 말한다.

어휘_ **heartsick** 슬픔에 잠긴, 마음 아픈 **keep the faith** 신념을 끝까지 지키다

정답_ (a)

19.

W: Good morning, Mike.

M: Did you check the e-mail about layoffs?

W: Yes, I did. How can they lay off 5 people in our department?

M: ___________________________________

(a) That's unreasonable. I need to talk to our manager.

(b) Yes. Jake quit his job last week.

(c) I think you should leave the office soon.

(d) It's amazing. Why don't we go out?

해석_ W: 안녕, 마이크.

　　　M: 정리 해고에 관한 이메일 확인했어?

　　　W: 그래, 확인했어. 어떻게 우리 부서에서 5명이나 해고할 수 있지?

　　　M: ___________________________

　　　　(a) 그건 부당해. 우리 부장한테 얘기해야겠어.

　　　　(b) 그래. 제이크는 지난주에 일을 관뒀어.

　　　　(c) 너 곧 퇴근해야 할 것 같아.

　　　　(d) 놀랍다. 우리 밖에 나갈래?

해설_ 동료가 5명이나 해고당한 사실에 불만을 토로하는 여자의 말에 이어질 응답으로 그건 부당하다며 동조하는 (a)가 적절하다.

어휘_ **lay off** 해고하다 **unreasonable** 부당한, 불합리한 **leave the office** 퇴근하다

정답_ (a)

20.

M: Let me see... I can't choose it.

W: I told you three times. The white shirt is better than the yellow one.

M: Just one question. Do you think the large size is better than the medium sized one?

W: ___________________________________

(a) No. The smaller one fits perfectly.

(b) Don't worry. I'll treat you today.
(c) Why don't you try on the medium size?
(d) If I were you, I would go to another store.

해석_ M: 어디 보자… 못 고르겠다.

W: 내가 세 번이나 말했잖아. 하얀 셔츠가 노란 것보다 나아.

M: 하나만 물어볼게. 큰 사이즈가 중간 사이즈보다 더 나은 것 같니?

W: ________________________

(a) 아니. 더 작은 게 딱 맞아.

(b) 걱정 마. 오늘은 내가 살게.

(c) 중간 사이즈를 입어 보는 게 어때?

(d) 내가 너라면 다른 가게에 갈 텐데.

해설_ 큰 사이즈가 더 어울리는지 의견을 묻고 있으므로 이에 관해 언급한 선택지를 고르면 된다.

어휘_ **fit** (꼭) 맞다, 어울리다

정답_ (a)

21.

W: What do you do on your spare time?
M: I usually go to tennis.
W: Really? I would like to go sometimes.
M: ________________________________

(a) I was there two weeks ago.
(b) I am going to the gym twice a week.
(c) Let's go together.
(d) I will tell you how to get there.

해석_ W: 넌 여가 시간에 뭐 하니?

M: 주로 테니스 치러 가.

W: 정말? 나도 가끔 가고 싶은데.

M: ________________________

(a) 난 2주 전에 거기 있었어.

(b) 일주일에 두 번 체육관에 갈 거야.

(c) 같이 가자.

(d) 거기 가는 방법을 알려줄게.

해설_ 여자도 가끔 테니스 치러 가고 싶다고 말했으므로 (c)가 자연스럽다.

어휘_ **go to tennis** 테니스 치러 가다   **gym** 체육관

정답_ (c)

22.

M: I can't understand French in the least.
W: Are you attending a French lesson?
M: Yes. What's more, my French pronunciation is getting worse.
W: ________________________________

(a) I know a good French tutor. Do you want me to introduce him to you?
(b) French is pronounced differently in my country.
(c) How did you answer a French exercise?
(d) My uncle is married to a French girl.

해석_ M: 프랑스어가 전혀 이해가 안 돼.

W: 프랑스어 수업 듣고 있니?

M: 응. 설상가상으로 내 프랑스어 발음이 나빠지고 있어.

W: ________________________

(a) 내가 좋은 프랑스어 개인 교사를 알고 있어. 그 사람 소개시켜 줄까?

(b) 프랑스어가 우리 지방에서는 다르게 발음돼.

(c) 프랑스어 연습문제에 어떻게 답했니?

(d) 우리 삼촌은 프랑스 여자와 결혼해 살고 있어.

해설_ 프랑스어가 어려워 괴로워하고 있으므로 이에 대한 조언이나 해결책을 언급한 선택지를 고르면 된다.

어휘_ **what's worse** 설상가상으로   **tutor** 개인 교사

정답_ (a)

23.

M: Where are you going now?
W: I was going to the mall.
M: Then why are you here?
W: ________________________________

(a) I just changed my mind.
(b) I am still on the other way.
(c) I will be back home.
(b) To go shopping there.

해석_ M: 지금 어디 가는 거야?

W: 쇼핑센터에 가는 중이었어.

M: 그럼 왜 여기 있니?

W: ________________________

(a) 그냥 마음이 바뀌었어.

(b) 난 여전히 반대편에 있어.

(c) 집에 돌아갈 거야.

(d) 거기서 쇼핑하려고.

해설_ 쇼핑센터에 가는 중이었는데 여기 있는 이유를 묻고 있으므로 마음이 바뀌었다고 응답한 (a)가 적절하다.

어휘_ change one's mind 마음[생각]을 바꾸다

정답_ (a)

24.

M: Are you going to go to school reunions party?
W: I forgot it! When is the party?
M: The party is January 24th at Jack's bar.
W: ___________________________________

(a) I've been looking forward to it.
(b) OK. I'll buy a bottle of wine for you.
(c) I don't know well but I'll try to help you.
(d) No matter what I'll leave that day open.

해석_ M: 동창회 모임에 갈 거야?
W: 깜박했다! 모임이 언제지?
M: 모임은 잭스 바에서 1월 24일에 있어.
W: ___________________________

(a) 난 그걸 기대해 왔어.
(b) 좋아. 널 위해 와인 한 병 살게.
(c) 난 잘 모르겠지만 널 돕기 위해 노력할게.
(d) 무슨 일이 있어도 그날은 비워 둘게.

해설_ 모임 날짜를 물어보고 확인했으므로 갈지 안 갈지에 대한 의사 표현이 이어져야 자연스럽다.

어휘_ school reunion 동창회   no matter what 무슨 일이 있어도

정답_ (d)

25.

W: Hi, Sam. Long time no see.
M: Hi, Carry. Long time no see. When did you get out of the hospital?
W: Yesterday. How have you been recently?
M: ___________________________________

(a) Let's meet together more often.
(b) Nothing special. What about you?
(c) I've been doing voluntary service for the poor for 10 years.

(d) I'm honored to meet you again.

해석_ W: 안녕하세요, 샘. 오랜만이네요.
M: 안녕하세요, 캐리. 오랜만이에요. 병원에서 언제 퇴원했어요?
W: 어제요. 요즘 어떻게 지냈어요?
M: ___________________________

(a) 좀 더 자주 함께 모여요.
(b) 특별한 거 없어요. 당신은요?
(c) 10년 동안 가난한 사람들을 위해 봉사 활동을 해왔어요.
(d) 다시 만나 뵙게 되어 영광입니다.

해설_ 어떻게 지냈는지 안부를 묻고 있으므로 이에 답하는 (b)가 정답이다.

어휘_ voluntary service 봉사 활동

정답_ (b)

26.

M: Hey! I've got a free baseball ticket from my senior.
W: Wow! It's a semifinals match.
M: Shall we go to a big game?
W: ___________________________________

(a) Are you kidding? It goes without saying.
(b) I'm sorry, but I'll try it.
(c) I think they will be a well-matched couple.
(d) How often do you go to the stadium?

해석_ M: 안녕! 선배한테 공짜 야구 경기표를 얻었어.
W: 와! 그거 준결승 시합이야.
M: 경기 보러 갈래?
W: ___________________________

(a) 농담하니? 두말하면 잔소리지.
(b) 미안해, 하지만 노력할게.
(c) 난 그들이 잘 어울리는 커플이 될 거라고 생각해.
(d) 얼마나 자주 경기장에 가니?

해설_ 경기 보러 가자는 제안에 당연히 갈 거라고 응답한 (a)가 적절하다.

어휘_ senior 선배, 상급자   semifinals match 준결승 시합   It goes without saying. 말할 나위도 없다.   well-matched 잘 어울리는

정답_ (a)

27.

M: You look pale. What's going on?

W: Am I? I've taken night duty since last month.

M: I am not sure that's the only reason. Why don't you have a physical exam?

W: ______________________________________

(a) I don't think it's serious.

(b) Wait. How should I get it done?

(c) The results of your physical examination will be done tomorrow at noon.

(d) Is it true that your mother entered the hospital?

해석_ M: 창백해 보인다. 무슨 일이니?

　　 W: 내가? 지난달부터 야근을 했어.

　　 M: 단지 그 때문만은 아닌 것 같은데. 건강검진 받아 보는 게 어때?

　　 W: ______________________________

　　 (a) 심각한 것 같지 않은데.

　　 (b) 기다려. 어떻게 끝내야 하지?

　　 (c) 네 건강검진 결과는 내일 정오에 나올 거야.

　　 (d) 네 어머니가 입원하셨다는 게 사실이야?

해설_ 남자의 건강검진 권유에 심각하게 생각하지 않는다고 응답한 (a)가 가장 적절하다.

어휘_ **look pale** 창백해 보이다　**take night duty** 야근하다　**physical exam** 건강검진　**enter the hospital** 입원하다

정답_ (a)

28.

W: I'd like to dry clean my coats.

M: OK, write down on this chart, your name and the kind of your clothes.

W: How long does it take for cleaning?

M: ______________________________________

(a) It's half past eleven.

(b) It takes around twenty miles.

(c) If you come two days later, it will be done.

(d) I'll have a day off tomorrow.

해석_ W: 코트를 드라이클리닝하고 싶어요.

　　 M: 알겠습니다, 이 차트에 손님 성함과 옷 종류를 적으세요.

　　 W: 드라이하는 데 얼마나 걸리나요?

　　 M: ______________________________

　　 (a) 11시 반이요.

　　 (b) 약 20마일 걸려요.

　　 (c) 이틀 뒤에 오면 다 돼 있을 거예요.

　　 (d) 내일 하루 쉴 거예요.

해설_ 드라이하는 데 걸리는 시간을 묻고 있으므로 정답은 (c)다.

어휘_ **dry clean** 드라이클리닝하다　**have a day off** 하루 쉬다

정답_ (c)

29.

M: Honey! What are you thinking? The light turned green.

W: Oh, I'm sorry. I was into the song.

M: We came close to hit the car.

W: ______________________________________

(a) I'll be more careful.

(b) You can say that agin!

(c) Put your seat belt on.

(d) Don't worry. Go for it!

해석_ M: 자기! 무슨 생각하고 있어? 신호가 파란불로 바뀌었어.

　　 W: 앗, 미안. 노래에 푹 빠져 있었어.

　　 M: 사고 날 뻔했잖아.

　　 W: ______________________________

　　 (a) 더 조심할게.

　　 (b) 나도 같은 생각이야!

　　 (c) 안전벨트를 매.

　　 (d) 걱정 마. 파이팅!

해설_ 하마터면 사고 날 뻔했다고 나무라고 있으므로 앞으로 더 조심하겠다는 (a)가 이어져야 자연스럽다.

어휘_ **be into** ~에 열중하다　**come close to** 하마터면 ~할 뻔하다　**Go for it!** 파이팅!

정답_ (a)

30.

M: Your camera looks expensive. Did you buy new one?

W: Yes. As you know my hobby is taking photos.

M: Did you take a photo lesson in schooldays?
W: _______________________________

(a) I've taken pictures since I was a child.
(b) No. I educated myself with a book.
(c) I was a troublemaker when I was young.
(d) People are posing in front of a statue.

해석_ M: 카메라 비싸 보인다. 새거 샀어?

W: 응. 너도 알다시피 내 취미가 사진 찍는 거잖아.

M: 학교 다닐 때 사진 수업 받았니?

W: _______________________________

(a) 어릴 때부터 사진을 찍었어.

(b) 아니. 책 보고 혼자 배웠어.

(c) 난 어렸을 때 말썽꾸러기였어.

(d) 사람들이 동상 앞에서 포즈를 취하고 있어.

해설_ 학창 시절 사진 수업을 통해 배웠냐고 질문하고 있으므로 이에 답한 (b)가 정답이다.

어휘_ schooldays 학창 시절 educate oneself 독학하다 statue 동상, 조각상

정답_ (b)

Part 3
31.
W: I wish I did not have to eat at school.
M: I agree with you. This bread is hard.
W: If I did not need to eat at school, I could eat at my home.
M: I wish I could eat at a restaurant once in a while.
W: It is a good idea. But we can not but eat this food.
M: That's terrible.

Q. What can be inferred from this conversation?

(a) Actually, hard bread is delicious.
(b) Eating at a restaurant is very expensive.
(c) Food of the cafeteria at school is not delicious.
(d) They are going to quit school.

해석_ W: 학교에서 급식을 하지 않았으면 좋겠어.

M: 동감이야. 이 빵은 딱딱해.

W: 만일 학교에서 먹지 않아도 되면, 집에서 먹을 수 있을 텐데.

M: 가끔씩 레스토랑에서 먹을 수 있으면 좋겠어.

W: 좋은 생각이야. 하지만 우린 이 음식밖에 먹을 수 없잖아.

M: 끔찍해.

Q. 이 대화를 통해 추론할 수 있는 것은?

(a) 실제로 딱딱한 빵이 맛있다.

(b) 레스토랑에서 먹는 것은 매우 비싸다.

(c) 학교 식당의 음식은 맛없다.

(d) 그들은 학교를 그만둘 것이다.

해설_ 두 사람 모두 학교 급식을 원치 않는 것으로 보아 학교 식당의 음식 맛이 별로임을 알 수 있다. 따라서 정답은 (c).

어휘_ once in a while 가끔씩, 때때로

정답_ (c)

32.
W: Hi, Mike! How are you?
M: I feel disgusted today. I think I have a headache.
W: That's terrible. Have you been to the drug store?
M: No, not yet. I'm going to my pharmacist this afternoon.
W: I hope he can give you some good medicine.
M: Me too. I think I'll rest for a while.

Q. What is correct according to the conversation?

(a) The man had an appointment with the pharmacist.
(b) The man is ill.
(c) Making an appointment with a pharmacist is important.
(d) The man is suffering from a stomachache.

해석_ W: 안녕, 마이크! 오늘 어때?

M: 오늘은 속이 메스껍다. 두통이 있나 봐.

W: 안됐구나. 약국에 다녀왔니?

M: 아니. 아직. 오늘 오후에 가보려고.

W: 약사가 좋은 약을 줬으면 좋겠다.

M: 그러게. 난 좀 쉬어야 할 것 같아.

Q. 대화에 따르면 맞는 것은 무엇인가?

(a) 남자는 약사와 약속이 돼 있었다.

(b) 남자는 아프다.

(c) 약사와 만날 약속을 정하는 것은 중요하다.

(d) 남자는 복통을 앓고 있다.

해설_ 남자의 첫 번째 대사를 통해 (b)가 정답임을 알 수 있다.

어휘_ **feel disgusted** 속이 메스껍다   **pharmacist** 약사

정답_ (b)

33.

M: Excuse me. I'd like to buy travel insurance.

W: Ok. There are two different types of insurance. One is accident insurance and the other one is comprehensive insurance.

M: I'll take the latter.

W: Good. To which country are you going and how long will you stay there?

M: I'm traveling in New Zealand for two weeks.

W: First, fill in this form. Have you brought your passport?

M: Yes, here you are.

W: While you are filling it, I'll copy your passport.

Q. What does the man want to do?

(a) Get a passport

(b) Travel to New Zealand

(c) Buy an airplane ticket

(d) Insure the journey

해석_ M: 실례합니다. 여행보험을 사고 싶은데요.

W: 네. 두 종류의 보험이 있어요. 하나는 상해보험이고, 다른 하나는 종합보험이에요.

M: 후자를 선택할게요.

W: 좋습니다. 어느 나라에 가시죠? 그리고 얼마나 머무르실 건가요?

M: 뉴질랜드에서 2주간 여행할 거예요.

W: 먼저 이 양식을 작성해 주세요. 여권 가져오셨나요?

M: 네, 여기 있어요.

W: 작성하시는 동안 여권을 복사하겠습니다.

Q. 남자는 무엇을 하기 원하는가?

(a) 여권 발급받기

(b) 뉴질랜드 여행

(c) 비행기표 사기

(d) 여행 보험 가입

해설_ 남자의 첫 번째 대사를 통해 그가 여행 보험 가입을 원한다는 것을 알 수 있다.

어휘_ **accident insurance** 상해보험   **comprehensive insurance** 종합보험   **latter** 후자   **fill in** (서류 등에) 써 넣다, 기입하다   **insure** 보험에 가입하다

정답_ (d)

34.

M: Excuse me. Can you tell me how to get to the National Theater?

W: Sure. Take bus 701 at the Hilton hotel.

M: Thank you, but I don't know where Hilton hotel is.

W: Just go across this road and walk straight ahead about half a mile.

M: That's a little long to walk. How much will it cost to go to the theater by taxi?

W: I think it will be about $4.

M: Then I'd rather take a taxi. Thank you very much.

Q. Which is correct according to the conversation?

(a) The man wants to go to the Hilton hotel.

(b) It costs $4 to take a bus.

(c) The Hilton hotel is about half a mile away from where the man and the woman are.

(d) Bus 710 goes to the National Theater.

해석_ M: 실례합니다. 국립극장에 가는 방법을 알려주실 수 있나요?

W: 물론이죠. 힐튼 호텔에서 701번 버스를 타세요.

M: 고맙습니다. 근데 힐튼 호텔이 어디에 있는지 모르는데요.

W: 이 길을 건너서 반 마일쯤 앞으로 쭉 가세요.

M: 걷기에 약간 멀군요. 택시로 극장 가는 데 요금이 얼마나 들까요?

W: 4달러쯤 될 것 같아요.

M: 그럼 택시를 타는 게 낫겠네요. 정말 고맙습니다.

Q. 대화에 따르면 맞는 것은 어느 것인가?

(a) 남자는 힐튼 호텔에 가길 원한다.

(b) 버스 타는 데 4달러가 든다.

(c) 힐튼 호텔은 남자와 여자가 있는 곳으로부터 약 반 마일 떨어져 있다.

(d) 710번 버스는 국립극장으로 간다.

해설_ 남자가 가려는 곳은 국립극장이다. 거기까지 택시 타고 가는데 드는 요금은 약 4달러쯤 된다고 했고, 국립극장으로 가는 버스는 701번이라고 했으므로 정답은 (c)가 된다.

어휘_ **National Theater** 국립극장

정답_ (c)

35.

W: What's the trouble?

M: I feel itchy in my arms and legs.

W: How long have you had that symptom?

M: For about 5 days. I think it's been since last Monday when my daughter brought a cat into my house.

W: I see. Let me run some tests on you.

M: Tests? What are those for?

W: I guess you may be allergic to cats. Some people are allergic to animals like cats and dogs. But don't worry about it. It doesn't seem that bad.

M: Thanks. Now I'm relieved of worry.

Q. What seems to be wrong with the man?

(a) The man feels itchy on his whole body.

(b) The man has an itch to raise a cat.

(c) The man has been sick since last Monday.

(d) The man might be allergic to cats.

해석_ W: 무슨 문제 있나요?

M: 팔다리가 가려워요.

W: 얼마 동안 그 증상이 있었나요?

M: 한 5일 정도요. 딸이 집에 고양이를 데려온 지난 월요일부터 이 증상이 생긴 것 같아요.

W: 알겠습니다. 몇 가지 검사를 할게요.

M: 검사요? 왜 하는 거죠?

W: 고양이 알레르기가 있으신 것 같아요. 어떤 사람들은 고양이, 개와 같은 동물들에 알레르기가 있죠. 하지만 걱정하지 마세요. 그렇게 심해 보이진 않아요.

M: 감사합니다. 이제 안심이 되네요.

Q. 남자에게 무슨 문제가 있는 것 같은가?

(a) 남자는 몸 전체에 가려움을 느낀다.

(b) 남자는 고양이를 기르고 싶어 안달이다.

(c) 남자는 지난 월요일부터 아팠다.

(d) 남자는 고양이 알레르기가 있을지도 모른다.

해설_ 여자의 마지막 대사에 고양이 알레르기가 있을지도 모른다는 말이 나오므로 (d)가 정답이다.

어휘_ **itchy** 가려운   **symptom** 증상   **run a test** 검사하다   **be allergic to** ~에 알레르기가 있다   **relieve** 안심하다   **have an itch to** ~하고 싶어 못 견디다

정답_ (d)

36.

W: Good evening, sir. Please let me check your belongings before you get on the plane.

M: Okay.

W: Anything made of metal has to be scanned. So would you put your belongings like your watch, ring or anything you have on you in this box?

M: Of course. Here it is.

W: Thank you. Well, everything is okay but the shaving foam.

M: Is that a problem to have it?

W: There is a chance it will explode during the flight.

M: Oh, I didn't know that. Then what should I do with it now?

W: We can keep it until you come back. But it will cost you $1 a day as charges for custody. You can get it back when you return.

M: I should just throw it away in that case. It's not worth that much.

Q. What does the woman want the man to do before he gets on the plane?

(a) Leave dangerous things behind

(b) Leave anything made of metal behind

(c) Throw away his shaving foam

(d) Pay $1 per day as charges for custody

해석_ W: 안녕하세요. 비행기에 탑승하시기 전에 소지품을 검사하겠습니다.

M: 좋아요.

W: 금속으로 된 것은 감지될 수 있습니다. 착용하고 계신 시계, 반지 같은 소지품을 이 상자에 넣어 주시겠어요?

M: 물론이죠. 여기 있어요.

W: 감사합니다. 음, 면도용 거품만 빼면 모두 괜찮습니다.

M: 그걸 소지하는 것이 문제가 됩니까?

W: 비행 동안 폭발할 가능성이 있어요.

M: 아, 그걸 몰랐네요. 그럼 그걸 어떻게 해야죠?

W: 돌아오실 때까지 저희가 보관해 드릴 수 있습니다. 하지만 보관비로 하루에 1달러의 비용이 듭니다. 물건은 돌아가실 때 돌려받으시면 됩니다.

M: 저 통에 버려야겠네요. 그렇게 비싸지 않거든요.

Q. 여자는 남자가 비행기를 타기 전에 무엇을 하기 원하는가?

(a) 위험한 것 두고 가기
(b) 금속으로 된 것 두고 가기
(c) 면도용 거품 버리기
(d) 보관비로 하루에 1달러 지불하기

해설_ 면도용 거품은 폭발 위험이 있어 빼야 한다고 했으므로 정답은 (a)다.

어휘_ **belonging** 소지품 **scan** 감지하다 **shaving foam** 면도용 거품 **explode** 폭발하다 **custody** 보관, 관리 **throw away** 버리다 **leave behind** 두고 가다, 뒤에 남기다

정답_ (a)

37.

W: What did you do on your weekend, Jake?

M: I went to a movie.

W: What movie?

M: I saw *Forrest Gump*. It was a great movie.

W: I heard the movie is so touching and a little funny. What did you like about it?

M: I liked everything about it, but especially the character was really interesting. He's feebleminded and he had some problem with his leg when he was young. But despite all of the difficulties, he overcame obstacles and achieved a lot of great things in his life.

W: Your opinion really makes me want to see the movie.

M: The movie is supposed to play until this Wednesday. You need to hurry up.

Q. Which is correct according to the conversation?

(a) The woman saw a movie on the weekend.
(b) The heroine in the movie is a mentally weak person.
(c) The man saw the movie on Wednesday.
(d) The man was moved by the movie.

해석_ W: 주말에 뭐 했니, 제이크?

M: 영화 보러 갔어.

W: 무슨 영화?

M: 〈포레스트 검프〉 봤어. 좋은 영화더라.

W: 영화가 무지 감동적이면서 약간은 웃기다면서. 넌 뭐가 좋았니?

M: 모든 게 다 좋았어. 하지만 특히 주인공이 매우 흥미로웠어. 그는 저능아이고, 어릴 때 다리에 문제가 있었어. 하지만 모든 어려움에도 불구하고 그는 장애를 극복했고 그의 삶에서 많은 대단한 것들을 이뤄냈어.

W: 네 말을 들으니 그 영화가 보고 싶어진다.

M: 영화는 이번 수요일까지 상영될 예정이야. 서둘러야겠다.

Q. 대화에 따르면 맞는 것은 어느 것인가?

(a) 여자는 주말에 영화를 보았다.
(b) 그 영화의 여주인공은 정신 질환자다.
(c) 남자는 수요일에 그 영화를 보았다.
(d) 남자는 그 영화에 감동받았다.

해설_ 주말에 영화를 본 것은 남자이므로 (a)는 틀리다. 또 영화에서 정신 질환자는 남자 주인공이므로 (b) 역시 맞지 않다. 따라서 정답은 (d)가 된다.

어휘_ **touching** 감동적인 **character** 주인공 **feebleminded** 정신 박약의, 저능한 **despite of** ~에도 불구하고 **obstacle** 장애물 **heroin** 여주인공 **mentally** 정신적으로 **be moved by** ~에 감동받다

정답_ (d)

38.

M: I'd like to talk with Mr. James.

W: I'm sorry, but he's not available right now.

M: Then can I talk to his partner Mr...

W: You mean Mr. Moore, right? But unfortunately they are together now and won't be back until 3 p.m.

M: I have something urgent and need to talk to either of them.

W: In that case, you should try their cell phones. Do you have their phone number?

M: I've already tried, but neither of them answers. What are they doing?

W: They're supposed to be reported about market research.

Q. Which is correct according to the conversation?

(a) The man is a partner of Mr. James.

(b) The man and Mr. James have an appointment at 3 p.m.

(c) Mr. James is a financial reporter.

(d) The man can't reach Mr. Moore now.

해석_ M: 제임스 씨와 통화하고 싶은데요.

W: 죄송하지만, 그는 지금 전화를 받을 수 없습니다.

M: 그럼 그의 동료와 통화할 수 있나요?

W: 무어 씨 말인가요? 하지만 유감스럽게도 그분들은 지금 함께 있고 3시까지 돌아오지 않을 거예요.

M: 급한 일이어서 둘 중 한 분하고 통화해야 해요.

W: 그런 경우엔 휴대폰으로 해보시는 게 좋겠는데요. 두 분 휴대폰 번호 아세요?

M: 이미 해봤는데 둘 다 전화를 안 받아요. 그들은 뭘 하고 있나요?

W: 시장조사에 대해 보고받기로 되어 있어요.

Q. 대화에 따르면 맞는 것은 어느 것인가?

(a) 남자는 제임스 씨의 파트너다.

(b) 남자와 제임스 씨는 3시에 약속이 있다.

(c) 제임스 씨는 경제 기자다.

(d) 남자는 지금 무어 씨와 연락이 되지 않는다.

해설_ 남자는 제임스 씨나 그의 파트너 무어 씨 둘 중 한 사람과 통화를 하길 원하는데 연락이 되지 않는다는 내용이므로 정답은 (d)가 된다.

어휘_ **market research** 시장조사 **financial reporter** 경제 기자

정답_ (d)

39.

M: Oh, gosh! The gas tank is almost empty.

W: No, it shouldn't be. I think the indicator is out of order.

M: Why do you think so?

W: Because I fueled the car right before I met you.

M: Hmm. Are you sure we don't need to fuel the car now?

W: Just trust me. I drove just 2 miles after fuelling.

M: Okay. But if you're wrong we'll be standing on the road to wait for help. And we'll be late for our conference.

W: Don't worry about it. We can surely run for another 50 miles.

Q. What is correct according to the conversation?

(a) The man fueled the car before he met the woman.

(b) They have a conference in 50 minutes.

(c) The woman drove 2 miles after she met the man.

(d) They will wait for help if the woman is wrong.

해석_ M: 앗, 이럴 수가! 연료 탱크가 거의 비었네.

W: 아니야, 그럴 리 없어. 표시기가 고장 난 것 같아.

M: 왜 그렇게 생각해?

W: 너 만나기 바로 직전에 기름 넣었거든.

M: 흠. 지금 차에 기름 넣을 필요가 없다고 확신해?

W: 나를 좀 믿어. 기름 넣고 겨우 2마일 운전했어.

M: 좋아. 하지만 네가 틀리면 우리는 도움을 기다리며 길에 서 있어야 할 거야. 그리고 회의에 늦을 거야.

W: 걱정 마. 50마일은 확실히 더 달릴 수 있으니까.

Q. 대화에 따르면 맞는 것은 무엇인가?

(a) 남자는 여자를 만나기 전에 차에 기름을 넣었다.

(b) 그들은 50분 후에 회의를 연다.

(c) 여자는 남자를 만난 후 2마일을 운전했다.

(d) 여자가 틀리면 그들은 도움을 기다릴 것이다.

해설_ 남자의 마지막 대사에서 여자가 틀리면 도움을 기다리며 길에

서 있어야 할 것이라고 했으므로 정답은 (d)다. 여자가 2마일
을 운전한 것은 남자를 만나기 전이므로 (c)는 틀리다.

어휘_ **indicator** 지침, 표시기 **out of order** 고장 난 **fuel** 연
료 보급을 받다, 연료를 얻다

정답_ (d)

40.

M: Where is the English literature section?

W: It's at D zone. Just turn around the corner.
What's the name of the book you want?

M: *Hucklberry Finn* by Mark Twain.

W: Just a moment. You can go to D zone and
then find number 275.

M: I see. Then, how can I check out the book?

W: You should join the site of the library
through the internet. After that, we'll issue a
card.

Q. Which is correct according to the conversation?

(a) The man is surfing the Internet.

(b) The man would like to return the book.

(c) The woman finds the book herself.

(d) The woman is working in the library.

해석_ M: 영문학 책 코너가 어디죠?

W: D 구역에 있어요. 코너만 돌면 돼요. 원하는 책 제목이 뭐
죠?

M: 마크 트웨인의 《허클베리 핀》이요.

W: 잠깐만 기다리세요. D 구역으로 가서 275번을 찾으시면
됩니다.

M: 알겠어요. 근데 그 책을 어떻게 대출받을 수 있죠?

W: 인터넷을 통해 도서관 회원 가입을 하셔야 해요. 그러고
나면 회원카드를 발급해 드려요.

Q. 대화에 따르면 맞는 것은 무엇인가?

(a) 남자는 인터넷을 검색하고 있다.

(b) 남자는 책을 반납하고 싶어 한다.

(c) 여자가 혼자 책을 찾는다.

(d) 여자는 도서관에서 일하고 있다.

해설_ 대화가 이루어지는 장소가 도서관이며, 남자가 찾는 책 코너
의 위치를 알려주는 것으로 보아 여자가 도서관에서 일하는
직원임을 알 수 있다. 따라서 정답은 (d). 남자는 책을 반납하

려는 것이 아니라 빌리려는 것이므로 (b)는 맞지 않다.

어휘_ **zone** 지역, 구역 **surf** 인터넷 상의 정보를 찾아다니다

정답_ (d)

41.

M: Hello. May I help you?

W: I want to stay in your hotel. Do you have a
single room for one?

M: Sure. When are you planning to stay here?

W: It's from July 15th to the 19th. Four days.
And how much is the room rate?

M: The single room is 59 dollars per night.

W: Please make a reservation. Could I use a
gym in the hotel?

M: Sure, but you should pay small extra fee.

Q. Which is correct according to the conversation?

(a) The woman confirmed a reservation.

(b) The woman reserved the room.

(c) The man paid by credit card.

(d) The man used the gym.

해석_ M: 안녕하세요? 무엇을 도와 드릴까요?

W: 당신네 호텔에 머무르려고 하는데요. 싱글 룸 있나요?

M: 물론입니다. 언제 머무를 예정이신가요?

W: 7월 15일부터 19일까지 4일간요. 방값은 얼마인가요?

M: 싱글 룸은 하룻밤에 59달러입니다.

W: 예약해 주세요. 호텔 헬스장을 이용할 수 있나요?

M: 물론입니다. 하지만 약간의 추가 요금을 내셔야 합니다.

Q. 대화에 따르면 맞는 것은 어느 것인가?

(a) 여자는 예약을 확인했다.

(b) 여자는 방을 예약했다.

(c) 남자는 신용카드로 지불했다.

(d) 남자는 헬스장을 사용했다.

해설_ 여자가 호텔에 예약을 하려는 상황이므로 정답은 (b)다.

어휘_ **make a reservation** 예약하다 **extra fee** 추가 요금
confirm 확인하다

정답_ (b)

42.

M: Sarah, what are you doing this Saturday?

W: I don't have any plans. Why?

M: How about going to the movies with me? I got two tickets for the movie *D-WAR*.

W: That sounds great. What time is the movie playing?

M: 4 p.m. We could have dinner afterward. I know a good Chinese restaurant around there.

W: It sounds perfect. Then dinner will be on me.

M: OK. I'll meet you 20 minutes before the movie.

Q. Which is correct according to the conversation?

(a) The woman likes Chinese movies.

(b) The man will buy dinner for the woman.

(c) They will meet at 3:40.

(d) The man is interested in war.

해석_ M: 사라, 이번 토요일에 뭐 할 거야?

W: 아무 계획 없는데. 왜?

M: 나랑 영화 보러 가는 거 어때? 〈디 워〉라는 영화표가 두 장 있는데.

W: 그거 좋은 생각이다. 몇 시 건데?

M: 4시. 영화 보고 나서 저녁 먹을 수 있어. 그 근처에 괜찮은 중국 음식점을 알고 있지.

W: 완벽한 것 같아. 그럼 저녁은 내가 살게.

M: 좋아. 영화 보기 20분 전에 만나자.

Q. 대화에 따르면 맞는 것은 어느 것인가?

(a) 여자는 중국 영화를 좋아한다.

(b) 남자는 여자에게 저녁을 사줄 것이다.

(c) 그들은 3시 40분에 만날 것이다.

(d) 남자는 전쟁에 관심이 있다.

해설_ 두 사람은 4시 상영 영화를 볼 예정이고, 영화 시작 20분 전에 만나기로 했으므로 (c)가 정답이다. 저녁은 여자가 사겠다고 했으므로 (b)는 틀리다.

어휘_ **afterward** 나중에

정답_ (c)

43.

M: Hello. Can I speak with Miss Jane?

W: Yes, this is she.

M: Hi, this is Tom. I'm calling to ask you about the apartment you advertised for rent. Is it still available?

W: Yes, it is. Please feel free to ask about it.

M: Ok, thanks. I saw the ad says the rent for the apartment is $600 a month. Does it include all utilities?

W: No, you will have to pay for all the bills except tap water.

M: And what about furniture? Is it furnished?

W: There is a queen-sized bed, a washing machine and a refrigerator in it.

Q. What is correct according to the conversation?

(a) The apartment was just sold.

(b) The tenant will have to pay the tap water bill.

(c) The rent is $600 a year.

(d) There is a king-sized bed in the apartment.

해석_ M: 여보세요. 제인 양과 통화할 수 있나요?

W: 네, 전데요.

M: 안녕하세요, 저는 탐입니다. 세를 놓으신다고 광고한 아파트에 대해 여쭤 보려고 전화드렸는데요. 아직 안 나갔나요?

W: 네. 서슴지 마시고 물어보세요.

M: 네, 감사합니다. 집세가 한 달에 600달러라고 나와 있던데요. 거기에 모든 공공요금이 포함돼 있나요?

W: 아니요, 수도세만 빼고 나머지 요금들은 따로 내셔야 합니다.

M: 가구는 어떤가요? 가구는 구비돼 있나요?

W: 퀸 사이즈 침대와 세탁기, 냉장고가 있습니다.

Q. 대화에 따르면 맞는 것은 무엇인가?

(a) 아파트는 방금 팔렸다.

(b) 세 든 사람은 수도세를 내야 할 것이다.

(c) 집세는 1년에 600달러다.

(d) 아파트에 킹 사이즈 침대가 있다.

해설_ 아파트 임대 광고를 본 남자가 전화상으로 여자에게 궁금한 점을 묻고 있는 대화 내용이다. 아파트는 아직 안 나갔으며, 집세는 한 달에 600달러이고, 퀸 사이즈 침대가 있다고 했으므로 정답은 (b)가 된다.

어휘_ **advertise** 광고하다   **feel free to** 주저 말고 ~하다
utilities 공공요금   **tap water** 수돗물   **furnished** 가구
가 갖춰진   **washing machine** 세탁기   **refrigerator** 냉
장고   **tenant** 세 든 사람

정답_ (b)

44.

W: May I help you set the table?

M: Yes, I'd like a table for 6.

W: I'm sorry, sir. There is no free table for 6
people right now.

M: Oh, I should have made a reservation. How
long do we have to wait?

W: I'm afraid you'll have to wait for about 30
minutes.

M: Wow, it's a little long to wait.

W: As you know, it's the weekend and it's
almost 7:00. It won't be easy to find a good
place without any waiting.

M: That's right. We should stay here and wait.

Q. Which is correct according to the conversation?

(a) The man was late for about 30 minutes.

(b) The man wants to buy a table for six.

(c) The woman suggested that the man wait for
the table.

(d) The man made a reservation at 7.

해석_ W: 자리 정하는 것을 도와 드릴까요?

　　M: 네, 6인용 테이블을 원합니다.

　　W: 죄송하지만, 손님. 6인용 테이블은 지금 빈 자리가 없습니
　　　　다.

　　M: 아, 예약을 했었야 했는데. 얼마나 기다려야 하나요?

　　W: 죄송하지만, 약 30분 정도 기다리셔야 합니다.

　　M: 와, 기다리기에 좀 긴 시간이군요.

　　W: 아시다시피, 주말이고 거의 7시라서요. 기다리지 않으면
　　　　좋은 자리 찾기가 쉽지 않을 겁니다.

　　M: 맞아요. 여기 있으면서 기다려야겠어요.

　　Q. 대화에 따르면 맞는 것은 어느 것인가?

　　(a) 남자는 약 30분 늦었다.

　　(b) 남자는 6인용 테이블을 사기 원한다.

(c) 여자는 남자에게 테이블 자리가 나기를 기다릴 것을 제안
했다.

(d) 남자는 7시에 예약을 했다.

해설_ 6인용 테이블을 원하는 남자 손님에게 여종업원이 지금은 빈
자리가 없으며, 주말이고 7시라 사람들이 많기 때문에 좋은
자리를 얻기 위해서는 기다려야 한다고 했으므로 정답은 (c)
가 된다.

어휘_ **wait for a table** (식당에서) 자리가 나기를 기다리다

정답_ (c)

45.

M: Brenda, you look so pale. Are you okay?

W: Not really. I don't know what's wrong with
me. I have a fever and feel a little nauseous.

M: I think you should take the day off and go to
see a doctor.

W: But I have important things to do today.
There is a deal with a construction company.

M: Honey, you need some care and to take a
rest. I'll call John and let him know about
your condition now. I'm sure he can take
care of your job.

W: Okay, thanks. I'll just stay in bed.

Q. Which is correct according to the conversation?

(a) The woman has a cold.

(b) The man is trying to let the woman relax.

(c) John will take care of the woman's job.

(d) The woman works in a construction
company.

해석_ M: 브렌다, 많이 창백해 보여. 괜찮아?

　　W: 아니. 뭐가 잘못된 건지 모르겠어. 열이 나고 메스꺼워.

　　M: 하루 휴가 내고 병원에 가 보는 게 좋을 것 같아.

　　W: 하지만 오늘 중요한 일이 있어. 건설회사와 거래가 있거
　　　　든.

　　M: 자기야, 당신은 치료를 받고 쉬어야 해. 존한테 전화해서
　　　　지금 당신 몸 상태를 알려야겠어. 그가 틀림없이 당신 일을
　　　　처리할 수 있을 거야.

　　W: 알았어, 고마워. 그냥 침대에서 쉴게.

　　Q. 대화에 따르면 맞는 것은 어느 것인가?

(a) 여자는 감기에 걸렸다.

(b) 남자는 여자를 쉬게 하려고 애쓰고 있다.

(c) 존은 여자의 일을 처리할 것이다.

(d) 여자는 건설회사에서 일한다.

해설_ 남자가 몸 상태가 안 좋은 여자에게 하루 쉬도록 설득하는 내용이므로 정답은 (b)다. 여자가 감기에 걸린 건지는 알 수 없으므로 (a)는 틀리다. 또 여자가 건설회사와 거래를 하는 것이지 거기서 일하는 것은 아니며, 존이 실제 여자의 일을 처리해 줄지는 알 수 없으므로 (c), (d) 역시 오답이다.

어휘_ **have a fever** 열이 있다 **nauseous** 메스꺼운, 역겨운 **take the day off** 하루 휴가를 내다 **take a rest** 쉬다

정답_ (b)

Part 4

46.

About 15 percent of an average American family's income is spent on food. Planning ahead will help to make sure that you will get the most for your money. The first step is to prepare a menu of meals for several days or even for a week or two. Next, make a grocery list of foods you will need to prepare the meals on the menu. Follow this list closely when you shop.

Q. What is the main topic of this talk?

(a) Preparing a menu of meals
(b) Planning ahead for grocery shopping
(c) American family's food shopping
(d) Saving money in preparing breakfast

해석_ 평균 미국인 가정의 수입의 약 15%가 음식에 소비된다. 미리 계획을 세우는 것은 돈을 가장 잘 활용할 수 있게 하는 데 도움이 될 것이다. 첫 단계는 며칠간, 심지어는 1, 2주간의 식사 메뉴를 준비하는 것이다. 그 다음엔 메뉴상의 식사를 준비하기 위해 필요한 식품 구매 목록을 만들어라. 쇼핑할 때 이 목록을 면밀히 따라가라.

Q. 이 담화의 주제는 무엇인가?

(a) 식사 메뉴 준비하기
(b) 식료품 쇼핑 미리 계획하기
(c) 미국 가정의 장보기
(d) 아침 준비에 드는 돈 절약하기

해설_ 미리 쇼핑 계획을 짜 두면 돈을 절약할 수 있다는 게 이 글의 중심 내용이다. 따라서 정답은 (b).

어휘_ **make sure (that)** 확신하다, 꼭 ~하다 **get the most for** ~을 최대한 활용하다(= make the most of) **grocery list** 구매할 물품 목록

정답_ (b)

47.

Do you have a favorite picture of one of our country's national parks, memorials or monuments? People are blessed with the beauty and splendor of our protected national parks, monuments and memorials on the site. Upload your photos before February 6. Then come back again and again to view new entries and cast your vote for the best picture. One vote per user per day! Voting begins February 7 and ends February 10.

Q. What is the purpose of this announcement?

(a) To advertise a photo contest
(b) To give directions to the national park
(c) To inquire about the information
(d) To celebrate monuments

해석_ 국립공원이나 기념비, 또는 기념물 중 좋아하는 사진을 가지고 있나요? 사람들은 웹사이트 상에서 보호 대상의 국립공원, 기념비, 기념물의 아름다움이나 화려함을 볼 수 있는 행운을 누리고 있는데요. 2월 6일 전에 가지고 계신 사진들을 업로드 시켜 주세요. 그런 다음, 새로 올라온 사진들을 보고 가장 좋다고 생각되는 사진에 투표하기 위해 다시 오세요. 하루 한 사람 당 한 표씩! 투표는 2월 7일 시작해서 2월 10일에 끝납니다.

Q. 이 광고의 목적은 무엇인가?

(a) 사진 콘테스트를 선전하기 위해
(b) 국립공원의 방향을 알려주기 위해
(c) 정보에 대해 묻기 위해
(d) 기념물을 축하하기 위해

해설_ 국립공원이나 기념물 사진 콘테스트가 있을 예정임을 광고하고 있으므로 정답은 (a)가 된다.

어휘_ **memorial** 기념관, 기념비 **monument** 기념물, 유물 **be blessed** 행운을 누리다 **splendor** 훌륭함, 빛남, 화려함 **upload** 소형 컴퓨터에서 대형 컴퓨터로 전송하다

entry 참가자, 등록 **cast a vote** 투표하다 **inquire** 묻다

48.

A structure fire Thursday evening at a house in the 1300 block of SE Fifth Avenue destroyed the residence of an Oak Harbor couple and killed two of their pets. Oak Harbor Fire Lt. Ray Merrill said no one was home at the time the department received the call at approximately 8:43 p.m. The interior of the residence was gutted and firefighters had to cut into the roof to extinguish hot spots in the insulation. In winter, we must care about the fire.

Q. What is the main point the speaker is trying to make?

(a) Preventing the fire must be demanded in a dry season such as winter.

(b) The boys playing with fire were arrested.

(c) Firefighters have a hard time living in winter.

(d) These days, the couples thoughtlessly spend money to buy a present.

해석_ 목요일 저녁 SE 5번가 1300 블록의 한 집에서 발생한 화재로 오크 하버에 사는 어느 한 부부의 주택이 전소되었고, 그들의 애완동물 두 마리가 숨졌습니다. 오크 하버 소방위 레이 메릴은 대략 저녁 8시 43분쯤 소방서에서 전화를 받았을 당시에 집 안에는 아무도 없었다고 말했습니다. 집 내부는 타버렸고, 소방관들은 단열재 안의 불이 가장 많이 붙은 지점을 진화하기 위해 지붕을 절단해야 했습니다. 겨울철에는 화재에 각별히 신경을 써야 합니다.

Q. 화자가 말하고자 하는 요지는 무엇인가?

(a) 겨울철과 같은 건조기에는 화재 예방이 꼭 필요하다.

(b) 불장난을 하고 있는 소년들이 체포되었다.

(c) 소방관들은 겨울철에 생활하는 데 어려움을 겪는다.

(d) 요즘에 커플들은 선물을 사는 데 돈을 무분별하게 쓴다.

해설_ 주택에서 발생한 화재 사건을 언급하면서 겨울철에는 화재에 특히 더 신경 써야 한다고 말했으므로 정답은 (a)다.

어휘_ **structure fire** 구조물 화재(구조물의 내부, 상부, 하부 구조재 등에 접한 화재) **destroy** 파괴하다, 전소시키다 **residence**

주택 **interior** 내부 **gut** (건물의) 내부를 파괴하다[태워버리다] **cut into** ~을 자르다 **roof** 지붕 **extinguish** 끄다 **insulation** 단열재 **dry season** 건조기 **thoughlessly** 무분별하게

49.

Inspired by a former classmate Parker's battle against cancer, Hilliard Davidson High School graduate Brian Shesky has organized a benefit to raise funds for cancer research. Parker was diagnosed with Hodgkin's lymphoma during his junior year at Indiana University. After chemotherapy, his disease went into remission. Within the past year, the cancer came back. Parker has undergone a stem cell transplant and is battling the disease again.

Q. Which is correct according to the report?

(a) Shesky has organized a benefit to raise funds for cancer research.

(b) Shesky was diagnosed with Hodgkin's lymphoma.

(c) A stem cell transplant seems to help the patients.

(d) Shesky gave his friend some money for a benefit.

해석_ 옛 급우인 파커의 암 투병에 의해 영감을 받은, 힐리어드 데이비슨 고등학교 졸업생 브라이언 셰스키는 암 연구를 위한 기금 마련을 위해 자선 공연을 조직했습니다. 파커는 인디애나 대학 3학년 때 호지킨 임파선 암 진단을 받았습니다. 화학요법을 받은 후 그의 병은 완화되었습니다. 지난해 암이 재발했습니다. 파커는 줄기세포 이식을 받고 다시 병과 싸우고 있습니다.

Q. 기사에 따르면 맞는 것은 어느 것인가?

(a) 셰스키는 암 연구를 위한 기금 마련을 위해 자선 공연을 조직했다.

(b) 셰스키는 호지킨 임파선 암으로 진단받았다.

(c) 줄기세포 이식이 환자들에게 도움이 되는 것 같다.

(d) 셰스키는 자선 공연을 위해 그의 친구에게 돈을 주었다.

해설_ 글 첫 부분에 셰스키가 암 연구 기금 마련을 위해 자선 공연을

조직했다는 내용이 나오므로 정답은 (a)다. 암과 투병하는 것은 셰스키가 아니라 그의 옛 급우인 파커이므로 (b)는 틀리다.

어휘_ **inspired by** ∼에 의해 영감을 받은 **benefit** 자선 공연 **diagnose** 진단하다 **Hodgkin's lymphoma** 호지킨 임파선암 **chemotherapy** 화학요법 **go into remission** 완화되다 **undergo** (수술을) 받다 **stem cell transplant** 줄기세포 이식

정답_ (a)

50.

What causes the differences in intelligence? This is one of the oldest and most enduring questions in all of psychology. As reasonable as it may sound, the question does not have a reasonable answer. There is some evidence that intelligence tends to run in families and may be due in part to innate, inherited factors. There are also data that tell us that a person's environment can and does affect intellectual, cognitive functioning.

Q. What is the speaker mainly talking about?

(a) Functions of intelligence
(b) Nature versus nurture
(c) Inherited factors of families
(d) From heredity to cognitive functioning

해석_ 무엇이 지능의 차이를 야기하는가? 이것은 심리학의 모든 분야에 있어서 가장 오래되고 가장 지속적인 질문들 중 하나이다. 이 질문이 합당하게 들릴지는 몰라도, 여기에는 합당한 답이 없다. 지능은 유전적인 경향이 있으며, 부분적으로 타고난 유전적인 요소에 의한 것일지도 모른다는 일부 증거가 있다. 또한 한 개인의 환경이 지적, 인지적 기능에 영향을 미칠 수 있으며 실제 영향을 미친다고 말해 주는 자료들도 있다.

Q. 화자는 주로 무엇에 대해 이야기하고 있는가?

(a) 지능의 기능
(b) 천성 vs. 양육
(c) 가족의 유전적 요소들
(d) 유전에서부터 인식적 기능까지

해설_ 지능의 차이는 유전적 요소에 의한 것이기도 하지만 환경적 요소에 의해서도 야기된다는 두 가지 얘기를 하고 있으므로 정답은 (b)가 된다.

어휘_ **intelligence** 지능 **enduring** 영속하는, 지속적인 **psychology** 심리학 **tend to** ∼하는 경향이 있다 **run in the family** (유전적 요소가) 가계를 따라 흐르다 **in part** 부분적으로 **innate** 타고난, 선천적인 **inherited** 물려받은 **factor** 요소, 요인 **cognitive** 인식의, 인식력 있는 **functioning** 기능

정답_ (b)

51.

A woman has described escaping from the wreckage of her home after it was hit by a plane which crashed yesterday, killing all 49 people aboard and one person inside the house. The cause of the disaster was under investigation, but other pilots were overheard around the same time complaining of ice building up on their wings — a hazard that has caused major crashes in the past.

Q. What is the report mainly about?

(a) The investigation about the cause of the accident
(b) A bad habit of overhearing
(c) The murder arisen in the plane for New York
(d) The crash accident by plane

해석_ 한 여성이, 어제 탑승객 49명 전원과 (사고 지점) 주택에 있던 주민 1명의 목숨을 앗아간 비행기 추락사고로 인해 무너진 그녀의 집 잔해 속에서 탈출했던 상황을 설명했습니다. 그 대참사의 원인은 조사 중에 있었습니다만, 사고가 났을 때쯤 다른 조종사들은 여태껏 대형 추락사고를 야기시킨 위험 요소인 비행기 날개에 쌓이는 얼음에 대해 불만을 얘기한 것으로 알려졌습니다.

Q. 주로 무엇에 관한 기사인가?

(a) 사고 원인에 대한 조사
(b) 엿듣는 나쁜 습관
(c) 뉴욕행 비행기에서 발생한 살인사건
(d) 비행기 추락사고

해설_ 비행기 추락사고로 무너진 집 잔해 속에서 한 여성이 탈출을 했고 그 사고 원인을 조사 중에 있다는 내용이므로 정답은 (d)가 된다.

어휘_ **wreckage** 잔해, 파편 **crash** (비행기가) 추락하다

overheard 우연히 듣다, 엿듣다   **wing** 날개   **hazard** 위험 요소   **murder** 살인 (사건)   **arise** 일어나다, 생기다

정답_ (d)

52.

A Lodi police officer staking out a gas station that has been robbed four times in the last three months made a different kind of arrest Friday morning after a woman allegedly propositioned him. The woman, 30-year-old Christina Marie Singh, of Manteca, allegedly asked for $30 in exchange for sex. Then, after she was arrested, she said she just wanted a ride to Jackson and wouldn't have really charged the officer, according to a police report.

Q. What is the report about?

(a) A change of official position
(b) The arrest of a woman
(c) A robbed gas station
(d) A woman's innocence

해석_ 지난 3개월 동안 네 차례 강도를 당한 주유소를 감시하던 로디 경관은 전하는 바에 의하면 한 여자가 매춘을 제안한 후 금요일 오전 강도 사건과는 무관하게 체포했습니다. 만테카의 서른 살 크리스티나 마리 싱은 전하는 바에 의하면 섹스의 대가로 30달러를 요구했습니다. 경찰 보고에 따르면, 체포된 후 그녀는 단지 잭슨과 섹스하기를 원했고, 그에게 실제 돈을 지불하라고 하지는 않았을 것이라고 말했다고 합니다.

Q. 무엇에 관한 기사인가?

(a) 공직의 변경
(b) 한 여성의 체포
(c) 강도당한 주유소
(d) 한 여성의 무죄

해설_ 강도질이 아닌 매춘 행위로 여자를 체포한 사건을 다루고 있으므로 정답은 (b)가 된다.

어휘_ **stake out** 감시하다   **gas station** 주유소   **rob** 강탈하다, 강도질하다   **make an arrest** 체포하다   **allegedly** 전하는 바에 의하면   **proposition** 유혹하다, 수작을 걸다   **in exchange for** ~의 대가로   **ride** 성교   **charge** 부과하다, 청구하다   **indicate** 암시하다, 보여 주다   **insist**

주장하다   **innocence** 무죄

정답_ (b)

53.

Two women were injured Sunday morning when their Toyota Camry left the road and crashed into a wall near the intersection of Bailey and Canal roads in Bay Point, the California Highway Patrol reported. Rosalinda Carranza, 49, and an unidentified woman were taken by ambulance to John Muir Medical Center in Walnut Creek where they were listed in stable condition Sunday night.

Q. What is the best title for this report?

(a) Have a balanced condition
(b) The danger of excessive traffic
(c) Stay in California Highway
(d) Two injured in Bay Point crash

해석_ 일요일 아침 여성 두 명이 그들이 타고 있던 도요타 캠리 자동차가 도로를 벗어나 베이 포인트의 베일리와 커넬 도로의 교차로 부근의 벽을 들이받아 부상을 입었다고 캘리포니아 고속도로 순찰대가 전했습니다. 49세의 로잘린다 카렌자와 신원이 밝혀지지 않은 한 여성은 월넛 크리크에 있는 존 뮤어 의료 센터로 후송되어 일요일 밤 안정을 찾은 것으로 알려졌습니다.

Q. 이 기사에 가장 적절한 제목은 무엇인가?

(a) 안정된 몸 상태를 가지다
(b) 과잉 교통의 위험
(c) 캘리포니아 고속도로에 머무르다
(d) 베이 포인트 충돌 사고로 두 명이 부상당하다

해설_ 자동차 충돌 사고로 두 명이 부상을 당했다는 소식을 전하고 있으므로 (d)가 적절하다.

어휘_ **patrol** 순찰대   **unidentified** 신원 불명의   **stable** 안정된

정답_ (d)

54.

In the developed world, recycling is a moral act, done primarily as expatiation for consumption. The average citizen rarely considers the economic value or cost of his or her sorted paper, cans, and bottles; sorting such materials is a civic duty. Meanwhile, in the developing world, recycling is an economic act, done primarily for income. The average citizen rarely considers the environmental benefit of selling his or her paper, cans, and bottles to the local scrap peddlers.

Q. What is the main idea of the talk?

(a) The average citizen rarely thinks they should recycle materials.
(b) In developed countries, few people are diligent.
(c) Between developed countries and developing countries, the perception of recycling is different.
(d) In poor countries, the people are arrogant.

해석_ 선진국에서 재활용은 도덕적 행위이며, 주로 소비에 대한 부연적 설명처럼 행해집니다. 대부분의 국민들은 분리된 종이, 깡통, 병의 경제적 가치나 비용을 거의 생각지 않습니다. 그러한 물품들을 분리하는 것은 국민의 의무입니다. 한편, 개발도상국에서 재활용은 경제적 행위이며, 주로 수입을 위해 행해집니다. 대부분의 국민들은 종이, 깡통, 병을 지역 고물상에 파는 것에 대한 환경적인 이로움을 거의 생각지 않습니다.

Q. 담화의 주제는 무엇인가?

(a) 일반 시민들은 물품들을 재활용해야 한다고 생각하는 경우가 드물다.
(b) 선진국에는 부지런한 국민들이 거의 없다.
(c) 선진국과 개발도상국 간에 재활용에 대한 인식이 다르다.
(d) 후진국에서는 국민들이 거만하다.

해설_ 선진국에서 재활용은 도덕적 행위이자 소비의 부연적 설명처럼 행해지는 반면, 개발도상국에서 재활용은 경제 활동이며 주로 소득을 위해 행해진다는 내용이므로 (c)가 정답이다.

어휘_ **recycling** 재활용 **moral** 도덕적인 **primarily** 주로 **expatiation** 상세한 설명, 부연 **rarely** 드물게, 좀처럼 **sorted** 잘 정리된, 분류된 **civic duty** 시민의 의무 **scrap peddler** 고물상 **perception** 인식 **arrogant** 거만한

정답_ (c)

Pancreatic cancer is one of the most dreaded of malignancies; the overall survival rate is barely 5 percent at five years, in stark contrast to the 80 to 90 percent five-year overall survival rate of prostate and breast cancer victims. Sadly, only 13 percent survive one year after diagnosis.

Q. Which of the following best summarizes the talk?

(a) Most of all malignancies are very fatal to patients.
(b) Breast cancer gives women a sense of frustration.
(c) Without curing well, the patients who have prostate cancer will die.
(d) Pancreatic cancer is more dangerous than any other cancer.

해석_ 췌장암은 가장 두려운 악성 종양 중 하나입니다. 전립선암과 유방암 환자들의 5년 전체 생존율이 80~90%인 것과는 완전히 대조적으로, 5년간 전체 생존율이 5%밖에 되지 않습니다. 애석하게도, 오직 13%만이 췌장암 선고를 받고 1년간 생존합니다.

Q. 담화의 내용을 가장 잘 요약한 것은?

(a) 대부분의 악성 종양들은 환자들에게 매우 치명적이다.
(b) 유방암은 여성들에게 좌절감을 안겨 준다.
(c) 치료를 잘 받지 않으면, 전립선암 환자들은 죽을 것이다.
(d) 췌장암은 다른 어떤 암보다 더 위험하다.

해설_ 췌장암이 가장 두려운 악성 종양 중 하나이며 생존율도 전립선암이나 유방암과 완전 대조적으로 매우 낮다는 내용이므로 (d)가 적당하다.

어휘_ **pancreatic cancer** 췌장암 **dreded** 두려운, 무서운 **malignancy** 악성 종양 **overall survival rate** 전체 생존율 **stark** 극명한, 완전한 **prostate cancer** 전립선암 **breast cancer** 유방암 **a sense of frustration** 좌절감

정답_ (d)

56

Anthony Kim matched the best score of the

week with a 5-under 67, taking a one-shot lead when Jim Furyk found the water for double bogey on the 18th hole at the Chevron World Challenge on Saturday. Kim was worried about rust coming off a five-week break, but his putter worked just fine in making six birdies at Sherwood Country Club.

Q. Which sport is the speaker mainly talking about?

(a) Football
(b) Golf
(c) Archery
(d) Shooting

해석_ 앤서니 김은, 토요일 Chevron World Challenge에서 짐 퓨릭의 18번 홀 더블 보기가 물에 빠지면서 한 점 차 앞서 나가면서 5언더파 67타로 이번주 최고 기록을 경신했습니다. 김은 5주 휴가 동안 무뎌졌을까 걱정했었지만, 셔우드 컨트리 클럽 경기장에서 버디 6개를 성공시키면서 그의 타구는 잘 들어맞았습니다.

Q. 화자는 주로 어떤 스포츠에 관해 이야기하고 있는가?

(a) 축구
(b) 골프
(c) 양궁
(d) 사격

해설_ double bogey(더블 보기), hole(홀) 등의 단어를 통해 골프 경기에 대한 내용임을 알 수 있다.

어휘_ **rust** (재능 따위가) 무디어짐　**come off** (장소를) 떠나다　**putter** 타구채

정답_ (b)

57.

Pathology is the cornerstone of modern medicine. The science, which seeks to understand disease and disease processes, has replaced the myth and superstition of traditional medicine with a rational basis for care of the unwell. Judging by the popularity of television dramas like *CSI* and *Silent Witness*, in which pathologists solve baffling murder cases, the speciality should be flourishing. Yet today many people have become actively hostile towards the profession.

Q. What can be inferred from this talk?

(a) These days many people underestimate the importance of Pathology.
(b) People will imitate a crime after showing a TV drama like *CSI*.
(c) The traditional medicine is now extinct.
(d) Pathologists who have the special license should serve the nation.

해석_ 병리학은 현대 의학의 초석입니다. 질병과 질병 과정을 이해하고자 노력하는 그 학문은 몸이 좋지 않은 사람들을 합리적인 기준으로 간호함으로써 민간요법에 대한 미신을 대체했습니다. 병리학자들이 미궁에 빠진 살인 사건을 해결하는 〈CSI〉와 〈Silent Witness〉와 같은 TV 드라마의 인기에 비춰 볼 때 그 전공은 번영되어야 합니다. 그러나 오늘날 많은 사람들이 그 직업을 매우 적대시하고 있습니다.

Q. 이 담화를 통해 추론할 수 있는 것은?

(a) 요즘 많은 사람들이 병리학의 중요성을 과소평가하고 있다.
(b) 사람들은 〈CSI〉 같은 TV 드라마를 보고 난 후 범죄를 모방할 것이다.
(c) 민간요법은 현재 사라졌다.
(d) 특별한 자격증을 소지하고 있는 병리학자들은 사회에 공헌해야 한다.

해설_ 병리학은 현대 의학의 초석이며 번창해야 하는 직업임에도 많은 사람들이 적대감을 가지고 있다는 내용이므로 (a)가 정답임을 알 수 있다. 병리학이 민간요법을 대체한 것일 뿐 민간요법 자체가 사라진 것은 아니므로 (c)는 맞지 않다.

어휘_ **pathology** 병리학　**cornerstone** 초석　**myth** 신화　**superstition** 미신　**unwell** 몸이 편치 않은　**popularity** 인기　**baffling** 불가해한　**speciality** 전공　**flourishing** 번영하는　**actively** 적극적으로　**hostile** 적대적인　**profession** 직업　**underestimate** 과소평가하다　**imitate** 모방하다　**extinct** 사라진, 멸종된

정답_ (a)

58.

Lincoln was born in Kentucky on February 12, 1809. His parents were poor farmers and uneducated. Lincoln attended school for no more than a year. But he read every chance he got. He did not go to law school. Instead, he studied on his own and earned a law license. In 1858, Lincoln ran for the U.S. Senate. He spoke against slavery. Lincoln did not win the Senate seat, but his words impressed voters. Two years later, he was elected as the 16th President of the United States.

Q. Which of the following is NOT true according to the talk?

(a) Lincoln's parents weren't taught in law school.
(b) Lincoln opposed slavery.
(c) After Lincoln had been in the Senate, he was elected as President.
(d) Lincoln isn't the 6th President of the United States.

해석_ 링컨은 1809년 2월 12일 켄터키에서 태어났습니다. 그의 부모님들은 가난한 농부였고 교육을 받지 못했습니다. 링컨은 겨우 1년밖에 학교를 다니지 못했습니다. 그러나 그는 기회가 날 때마다 책을 읽었습니다. 그는 법대에 다니지 않았습니다. 대신 그는 독학을 하여 변호사 자격증을 취득했습니다. 1858년에 링컨은 미 상원의원에 출마했습니다. 그는 노예 제도에 반대하는 연설을 했습니다. 링컨은 상원의원에 낙방했지만, 그의 연설은 유권자들을 감동시켰습니다. 2년 후, 그는 미국의 제16대 대통령으로 선출되었습니다.

Q. 담화에 따르면 사실이 아닌 것은 어느 것인가?

(a) 링컨의 부모는 법대에서 교육받지 않았다.
(b) 링컨은 노예 제도에 반대했다.
(c) 링컨은 상원의원이 되고 나서 대통령으로 선출됐다.
(d) 링컨은 미국의 제 6대 대통령이 아니다.

해설_ 상원의원에 낙방한 후 2년 뒤에 미국의 제16대 대통령으로 선출됐으므로 (c)가 틀리다.

어휘_ **uneducated** 교육을 받지 못한 **law license** 변호사 자격증 **run for** ~에 출마하다 **slavery** 노예 제도 **impress** 감동시키다 **voter** 투표자, 유권자

정답_ (c)

59.

A big rig driver who crashed into other vehicles that had stopped for a draw bridge on Highway 12 last summer was fined $280 Friday for the death of a man in that crash. Edwin Soper, 57, of Diamond Springs, will also be on probation and pay restitution, which will be determined at a later date. He received no jail time, a punishment that upset the victim's widow.

Q. Which is referred to in this report?

(a) A big rig driver crashed into a street tree.
(b) A big rig driver felt good, despite the car's collision.
(c) A big rig driver received no jail time.
(d) In spring, car accidents often happen.

해석_ 지난 여름 12번 간선도로의 가동교 때문에 멈췄던 다른 차량들과 충돌한 대형 트럭 운전 기사는 그 충돌로 인해 발생한 한 남자의 사망 사고로 금요일 280달러의 벌금을 부과받았습니다. 다이아몬드 스프링스의 57세 에드윈 소퍼는 또한 집행유예를 선고받게 될 것이며, 손해 배상을 하게 될 것입니다. 이는 추후에 정해질 것입니다. 그는 형을 선고받지 않았고, 이러한 처벌이 희생자의 미망인의 심기를 불편하게 했습니다.

Q. 이 기사에 언급된 것은 어느 것인가?

(a) 대형 트럭 운전사가 가로수와 충돌했다.
(b) 대형 트럭 운전사는 자동차 충돌에도 불구하고 기분이 좋았다.
(c) 대형 트럭 운전사는 형을 선고받지 않았다.
(d) 봄에는 차 사고가 자주 발생한다.

해설_ 마지막 문장에 남자가 형을 선고받지 않았다는 내용이 나와 있으므로 정답은 (c)다.

어휘_ **rig** 버스, 트럭 **draw bridge** 가동교(可動橋), 들어 올리는 다리 **fine** 벌금을 과하다 **on probation** 집행유예로 **restitution** 손해 배상 **at a later date** 추후에 **jail time** 감옥형 **punishment** 형벌, 처벌 **victim** 희생자 **widow** 과부, 미망인 **collision** 충돌

정답_ (c)

60.

Wind peeled the roof off a home on Old

Anderson Quarry Road at 6:30 Sunday evening. Libby Trivette was home alone when the entire house shook and she heard a pop. The roof from the front section of the home landed on the rear of the home, damaging the back porch. Trivette called the Boone Fire Department because the top part of the chimney was blown away. Firefighters responded and determined the wood-burning stove safe to continue to use.

Q. What kind of damage can be inferred from the report?

(a) Snow damage
(b) Rain damage
(c) Wind damage
(d) Earthquake damage

해석_ 일요일 저녁 6시 30분에 불어닥친 바람이 올드 앤더슨 쿼리 로드에 위치한 어느 집 지붕을 벗겨냈습니다. 온 집이 흔들리고 '펑' 하는 소리가 날 때 리비 트리베트 씨는 집에 혼자 있었습니다. 집 앞부분에서 떨어져 나간 지붕이 베란다를 손상시키며 집 뒷부분으로 떨어졌습니다. 굴뚝의 윗부분이 날아가 버려 트리베트 씨는 분 소방서에 연락했습니다. 소방수들이 출동했고, 그들은 장작 난로는 계속 사용하기에 안전하다고 결론지었습니다.

Q. 기사를 통해 어떤 종류의 피해를 추론할 수 있는가?

(a) 폭설 피해
(b) 비 피해
(c) 폭풍 피해
(d) 지진 피해

해설_ 바람이 집의 지붕을 벗겨 버렸다는 내용으로 보아 그 지역에 폭풍이 불어 닥쳤음을 알 수 있다. 따라서 정답은 (c).

어휘_ **peel off** 벗기다   **pop** '펑' 하는 소리   **rear** 뒷부분   **back porch** 뒷베란다   **chimney** 굴뚝   **blow away** 날려 버리다   **wood-burning stove** 장작 난로

정답_ (c)